*Dosh — Some fu...
among a few golf fri...
You Bill*

2010

THIS
GOLFING LIFE

Also by the Author

The Green Road Home
To the Linksland
Bart & Fay (a play)
Wonderland

THIS
GOLFING LIFE

MICHAEL
BAMBERGER

Grove Press
New York

Pages 261–264 constitute an extension of the copyright page.

Published simultaneously in Canada
Printed in the United States of America

FIRST GROVE PRESS EDITION

Library of Congress Cataloging-in-Publication Data

Bamberger, Michael, 1960–
    This golfing life / Michael Bamberger.
      p. cm.
    ISBN-10: 0-8021-4275-3
    ISBN-13: 978-0-8021-4275-7
    1. Golf. 2. Golfers. I. Title.
GV965.B23 2003
796.352—dc22   2005048340

Grove Press
an imprint of Grove/Atlantic, Inc.
841 Broadway
New York, NY 10003

Distributed by Publishers Group West

www.groveatlantic.com

06 07 08 09 10   10 9 8 7 6 5 4 3 2 1

For *FRED ANTON,*
a better than average putter,
and a true friend.

CONTENTS

CHAPTER ONE

GREEN (1985)

THE GOLFER IS ALWAYS IRRATIONAL about the place in which he first falls in love. Ask anyone. For me, it was at the public golf course in Bellport, New York, one town east of Patchogue, the Long Island village where I grew up. Bellport is sixty-five miles east of Manhattan, and its municipal course is flat and short. Nothing famous has ever happened there. Fred Couples played it once, shot an even par 71, and people talked about that for years. During a hot, dry summer, it gets baked along the edges. But it's my home course. It's home. After you've been at the game for some years, you play better courses than your first course, courses that are more famous and challenging. But nothing is like the place where you first break 100 and the place where you first get the bug. The Bellport course at night is pleasing, too, but I can't go into that, except to say this: One hole fronts Bellport Bay—a nice spot.

I found my way to the Bellport course, by bus, in the summer after I turned fourteen, in 1974. I knew nothing about golf— mornings then began with baseball box scores and Red Smith— until a gym teacher named Mr. Greenlee instructed us in the art of hitting plastic golf balls off plastic mats in his gym in our eighth-grade winter. Why I got hooked I do not know. My guess is that the predisposition for golf is in your DNA. Or maybe it comes from the same place that religious zealotry does. You know, some need. However it happened, it happened. My parents, who fled Nazi Germany as children, knew nothing about the game, but they helped sustain my early interest. My mother found mismatched clubs at the Salvation Army on Main Street in Patchogue and sewed little golf-bag emblems on my shirts. A few years later, my father pointed me to Herbert Warren Wind's golf reports in *The New Yorker.* Just the idea of Herbert Warren Wind was too much for me. Hanging around golf and writing about it? Please.

Golf at Bellport was affordable. In ninth grade, I got a junior membership, which cost fifty dollars and allowed you to play Monday through Thursday after 2:30 p.m., except on Wednesday, Doctors' Day, when the starting time for Class F members was 3:30 p.m. For a middle-class family like mine, fifty dollars was reasonable. My dentist's wife, Mrs. Libin, lent me her matched clubs, with pink grips and blue-painted woods, and gave me stacks of Dr. Libin's old *Golf Digests*. There were whole worlds in them.

I often played alone and sometimes with a friend or two. We found golf balls in the woods and in the creek that ran through the golf course and bought cold bottles of Yoo-Hoo for thirty-five cents at the halfway house, which was an actual house, with brown shingle walls, just beyond the eighth green. In summer, the halfway house was staffed by good-looking college girls, and there were always guys hanging around, too. As we walked to the ninth tee, perspiring Yoo-Hoos in hand, we were sure that fantastic and unknowable fleshy acts were going on beyond the brown walls.

I went to the golf course almost every day after school. I'd pedal down to Main Street with my golf bag on my back, lock my bike to a parking meter in front of the old Bee Hive (the only store in Patchogue with an escalator), and take a public bus to Bellport, also for thirty-five cents. The bus stopped directly in front of the golf course, on South Country Road. The only inconvenient thing about the bus was that the driver required a cover for my golf bag and I didn't own one. One day the driver said to me, "If I come to a sudden stop and one of them clubs goes flying and somebody's eye gets poked out, it's not you that's gonna get sued, it's me." In those days, in the mid-1970s, there was a lot of misinformed class resentment about golf and golfers. After that warning, I carried a brown paper shopping bag in my golf bag and put it over the clubs upside down when riding the bus. That satisfied the driver. Coming back, I'd often hitchhike and sometimes was picked up by Dr. Libin himself. I'd rest the clubs on the back seat of his Cadillac and cruise home in air-conditioned splendor.

I wanted to work in the game. There wasn't much of an opportunity to caddie at Bellport, where most golfers used a pullcart, but one golfer who did use a caddie was the principal of my high school, Frank Juzwiak, and I carried his bag through my high school years. Mr. Juzwiak played first thing Sunday morning, and the men in his group were real golfers. They played quickly, no fussing around, and by the rules. They gambled, with just enough at stake that everyone became quiet and edgy late in the round with the outcome on the line. One of the regulars in the group, Sal "Mags" Maglio, was Bellport's retired greenkeeper, and he talked simply and knowledgeably about how grass grows and where bunker rakes should be placed. (Always outside the bunker.) They discussed the Masters and the U.S. Open, although not the weekly tour stops, and Trevino and Nicklaus. They knew the culture of golf and the foibles of life. They spoke as men, and all you had to do to learn something was to shut up and listen. Mr. Juzwiak had me hold his pipe between shots. Sometimes, as he handed me the pipe, a string of saliva would stretch from his lower lip to the stem, break off, and come to rest on the stubble of his unshaven chin. This was not the Mr. Juzwiak I would see in school. I realized something: The game was a leveler.

Sometimes Mr. Juzwiak would ask me about our high school golf team and how our coach, John Sifaneck, was doing. Sifaneck, a math teacher and also the Patchogue-Medford High School bowling coach, was the first adult to treat me as a grown-up. He had caddied his way through high school and college, and his caddie-yard stories had a lot to do with me wanting to become a looper, too. He had a crooked nose, a short backswing, and a playful manner. He was an expert on gambling—he was a hustler. We played regularly during my college summers. He loved golf. He lived in a windbreaker.

One day in 1985 he got a bad call from his doctor. He was a lifelong diabetic and now was being told he'd need to have a leg amputated. A surgery was scheduled.

Some days later, he was playing golf at Bellport and he reached the sixth hole, nearly two hundred yards from the back of the tee, with willows and beach grass running down the right side of the hole and a green shaped like a boomerang. He knew his golfing life, as he knew it, was coming to an end. With the flagstick in the back right corner of the green and a five-wood in his hands and the breeze in his face, Sifaneck made a hole in one, the first of his life.

And then he was in the hospital, where a doctor told him that he'd have to lose not one leg but both. As he was being wheeled on a gurney to the operating table, Sifaneck had a massive heart attack and died. I had a hard time imagining Sifaneck without legs, without golf. His ashes were dispersed one blowy day on Bellport's sixth green, with his family and his golf friends gathered around.

⚑

Nineteen eighty-five was one of my golf years, a year in my life I devoted to the game. I was twenty-four, turning twenty-five in April, with a college degree and two years as a reporter on a weekly paper on Martha's Vineyard, and all I really wanted to be was a tour caddie. I was surprised how willing Brad Faxon was to grant me a tryout. I had written to him, then called him after two rounds of the 1985 Bing Crosby National Pro-Am, as the Pebble Beach tournament was then known. Brad, a PGA Tour sophomore, was a year younger than I. He was a stroke off the lead.

"I'm not sure how long this could work out, but I'll give you a chance," Brad said. "Caddying is not the most lucrative profession in the world, you know."

"I know," I said.

"Seems like certain caddies are always borrowing money," he said. He paused. The caddie culture then was dominated by black men from the Deep South, some of them running from alimony payments and crying babies. "And the work itself—it's not as easy as it looks. Carrying the bag, that's the least of it."

"I know."

"And although the golf tour goes to a lot of beautiful places, the caddies usually wind up staying in cheap dives off the highway," Brad said.

"I love a good cheap dive," I said. It was one of those absurd lies people say, or I do, anyway.

"And although there are a lot of parties and dinners for the players, the officials, and the press, there isn't anything like that for the caddies, you know," Brad said. There were still press tents then, not media centers.

"I know."

"Okay," said Brad. His deep voice and mature manner belied his youth. He sounded much older than twenty-three. "I just want you to know what you're getting into."

"What I'm worried about is doing a good job so I can keep my job," I said. "What do you think makes for a good caddie?"

"Well," Brad said, "you've got to have all the basics."

I reached for a scrap of paper in my parents' chilly basement, cradled the heavy black 1940s phone on my left shoulder, and started scribbling fast.

Basics, I wrote down.

"You know: Keep the ball clean, the clubs clean, give accurate yardages, keep things dry in the rain, keep things organized," Brad said.

Ball clean, club clean, yards good, dry rain, organ, I wrote down.

"That's the easy stuff," Brad said.

EZ.

"It's the intangibles, the stuff you can't articulate, those are the things that separate the good caddie from the poor one," Brad said.

Intangibles toughest, I wrote down.

"Does that help?" Brad asked, obviously anxious to get back to something, probably the practice tee or the putting green or one of those player parties.

"Oh, yes," I said, "yes, yes, yes."

⚑

Brad was a name player. He had played on the 1983 Walker Cup team, he was an All-America golfer at Furman as a junior and senior, and as a senior he won three college awards as player of the year. He wasn't the next Nicklaus. Tom Watson—my golfing hero—was at the height of his powers then, and even he wasn't the next Nicklaus. Still, I had no right calling him (not that I knew that then). In 1984, his rookie season on the PGA Tour, he had finished in eighty-second place on the money list, making $71,688. Of the top 125 players, no one was younger than Brad. He didn't intend to take my call. He just picked up a ringing phone in his hotel room, that's all.

We arranged to meet in Florida, at the Honda Classic, when the tour moved east in February to the Tournament Players Club at Eagle Trace, in Coral Springs. I flew to Miami because I didn't know the Fort Lauderdale airport was much closer to the course, rented a car and drove north, hoping to join the circus. I was close to broke and feeling reckless when I took a room at the tournament hotel, a Holiday Inn. The players, at least those who had played the previous week in the Doral-Eastern Open, were making the drive from Miami, too. Bill Kratzert was checking in, his big orange PowerBilt golf bag on his shoulder. George Archer and Hubert Green, two tour stalwarts, were by the hotel's front door.

"You wearin' a girdle, George?" Green asked Archer. I was eavesdropping on a conversation between two pros, and my heart was racing. It was a warm, soft Florida night.

"Nah," Archer said. "This thing is enough of a pain." He pointed to a white bandage around his forearm.

"Ya look so skinny, George, that I figured you must be wearin' a girdle." He poked Archer in the stomach, and the two men laughed at nothing.

In those days, a caddie made between $200 and $300 a week, plus 5 percent of his man's earnings, 10 percent for a win. A player got $90,000 for winning a standard-issue tour event, and last money was usually about $900. It sounded like a fortune then, but it was actually before the big money reached the tour. Golf was still minor, which is why the players were staying at a $59-per-night Holiday Inn. If Brad finished in the middle of the pack, I had a chance to break even for the week. I wasn't so worried about that, though. If I could get a job in the circus, regular work, everything else, I figured, would follow from that.

My first morning at Eagle Trace, on the Monday of Honda week, I bought a yardage book—the wrong one, it turned out—from Angelo Argea, Jack Nicklaus's former caddie. Angelo was cashing in on his celebrity by making a book, a map of the course, to compete with the one made by a caddie named George Lucas. The Lucas book, I later learned, was the only book the caddies trust, but for six bucks, anyway, I got to meet Angelo.

"Who you working for?" he asked.

"Brad Faxon."

"How long you been with him?"

"This is my first week."

"Friend of his from home, I suppose? You know Brad from Massachusetts?"

Brad was actually from Rhode Island.

"Well, sort of. I guess you could say that."

"You from Massachusetts yourself?"

"I've lived there."

"But you're not from there."

"Well, no, not from there."

"Where you from?"

"New York."

"New York City?" He was quizzing me, I imagine, because I came from nowhere.

"Well, no. New York State."

"Where?"

"Patchogue. On the South Shore of Long Island."

"Why didn't you just say that?"

"It didn't occur to me you would have heard of it."

"Oh, sure, we've heard of it. We've heard of everything out here," Angelo said. "Patchogue. Just say that. Out here we like to know where people are from."

On Tuesday, I got to the golf course early, shortly after sunrise, and Brad's sack was already there, a big black Titleist bag, with his name stitched on in white letters, a fresh towel wrapped around the necks of his clubs, as if his sticks were a boxer, pre-fight. The dew on the grass left my canvas sneakers soaked.

"You looking for Brad?" a real caddie asked.

"Yes," I said.

"Just sit tight; he'll be back in a couple of minutes."

I was fooling nobody. My discomfort was on display.

Brad suddenly arrived. "Warm up these eggs, would ya?" He handed me a sleeve of new balls. The term was new to me.

We started walking to the first tee for a practice round. Brad led the conversation.

"You're a southpaw, eh, Mike?" Brad asked, noting the bag on my left shoulder.

"Just in caddying and hockey. Everything else I do righty."

"What happened to your Rangers last night?" I didn't realize he knew I was a New Yorker.

"They got whooped, huh?"

"Twelve to four," Brad said.

He continued his recitation of that morning's *USA Today* sports section (he was as devoted to the Boston Red Sox as I was to the New York Mets) until he reached the first tee, and then he became all business. He spent five hours on the practice round, hit putts for an hour or two, went to the range for over an hour. The next day, it was more of the same. On Thursday, the first round of the tournament, his tee time was 7:38 a.m., playing with two other young pros, Mike Donald and David Ogrin.

Brad made all pars on the front nine, despite many crooked shots. In the practice rounds my caddie game was fine, but now, with the lights on, it was obvious I didn't know what I was doing. As Brad had said, the work was harder than it looked. You had to know where each player was at all times, without asking. You had to know which player was likely to putt last, for that caddie is responsible for putting the flagstick back. You had to be able to anticipate. On some holes, Brad wanted his driver as he came off the green, but other times it was a three-wood or an iron. He changed balls every three holes, because the balls then, with their soft balata covers, would crack and get bent out of shape, even on good shots. I was to have a new egg ready and warm. On the ninth hole, the players needed their scorecards, which the caddie typically held, to give to the scorekeepers. (The idea of updating every player's score after every hole came years later, with faster computers and more volunteers to process more information.) Then, as now, the caddie had to have his player's snacks ready: a Snickers bar or a banana or something. (The "energy bar" came later.) The caddie had to be able to fold and put away a rain jacket or sweater or windbreaker without any fuss. And this was all before you even started to think about advising your player, let alone giving him the most basic information he'd need, like distance to the front edge of the green.

I was overloaded.

On the ninth hole, a long par-4, Brad pushed his drive badly into the rough. His second shot was 220 yards, blind and uphill. He could not see the flagstick from where he stood. He climbed to the top of the hill to get a better look, and I traipsed after him. He positioned me in a line between his ball and the hole so he'd know where to play his shot. He returned to the ball, taking a five-iron with him, and addressed the ball, using me for his line. He set up and waved me to the side. He had his line. He made a furious swing, and the ball squirted out of the grass like a knuckleball and made it a little more than halfway to the green. He smashed his club into the ground, climbed up the hill, and said to me, "Don't ever stand in my view while I'm making a shot again." I was in his peripheral vision. He was not hostile, just curt.

We continued the walk to his ball in silence. Brad hit a sand wedge to ten feet and made the putt for par.

Everything was happening too fast for me. I didn't have his new egg, ready and warm, for the tenth hole. I didn't have his driver ready. I felt my pockets for his scorecard. I couldn't find it. Brad was standing beside me, waiting, as I pulled the driver out of his bag, fumbling with the head cover.

"New ball?" he said.

"I'll have to get one out of the bag," I said.

"Scorecard?"

I stared at him blankly, not knowing what to say, and went into a cold sweat. I had no idea where it was.

He yanked it out of the breast pocket of my caddie bib.

We went to the tenth tee. Brad reached into the bag and grabbed a new package of balls, which he handed to me. He took off his sweater and handed me that, too. It was a warm morning, fast getting warmer. He took out a banana and started to peel it. When it was his turn to play, he handed me that, too.

After his tee shot, another poor one, he wanted to get rid of his driver as quickly as he could. He looked at me juggling the sweater, the package of balls, the half-eaten banana, his driver with a real wooden head.

"Your hands are too full," he said. He took back his banana.

As I made a lopsided trot down the fairway—a good caddie always beats his man to the ball—I could hear Brad talking to Mike Donald's caddie, Greg Rita, about what weeks he was available down the road.

Brad made the cut—and in the Friday round I actually helped him on one hole—but I knew I was going to be fired. As he got out his checkbook, he said, "Well, I *am* going to pay you." I could only wonder: Was my caddie career—my stint in the circus—over before it ever really got started?

I did what people do. I stuck with it. I found work with other players: Bill Britton, a struggling pro from Staten Island; Al Geiberger, nearing fifty, with a beautiful waltz of a swing; Steve Elkington, for one week, in his first professional event, the 1985 Dutch Open. I'd see Brad Faxon here and there, and we'd have little friendly conversations. I think he was impressed that I was finding regular work. Mike Donald, Brad's playing partner that first week at Honda, played practice rounds with Bill Britton, so I got to know him a little. At the U.S. Open, during a practice round, I was in the same group as Tom Watson, my hero, and his famous caddie, Bruce Edwards, who treated me as if I belonged out there. I wasn't totally unnerved, being so close to greatness. (Part of that was because of my newspaper work on Martha's Vineyard, where I reported on the summer activities of Mike Wallace and lived next to Bart Giamatti, then the president of Yale.) Watson and Bruce and I (*yeah, right*) were at Oakland Hills, on the outer rim of Detroit, as Herbert Warren Wind liked to write it. A guy in the gallery yelled out to Watson, "Hey, Tom, I'm from San Diego!" Watson is from Kansas City. He yelled back to him, good nature in his voice, "San Diego—what the hell are you doing here?" He turned to our little group marching down the fairway and said, "San Diego—who the fuck cares?" It was funny, in a mean way. Hearing it was the privilege of being an insider.

I caddied in the U.S. Open (for a young pro named Larry Rentz) and the British Open (for a young pro named Jamie Howell on his honeymoon) and the PGA Championship (for Kevin Morris, a club pro from New York who made the cut). I caddied in most of the big events, although not at Augusta. (During Masters week, I was caddying for Bill Britton at the Magnolia Classic in Hattiesburg, Mississippi, watching the CBS telecast in the caddie shack as Curtis

Strange kept dumping balls in the water and Bernhard Langer won his first green coat. Someday, I vowed, I would caddie in the Masters.) One week in March, unable to secure a bag for the Players Championship, I worked for CBS, as out-of-work caddies often did, and was in the vicinity of two TV golf legends, Frank Chirkinian, the producer of golf for CBS, and his director, Chuck Will. I played in the annual player-caddie softball game and in the annual caddie golf tournament. I found a home *out there,* as the caddies refer to the tour.

When the season, or my portion of it, was over, I went back to my parents' house in Patchogue and wrote a book, my first, about my caddie days, called *The Green Road Home.* The last line was for John Sifaneck, my old high school coach: "He loved the game, and his enthusiasm was contagious." He was forty-four when he died, the age I am now. He left behind his wife, two children, one hole in one, and, in me, the golf-bum spirit. There's a boulder and a plaque at Bellport to remember him and his last great shot.

That's where I am, too: one wife, two children, one hole in one. I live in Philadelphia now and when I visit my parents in summer the first place I go after dinner is Bellport. I'm no longer a member and since I don't live in the village I have no access to the Bellport course, short of sneaking on. I'm not going to tell you my way on. I will say that on those summer nights I seem always to play well. I'm a dressed-up duffer, really, but on my home turf I feel light on my feet and my backswing is slow and the ball flies like it does nowhere else for me. There's a certain brackishness to Bellport. I love having that soggy air in my lungs. It fills me with hope and happiness. It reminds me of my dreams.

CHAPTER TWO

THE PAPER (1986–90)

SOMETHING BIG CAME OUT OF MY CADDIE BOOK: I got to meet
Herbert Warren Wind. I sent him the manuscript, and he wrote a
generous blurb for it and invited me to see him in his office, on the
eighteenth floor of the old *New Yorker* building. He was tweedy
and kind. He invited me to call him Herb. On a wall in his cramped
office was a letter from Bing Crosby to him. Crosby wrote, "You
ask me if I'm playing much. Only days." William Shawn was still
the editor of *The New Yorker,* and Herb went to the Yale Club for
lunch regularly. It wasn't all that long ago, but it was a different
era. Commenting on the length of his pieces, Herb said, "It takes
me a thousand words to clear my throat." He wrote in longhand. I
wrote the book on a Royal typewriter.

It improved my life. I bought a sofa with my first royalty check,
and the book helped me get a job. I was young (twenty-six) and
inexperienced (just two years on the weekly *Vineyard Gazette* and
none on a daily) when I applied to *The Philadelphia Inquirer,* looking for a position as a news reporter. The paper had an opening
covering suburban high school sports, and the only reason I got
the job, from what I later heard, was that the editor, a legend of
newspapering named Gene Roberts, liked how I "got around the
country on the cheap doing that caddie thing." Roberts was a

southerner, and so was Joe Logan, the staff writer who reviewed my book for *The Inquirer.* The review was close to a pan and it came out while I was interviewing for the high school job, so I figured my fate with the paper was sealed. Later, when Logan and I became fellow reporters and friends, I lodged a complaint with him.

"You ripped me," I said.

"Ah didn't rip ya," Logan said, drawling gently. "Ah lukewarmed ya."

In my nine years at the paper, I was never the golf writer, but I was able to get golf stories into the paper regularly. Under Roberts, that was all the reporter had to do: get good stories in the paper. It made the job pretty easy.

In one piece, I tried to make the case that Philadelphia was the golf capital of the country. I interviewed Ben Crenshaw, who said his dream was to play and study all the great Philadelphia golf courses. He said no region in the United States, with the exception of metropolitan New York, had as many first-rate golf courses as did Philadelphia and its suburbs. Herbert Warren Wind said that only metropolitan Chicago rivaled Philadelphia for its number of outstanding courses. And Robert Trent Jones, then the dean of American golf course architects, told me that no single area in the United States could rival Philadelphia for the depth of its golf excellence.

They all knew what Frank Hannigan, a former executive director of the United States Golf Association, had once written: "There are courses thought of as indifferent in the realm of the Golf Association of Philadelphia which would be considered works of art if transplanted to many another section of the country."

I devised a poll of Philadelphia-area golf experts to identify and rank the ten best Philadelphia golf courses. The top three courses—Pine Valley, Merion, and Aronimink—were all courses with significant national reputations. All ten courses were built between 1908 and 1928, a period Crenshaw called "the golden age of American golf course architecture." That period, he explained, and particularly the Roaring Twenties, was a time of great wealth in Philadelphia. The surrounding countryside was just beginning to turn into a suburban dreamland. The architects nabbed prime pieces of land before it was too late, rolling terrain with winding streams and stately trees and lush meadows and rich dirt. The ten courses—the three above plus Philadelphia Cricket, Rolling Green, Whitemarsh Valley, Philadelphia Country, Huntingdon Valley, Torresdale-Frankford, and the North Course at Philmont—were built by seven architects: George Crump, Henry Colt, Hugh Wilson, Donald Ross, A. W. Tillinghast, George Thomas, and William Flynn. They had all studied the great aboriginal Scottish links and helped bring the Scottish pastime to America. Trent Jones considered that list of architects and deemed them "the giants of the business." It was fairly common, in certain Philadelphia golf circles, to hear some golf people talk about "Bill Flynn" as if he were still alive. They discussed his work at Shinnecock Hills in the early 1930s as if it were a current event. I was never bored.

The history of golf in Philadelphia was nearly as significant as its architecture. Bobby Jones completed his Grand Slam in 1930 at Merion. Sam Snead lost a U.S. Open at Philadelphia Country in 1939, with a massive meltdown near the end. In 1950, Ben Hogan won the U.S. Open at Merion in a playoff a year after an accident that should have claimed his life. Frank Chirkinian produced the first golf telecast, the 1958 PGA Championship at the Llanerch in suburban Philadelphia, won by Dow Finsterwald. Lee Trevino defeated Jack Nicklaus in a playoff for the U.S. Open at Merion in 1970. For years, there was a PGA Tour stop at crafty Whitemarsh Valley, beloved by Crenshaw and Tom Kite and Jack Nicklaus and other players considered to be not just golfers, but, better yet, shotmakers. Scottsdale, Arizona, had nothing on Philadelphia.

⚑

I had heard that the man who caddied for Bobby Jones when he completed the Grand Slam in 1930 at Merion was still alive, and one August day in 1989 I paid him a visit. His name was Howard Rexford and he was seventy-eight, a retired restaurateur with a loaf of white hair and double-knit trousers, sans belt, a style that even then was deliciously passé. He had a booming voice, an infectious giggle, and, wedged in his back teeth, a cheap cigar.

In September of 1930, he was a nineteen-year-old caddie called Rex, skinny as a driving iron. He was one of the 350 loopers at Merion, and all of them wanted to caddie for Jones in what was then called the National Amateur. Earlier in the year, Jones had won the British Amateur, the British Open, and the U.S. Open. The regal, Harvard-educated Georgian—the embodiment of the Golden Age of Sport—would be coming to Merion with a chance to do what nobody had done before, win all of golf's four major events in a single year. For Jones, it was three down with one to go. Rexford recreated for me the two-sentence, nine-word conversation that defined the rest of his life. It was between Harry J. Haas, chairman of Merion's caddie committee, and Joe Markey, Merion's caddie master. Young Rex had just caddied for Haas, a vice president of Philadelphia National Bank. Haas perused the club's caddie-payment slip, which contained a litany of potential complaints.

Caddie (please check):
1. Lags behind
2. Occupies benches
3. Swings clubs
4. Doesn't clean balls
5. Doesn't replace turf

Haas had no complaints about Rex, the son of an ink salesman, a graduate of a local Catholic high school. The banker signed the chit: a ten-cent tip atop the ninety-cent caddie fee. Haas handed the slip to Markey and said, "This boy I want for Bob Jones." The sun was at high noon. Markey squinted.

"Okay, then," said the caddie master.

Two weeks later, Jones won the Amateur with Rexford on his bag. Fifty-nine years after that, in the summer of 1989, Rexford was recalling once again how Jones played a brassie out of the fairway bunker on the par-5 fourteenth. He remembered the sweet scent of Jones's cologne, the crisp part in Jones's slicked-back hair, the sharp crease in his flannel knickers. Somewhere underneath his white loaf, the former caddie could still hear Jones's slow drawl: "Okay, Howard, ahundra-an-nineda yahds from the bunka." He remembered the strong grip of Jones's meaty right hand when they said goodbye.

Rexford said Jones was a quick player who took one waggle and swung. His action was athletic but unhurried. With his hickory-shafted driver, he hit dead-straight line drives of 230 yards on the brownish green fairways that received only natural rainfall.

Jones seldom talked on the golf course. Every so often, Rexford recalled, Jones would make an observation to Grantland Rice, the sports columnist, or to O. B. Keeler, who later became Jones's bi-ographer, or to Jones's father. He was cordial to his opponents, but not chatty. He was nine years older than Rexford and his concen-tration was intense, but he was always calm. "Of course, he was in the driver's seat in every match he played," Rexford said. "No match went beyond the fourteenth hole."

When Jones closed out Eugene Homans on the eleventh green in the thirty-six-hole match-play final, bedlam ensued. As Rexford sat in front of me, he closed his eyes and imagined the six marines who sprang out of the trees, surrounding Jones and escorting him to the clubhouse through throngs of spectators. Newsmen peppered Rexford with questions, and when they were done, the caddie waited for his player outside Merion's sprawling white clubhouse. When Jones emerged from it, he approached Rexford and, in one motion, shook his hand and discreetly placed a roll of bills in it. When they parted, Rexford dashed into the woods and counted the money. There were fifteen ten-dollar bills. He put the money inside his shoe.

"I didn't do much, didn't say much," Rexford said. He was a robust man but oddly quiet when he said that. "I carried the bag, told Jones the distances. He chose the clubs."

Rexford became an accomplished golfer and a busy man. He won seven club championships, made seven holes in one, and owned a golfers' hangout called the Black Horse Tavern. He did well with it. But when I saw him, he was an old man, retired, who knew that nothing in his life equaled his two-week brush with greatness. How many people in this world can say they keep their telephone bill in a crystal fruit bowl given to them by Bobby Jones as a wedding gift? After the 1930 Amateur, Rexford did not see Jones for three decades, until 1960, at a crowded golf banquet in Philadelphia. Jones saw his old caddie and said, "You must be Howard Rexford. You must sit with me for the dinna." And he did, the regal golfer and the scrappy caddie side by side on a dais at a rubber-chicken dinner. There were hundreds of people at the dinner, and Rexford was the man with whom Jones most wanted to sit. Rexford was going to take that memory all the way to his end, too.

When I moved to Philadelphia to take the job on *The Inquirer,* golf was still an odd enough pastime that people would say things like, "Oh, you're a golfer? Then you should meet so-and-so. He's a crazy golfer. He plays once a week!" In that vein, I met Bill Eddins and Jonathan Storm, then both editors at the paper, and Bob Warner, a city hall reporter on *The Philadelphia Daily News.* They were members of something called the Philadelphia Newspapermen's Golf Association, which gathered at various courses on Mondays, typically lush private courses that were closed on Mondays, like Llanerch, to spend a workday playing golf and leading, for six hours, the country club life. It was a way, as the old newspapermen used to say, to take a slide. Naturally, I joined. The association was left over from another era, when Monday was a day off after working the weekend, when newspaper work was generally regarded to be a working-class profession, and when there were guys at the papers who knew the caddie masters and the club pros and the greenkeepers, the men who got the group on courses that otherwise would have been off limits. To prove to the clubs we were an organization with "class," there was a list of rules we were required to follow. We had to wear long pants, even though all the clubs allowed shorts, and we had to ride a cart, because carrying one's own bag was considered, although I never heard anybody use this word, déclassé.

For a while, Warner, Storm, Eddins, and I played almost every Monday. On other days, Eddins and I traveled all over the Philadelphia suburbs playing one public course after another, most of them mediocre, but we didn't care. The golf in Philadelphia that Robert Trent Jones and Herbert Warren Wind and Ben Crenshaw knew about was all private-club golf. That's how Philadelphia got its golf reputation. In the late 1980s, the public courses owned by the city of Philadelphia were in horrid condition, and a good number of the courses in the suburbs and surrounding countryside still felt like the dairy farms they once had been.

The king of the farm courses was a place called Pickering Valley, where six brothers named Thompson—Tommy, Jimmy, Johnny, Jerry, Benny, and Stevie—sold their 350 milkers and without knowing a thing about golf turned the grazing land into a public course.

"We did some market research to find out about golf," a Thompson (I think it was Jerry) told me.

One of them called a friend who played golf.

"Hey, you all need another public golf course 'round here?"

"Guess so. You got lines most everywhere you go."

So they built a course, one with big greens, thinking that if the golfers hit more greens in regulation (in one shot on a par-3, two shots on a par-4, and three shots on a par-5), they'd feel better about themselves and be more likely to return. They made the course reasonably long but not backbreakingly so. It measured 6,487 yards from the back tees.

"And that's a true measurement," said one of the Thompsons (I think it was Jimmy). He then made an admission no golf-playing golf entrepreneur would ever make: "You can cheat on the driving range, call 185 yards 200 yards, make the people feel good. But you can't do that on the course. Just isn't right."

The pro shop was an old milking station, there was a plan to convert a barn with no roof into a locker room, and there was a wait to play it every Saturday, Sunday, and holiday in good weather. After years in the business, none of the Thompsons was ever tempted to play. Still, they had picked up something about the game.

"Golf is good for a man, good for his character," one of the Thompson brothers told me. "Before he heads out to play, he's filled with good spirits, he's comradely. Not necessarily when he comes in, but when he heads out, he's feeling just fine."

⚐

The two men who ran golf for CBS—the legendary producer Frank Chirkinian and his director Chuck Will—were both from Philadelphia. Chirkinian grew up in a section of the city called Oxford Circle, the son of an Armenian silk weaver who had come to the United States in 1920. In an interview before the 1988 Masters, Chirkinian gave me a tremendous insight into why Augusta made for such superb TV. He thought of the tournament as a play: The Thursday and Friday rounds were Act I, the Saturday round was Act II, and the Sunday round was Act III. The actors, of course, were the players, and you could never know who the hero would ultimately be until it was all over. Augusta National, the course, was the epitome of stages, the greenest and most beautiful outdoor stage in the world. It was a stage with no parameters, and the play performed on it had no scripted lines. In fact, in TV production, the CBS people referred to the tournament, the first major of the year, as "the show." Chirkinian was so enamored of the Masters, he moved to Augusta and joined the Augusta Country Club.

As a kid in Philadelphia, Chirkinian's dream was to become a saloon singer; he wound up working for WCAU radio. That was in 1950. He never left broadcasting. When he produced the 1958 PGA Championship, he used ten cameras. The CBS suits thought that was excessive, but that's what Chirkinian felt he needed. Decades later, ten cameras was still the norm for most televised golf tournaments. For the Masters, he used closer to thirty.

"Frank humanized golf," Chuck Will told me. After my brief stint working for him as a spotter at the 1985 Players Championship, when I was an unemployed caddie, we became friends. We would see each other at the Bala Golf Club, where Chuck and Frank were both members. Chuck trained for his work in TV by selling cardboard boxes and playing years of scratch golf. "Frank captured the faces," Chuck said. "In 1985, Curtis Strange hit a four-iron into the pond at fifteen with the tournament in his grasp. Curtis's tan went white. Frank caught that. It was the image of the tournament."

Will and Chirkinian were an effective better-ball golf team at Bala, Will shooting right around par, Chirkinian able to break 80. But in their professional life, Chirkinian was the boss, and Will referred to himself as "Frank's caddie." Will had a soft spot for caddies.

One morning in Chuck's trailer during the week of the '85 Players Championship, there was an old tiny black caddie named Beaufort, out of work and out of luck. He was there for the same reason I was, looking for a gig and a paycheck.

"You come in here and you tell me you want a job," Will said to him, pulling out an index card with two dozen names on it. Next to each name was an amount of money. Thin black lines were drawn through most of the names.

"You see this?" Will asked Beaufort. "This card dates back to 1980. One-nine-eight-oh. That's five years ago. It says here I lent you forty dollars in 1980, and your name is not crossed off, which means you did not pay me back. You come in here looking for a job, but you don't pay me the forty dollars you owe me, and you don't even have the decency to mention it."

"I can't pay you back right now. I don't have the money," Beaufort said. "If I had a job, I could pay you back."

"I don't give a shit about the money," Will said. "My accountant wrote it off as a loss years ago. It's not the money. 'I could pay you back, I could pay you back.' Go on, get out of here. I don't have any work for you."

Beaufort turned on his worn sneakers. He hadn't had a good bag in years.

"Understand that it's not the money," Will said softly as Beaufort was at the door. His tirade was over. "It's the principle of the thing, right? You understand that. See you sometime down the road."

The door closed and Will sat and exhaled slowly. Of course it wasn't about the money. It was about the community of golf to which Will and Beaufort both belonged.

٢

Bob Warner, the city hall reporter from *The Daily News* and one of my fellow newspapermen in the Philadelphia Newspapermen's Golf Association, became a good friend. Bob's wife, Jeannie Hemphill, was from an old-stock Philadelphia family, and on that basis Bob was able to slip through the cracks and become a member of one of Philadelphia's old-line clubs, the Philadelphia Cricket Club, which had, in the late 1980s, no cricket but excellent squash, tennis, swimming, bridge, trapshooting, and golf. Two U.S. Opens had been played at the club. I loved the club's A. W. Tillinghast course from the first time Bob invited Storm and Eddins and me to play it. Newspaper reporter was, decidedly, not a common profession at the Cricket Club, but the waiters served Bob, and his three inky guests, just the same. Bob had a lot going for him: nice table manners; Exeter and Princeton; a good squash game; a beautiful home in the city's Chestnut Hill section, near the main clubhouse; his wife. That he was willing to risk his standing at the club by putting me up for membership impresses me still. One night at the bar of a neighboring club, in the period when my application was pending, a slightly lit Cricket member said to me, "Well, it'll be interesting to see what the admissions committee does with a Center City Jew." I slipped in, too, doubling the population of newspaper reporters in the club. As a bachelor under thirty (special rates in that category), with no mortgage, I could swing the initiation fee and dues, though barely.

By 1989, at age twenty-nine, I was off the high-school sports beat and was a news reporter at *The Inquirer.* When Bart Giamatti, the commissioner of baseball, died suddenly of a heart attack, shortly after banishing Pete Rose from baseball, I was assigned to write the story. (I had known the summertime Giamatti, from when we lived next to each other on Martha's Vineyard; on Sunday afternoons, he'd sit, shirtless, in a beach chair set up on his crabgrass lawn and listen to the Red Sox on a portable radio. We had small cottages deep in the woods.) Right about the time of Bart's death, the paper was looking for a new beat writer to cover the Philadelphia Phillies for the 1990 season. On the basis of my Giamatti obit, and my childhood devotion to the New York Mets, I got the job. In 1990, on the day after Father's Day, the Phillies manager, Nick Leyva, and I sat in his office and watched Mike Donald lose a nineteen-hole playoff to Hale Irwin for the U.S. Open title.

Lenny Dykstra was then the Phillies centerfielder and leadoff hitter and liveliest wire. He loved to play golf for big stakes. Once, at the Cricket Club, it was Lenny and I against two Mercedes salesmen. Lenny played his guy a $500 Nassau ($500 for the front nine, $500 for the back, $500 for the overall match), plus all manner of side action. I suggested to the salesman assigned to me that we play for one tenth of that, with no side action, which was still out of my league. Lenny and I lost the first hole. We lost the second when my four-foot putt to halve the hole did not touch any part of it. I was quaking.

On the third tee I said to Lenny, "I'm really sorry about that."

He said, "Don't worry about it. We're better than these guys." It was said with conviction, by a guy who was then one of the best hitters in baseball. He made his living being confident. It was a revelation for me.

I made a birdie on three. Lenny made a birdie on four. The match was even, and we ended up winning every which way. Lenny made well over $2,000, and he was paid in cash in the Cricket Club parking lot, in front of his red convertible Mercedes. (In deference to the club's Quaker roots, the $2 Nassau was the regular game.) I pocketed my $150. Some years later it was no surprise to learn that Lenny's gambling problems had come to the attention of the commissioner of baseball.

I had been seeing, for some time, a California girl with lively green eyes who had moved to New York after college. Christine's interest in golf was passing, but she was born to travel and saw that the game could take you to nice places: Fishers Island in Long Island Sound, the Homestead in Virginia, the Leatherstocking course of the Otesaga Hotel in Cooperstown. We traveled to nice places. The eighteenth tee at the Leatherstocking course was a tiny island out in a lake, and for your tee shot you could bite off as much water as you dared. It was all about greed: The more you cut off, the closer to the green you were. I deposited my four remaining golf balls in the lake by virtue of my bogeyman, the quick pull-hook, and with no more balls left, I went temporarily insane. Had I asked Christine for her hand in marriage that day, I'm sure I would have received a quick no.

I wisely waited, and we were married a week or so after the 1990 World Series. I was fortunate that the Oakland A's swept that series, giving me a few free days to sow my final bachelor oats. I found the idea of a bachelor party appalling, but some friends and I did get together for a day of men's golf at the Cricket Club a few days before the wedding day, playing for an odd-looking metal golfer, eventually attached to a slab of wood, to which I assigned a grand name: the Shivas Trophy, named for the peculiar, irresistible Scottish golf professional Shivas Irons, from the Michael Murphy book *Golf in the Kingdom*. The first name on the trophy was your correspondent's (a sparkly 82 with a 12 handicap). A group of friends and I have been gathering each fall to play for the Shivas Trophy ever since, but I haven't even sniffed it.

Covering baseball full-time can rob you of your love for it. Fortunately, I had signed up for only one year. My newspaper heart was in news. I told the sports editor, a closet poet named David Tucker, that I wanted to take a leave from the paper in 1991, so that I could become a caddie on the European golf tour. (Christine would be in charge of reading the train schedule and finding cheap digs.) I told Tucker I hoped to write a book about the experience, a sort of sequel to my first book.

He dropped his whole poet thing and went into management mode. "That's a terrible idea," he said. He wanted me to take the beat for another year. Why I cannot imagine. "Don't write that book. That's a dilettante's book." He had no use for golf. It was a baseball beat writer for 1991 he needed. Someday, I knew, kids were coming, a mortgage, a lawn in need of raking. I saw a chance, maybe a last chance, to devote myself to golf for a year.

Off we went to Europe, my bride and I, a golf bag over my left shoulder.

CHAPTER THREE

WHIPLASH (1991, PART 1)

IN FEBRUARY OF 1991, I made wallet-sized copies of the first half of the European golf tour schedule, from the start of the year until the tour reached Scotland. One copy was for myself, the other for my bride, Christine. On the 24th of February, we took a cab to Kennedy Airport for a flight to France with little more than a loose plan in place: I'd loop my way to Scotland as a caddie on the European golf tour, and once there, we'd really go exploring. Our itinerary, to the degree we had one, looked like this:

DATES	TOURNAMENT	LOCATION
February 28–March 3	Mediterranean Open	St. Raphael, France
March 7–10	Balearic Islands Open	Majorca, Spain
March 14–17	Catalonia Open	Tarragona, Spain
March 21–24	Portuguese Open	Porto, Portugal
March 28–31	Florence Open	Florence, Italy
April 11–14	Jersey Open	Jersey, United Kingdom
April 18–21	Benson & Hedges Championship	St. Mellion, England
April 25–28	Madrid Open	Madrid, Spain
May 2–5	Cannes Open	Cannes, France
May 9–12	Spanish Open	Madrid, Spain

DATES	TOURNAMENT	LOCATION
May 16–19	Italian Open	Milan, Italy
May 24–27	PGA Championship	Virginia Water, England
May 30–June 2	British Masters	Woburn, England
June 6–9	Murphy's Cup	York, England
June 13–16	Belgian Open	Waterloo, Belgium
June 20–23	Irish Open	Killarney, Ireland
June 27–30	French Open	Paris, France
July 3–6	Monte Carlo Open	Monte Carlo, Monaco
July 10–13	Scottish Open	Auchterarder, Scotland
July–September	Explore Scotland	

Suddenly, we were at a train station in St. Raphael, France. I had just caddied for an American golfer playing in Europe, Peter Teravainen, and he had made the cut, so now I had a job for the next week, in Majorca, Spain. There was a man at the train station, a caddie. He seemed to like my wife. He kept saying to her, "If you want to eat, eat now. No food till we get to Port Bou." He was a trim man, with long white sideburns and a tiny head, and his clothes—his sneakers and pants and vest and cap—all bore the crest of a great sporting goods manufacturer, Wilson, the brand favored by the man's boss, a young Fijian golfer named Vijay Singh, and therefore by Vijay's caddie. His voice, warm and slightly drunk, sounded vaguely familiar. I had never met this little man, and yet I felt I knew him. Who was he? Where had I heard that burr? He looked at my golf bag. I looked at his crests. He looked at my wife. No introductions seemed necessary. Why were we there, newly-weds, sitting on the cold floor of a train station in St. Raphael, a small seaside cathedral town in the south of France? Because the wooden benches were filled with sleeping soldiers returning from war. Because we had nowhere else to be—we had given up our apartments, our jobs, our former lives. Because, just like the little man standing before us, we were waiting for the overnight train to Port Bou, working our way to the next stop, and trying to beat a night's rent doing it.

I wondered if Vijay's caddie would be in our compartment. A private cabin was not in our budget. A month earlier, we had been rich. I had my job on *The Inquirer,* and Christine had been an account manager on brands you've heard of for a New York advertising agency. We rode in taxicabs. But after the World Series and our wedding, and before pitchers and catchers reported for spring training in February of 1991, she quit her job and I took a leave from mine so that I could become a caddie on the European tour and so that she could join me. Convincing her was not work. The tour stopped in Paris and Madrid, London and Florence, Brussels and Milan, the Scottish Highlands, the north coast of Portugal, the south of France. We wanted adventure. We wanted to be overseas. The very word excited us.

As my wife and I were packing, deciding what to bring and what to leave behind, I was afraid to tell my friends, family, colleagues, and bosses the truest purpose, the ultimate goal, of my trip. I feared that it sounded so small. Now I realize the true size of its scope, and I'd like to tell you because I think you will understand and because I am no longer afraid: I wanted to improve. I remember the day I realized I needed help. I was on the practice tee of a Palm Beach resort, lashing at striped balls with a sort of desperate energy. Next to me was an old hunched man, a man of wealth and accomplishment long done pushing ninety, slapping one meek ground ball after another in the general direction of the fifty-yard marker. A youth working the range, a collegian of mindless good cheer, watched a single swing and announced, "You're hitting them well today, Mr. Hartmann." And Mr. Hartmann turned slowly on his spikes, leaned on his driver, and said, "Young sir, I am running out of time." And right then I came to a realization: I am Mr. Hartmann; I am that man!

But why did I have to become a caddie on the European golf tour in order to seek betterment? Why couldn't I just go to one of those golf schools in Arizona or Florida or New Mexico? Because the golf schools are held on courses financed by the sale of condominiums. Because they are run by men trying to make money.

Because the instructors are experts in a narrow area, the golf swing. I wanted to be part of the game again.

The European tour of that era struck me as a vast and unexplored territory. In the back pages of *Golf World* there always seemed to be a picture of a ruddy-faced professional wiping windblown hair out of his eyes with one hand as he reached for a driver with the other, and the cutline had something about so-and-so's play in the French Open or the Spanish Open or the Irish Open. This was the period in which Europe was producing players unlike anything we had in the United States: Ian Woosnam, the tiny, strong Welshman with a temper; Bernhard Langer, the German stoic maniacally dedicated to precision; Sandy Lyle, a large, amiable Scotsman who played large, amiable golf; José María Olazábal, a Spaniard engrossed in a quest for mastery and uninterested in swing mechanics; Nick Faldo, an Englishman obsessed with swing mechanics in his quest for mastery; and Severiano Ballesteros, the Spanish artista, to me the most captivating golfer in the world.

One morning, in our first week on the European tour, in France, on the Côte d'Azur, I left our little hotel, shabby but adequate, shortly after six, seeking coffee and a croissant and a ride to the course. The fog was lifting off the streets of St. Raphael and daylight was breaking. Across the street and out of the glimmer a body emerged, a trim little man wearing a cap. I couldn't tell if the body belonged to a player or an official or a caddie, but it definitely belonged to golf. He called out to me with a hint of a brogue, "All right?" It was a welcoming.

⚑

"I play a full schedule," Peter Teravainen said on our first day together. We were climbing up and down the hills of a contrived Robert Trent Jones development course—the venue for the Mediterranean Open—and I had his bag on my back. I was a caddie again, and I was happy. "I feel that if there's a golf tournament somewhere and they're offering money and I can get it, I should be there."

I had known his distinctive Finnish name for a long time—you'd see it in the agate type of newspaper columns, playing here and there around the world, seldom finishing much better than thirtieth. I knew that Peter Teravainen had been born and raised in Massachusetts and educated at Yale and that he was living in Singapore. He was starting his tenth year on the European tour, exiled to it because he couldn't earn a spot on the lucrative U.S. tour. To play the PGA Tour, you have to be a good putter, and Teravainen was not a good putter. The European tour suited him. He believed that the life of a touring professional must include struggle: play hard, sleep rough, travel cheap, carry cash.

Since turning professional in 1979, Peter had one goal above all others: to make a living solely by playing tournament golf, and to make it without the accoutrements common to the modern pro. When I met him, he had no teaching guru, no travel agent, no manager, no psychologist, no equipment endorsements, no professional caddie, no clothing contract. His style was all his own. The collars on his shirts were stiff enough to accommodate a tie. His favorite pants, made of a material not found in nature, were slate gray and shiny, with an off-white pinstriping, tight at the hips and thighs, then slightly flaring from the knees to the tops of his shoes. A great pair of trousers.

Teravainen belonged to the brute force school; off the tee, he was as long as anybody. Occasionally during his swing he grunted. He had so much unspent energy at the traditional concluding point for a full swing that he sometimes swung the club again, hard and in reverse, returning to his starting point. Among his colleagues, his swing had a nickname: the Whiplash. Once, in a tournament in Switzerland, Peter swung so hard he fainted and in the fall sprained an arm. His swing was unteachable. It came from within.

Peter told me that he was an easy loop, but that was only his opinion. I fast realized that he was superstitious, fastidious, and finicky. I also fast realized that whatever caddie skills I had developed during my stint as a caddie on the PGA Tour in 1985 had been pushed to the farthest recesses of my brain. I had to get my caddie legs back in a hurry and to reacquaint myself with the caddie mentality.

Early on, Peter told me that the clubs were rattling too much when I walked. I wanted to say, "Peter, don't you realize that the rhythmic clinking of clubheads is one of the great sounds produced by the game?" Instead, I wrapped the towel around the clubs in a serpentine pattern, held a hand around the towel, and kept the clubs, and myself, quiet.

We did odd things. I caddied for Peter through a sandstorm in Majorca. On another occasion, he and Christine and I—and forty or fifty hard-drinking loopers—took an all-night caddie bus from Tarragona, Spain, to Porto, Portugal. (Peter was pathologically frugal.) He paid me £225 a week, plus 5 percent of his after-tax winnings, and always in cash. One month into our journey, I had American dollars, British pounds, French francs, Spanish pesetas, Portuguese escudos, and Italian liras jumbled in my wallet, and my change purse weighed a kilo or two. He calculated by percentages to the pence.

He took pains to treat me not as a "writer" but as a caddie. In Monte Carlo, Christine and I had a rental car, and Peter did not. One night I offered him a ride to the golf course for the following morning. We agreed to leave at half past seven. When I returned to my hotel room around eleven that night, there was a note from Peter: "I want to leave at seven so I can have breakfast at the club." It was rude, really, even if I was just an employee. Christine wrote on the back of the note, "Pete, the car leaves at 7:30. If you need it sooner, bus it.—The Bambergers." I would have loved to return that note to him. Of course, at 7:00 a.m., I was waiting outside his hotel.

Generally, he was fair. At the Florence Open, he sent me up to a blind green. "Tell me if the pin is on the upper shelf or the lower shelf," he said. I climbed the hill to the green and saw no shelves at all, just a gentle slope from top to bottom, and the hole in the center of the green. "It's in the middle," I yelled back to him.

I could see him shaking his head in the fairway as he propped himself up on his sand wedge. He made no effort to hide his disgust. "Can't be in the middle. Top shelf or bottom shelf?"

I could think of no answer that would satisfy him. "To me, it looks middle," I said.

Peter hit his shot, not well but onto the green. He didn't know how firmly to hit the wedge. He two-putted for his par, and when he came off the green, he said, "You're right, the green has no tiers."

Only once did I think he was being out-and-out unfair. During the third round of the Italian Open, on the eighth hole, a par-5, he hit his second shot over the green and into the woods. He hit a delicate shot out of the woods, a very tricky play, and the ball slid just past the hole, narrowly missing the pin. As it passed the hole, the ball showed no signs of weariness. As it approached the short fringe grass between the green and the greenside bunker, I said, "Sit down, golf ball," just once and in a low voice. I have talked to golf balls all my golfing life. I accept that a golf ball is inanimate; I understand that a golf ball does not have ears or a brain or even a nervous system. But it is, nonetheless, pleasing to see a golf ball pop right out of a lake at the exact moment you've yelled, "Skip, golf ball, skip!"

At almost the exact moment I said, "Sit down, golf ball," Peter's playing partner said the same thing. The ball refused its orders and rolled into the bunker. Peter watched in stunned, silent, angry amazement, and then he made a bogey. Coming off the green, he started yelling, "Never talk to my golf ball, never talk to my golf ball, goddamnit, never talk to my golf ball!"

Peter's playing partner came up to me and said, "Is he talking to me or to you?"

"Me," I said.

What did Peter think, that the golf ball was doing the opposite of what I asked it to do? Besides, the round was our thirty-third competitive round together, and he had never before said anything about not talking to his golf ball, which I had been doing from the start. The other caddie, very prominent in looper circles, said to me on our way to the ninth tee, "Does he always treat you like that?" Walking down the ninth fairway, keeping my distance from my boss, I started to fantasize about firing him. Nah, not here, I reasoned, too close to the clubhouse. Stick him with the bag when he's miles away.

But for some odd reason, I became fond of him. When Peter was a young pro, a few years out of Yale and trying to get into PGA

Tour events in the United States in Monday qualifiers, Mike Donald once called him a quitter. He'd be five over par through fifteen holes and would mail it in from there.

The day Mike said that, Peter swore he would never quit again, and that's how he approached his whole unlikely career. I loved watching him line up putts. He would stand halfway between the ball and the hole, just off the line of the putt, put his hands on his hips for symmetry and balance, and then strangely throw his shoulders and head back and shake his head from side to side as if he were watching a tennis match, with a contorted face that said, "Goddamnit, I've got to figure out what this putt does." At the Scottish Open, our last tournament together, he played beautifully, even par for two rounds in bad weather with a birdie to finish, and missed the cut by a shot. In a postmortem, he said to me, "Having a regular caddie has helped me this year." I was flattered; it was the most direct compliment he had ever paid me. He was then number forty-six on the European tour's Order of Merit. "I'd like to work with a guy on a steady basis, if I found a guy I liked. I could raise my wage, to keep a guy I really liked," Peter said. Had I heard that right? "Sometimes you have to spend money to make money," he said. I was amazed. At the British Open, the week after the Scottish Open, a marketing man from Tommy Armour Golf said to him, "You give us a few years, Teravainen, we'll give you a complete make-over." They had given him a pastel blue cotton sweater, sheer and delicate—a very fine sweater. I thought he looked uncomfortable in it.

CHAPTER FOUR

STARK (1991, PART 2)

IN SCOTLAND, IN THE SUMMER OF 1991, I fell under the spell of a teaching pro named John Stark. The first thing he said was, "Tell me precisely what is it you seek to accomplish." We were sitting in his crammed office, in the back of his pro shop at the Crieff Golf Club, in central Scotland. I had expected a trim man in a tweed coat, but my expectations were wrong. Stark was a behemoth, two or three inches over six feet and a stone or two over two hundred pounds, with a deep, booming voice and a rich Scots dialect. He wore white loafers, shiny blue nylon sweatpants, and a white golf shirt a size or two too small. Around his neck hung a gold chain, and the borders of his teeth were lined with gold, too. He had a heavy, compassionate face and thick white hair combed off his broad forehead. He smoked a cheap cigar. He was sixty years old, and he looked it, except in his eyes—he had ageless, piercing, wise blue eyes.

"I want to get better," I said, quietly.

Stark stared at me. My God, how he stared at me! I felt as if the master teacher were looking right into my golfing past: Here I am in Mr. Greenlee's eighth-grade gym class, whacking balls with wild, happy abandon; here I am in the summer before my freshman year of college, at the height of my modest golf powers, which is to say, able to break eighty from time to time at Bellport, which I knew so well; here I am some years later, on the practice tee of a Palm Beach resort, hearing old Mr. Hartmann say to a youth working the range, "Young sir, I am running out of time," and feeling solidarity with him. No, Stark wasn't staring at me, he was staring right through me: He saw my suffering, my dissatisfaction, my false pride, my humiliation, my longing, my urgency.

He lit his cigar, and we sat in silence for a long moment. In time, he spoke; I remember the weird way his lips started moving, well before his words came out. I will tell you what he said, but before I do, I'd like to explain how I found my way to that back room, amid the boxed shoes waiting for feet, the unfinished woods waiting for paint, the naked shafts waiting for grips. I think I should tell you how I came to have an audience with Mr. J. M. Stark, golf professional, whose dangerous and powerful vision was so immediately apparent.

I had been looking for a teacher. In my mind, I was a 70s shooter in the midst of a long, long slump, but in reality I had to play well to shoot 82 and more often shot 92. I could play to my handicap, twelve or thirteen, only on my good days, and that was an unsatisfying way to go through life. I longed to feel again the thrill of discovery, the thrill of improvement. I felt I needed a fresh start and a teacher to set me on a new course. A British Ryder Cup player from the Palmer era, whom I had met in England while caddying for Teravainen, told me about Stark. "He teaches no two people the same way, and he knows the game from the outside and the inside," I was told. "He's a mystic, something of a recluse, and if you get him to take you on, you'll be lucky indeed." Intrigued, I wrote to John Stark and inquired about becoming a pupil. He invited me in for "a little chat"—that's how he put it. So, during the weekend of the Scottish Open, after Peter missed the cut, I went up to see Stark at the club where he had worked since 1961, in the town of Crieff. I left my clubs behind; I didn't want to appear presumptuous.

"You want to get better, a worthy goal," Stark said. "But what makes you think tuition is the way to improvement? I've seen many players ruined with instruction, I've seen instruction rob a player of all his natural instincts for the game."

Stark leaned back in his desk chair, which was too small to accommodate him. I didn't know if he wanted me to respond. The rhythms of Scottish and American conversation are different. The Scots pause more, and ask more questions, questions not always meant to be answered. I waited, and eventually Stark continued.

"When I was a boy, there was no teaching of golf in Scotland, not in a formal sense, and I don't think the quality of the play in this country was any worse for it. Your father showed you a couple of things when you played with him in the summer evenings. You caddied, and if you had a player you liked, you emulated him. If you were lucky enough to see a Henry Cotton, you didn't ask him how many knuckles of his left hand were visible at address. You'd follow him around, watch how he approached the game, watch his swing, and then you'd try to do the same. You'd fiddle around, perform experiments, amalgamate what he was doing with your own ideas, and come up with something distinctly your own."

A young shop assistant came in with instant coffee, and Stark stirred it with a letter opener.

"You Americans have made the game so bloody mechanical and plodding. You've made these mechanical courses, where all you do is hit the ball from point A to point B. Target golf, aye, they got that name just right. The best of your countrymen have become good golf robots, all swinging the club the same way. You've made us change the way we think about the game. As a result, there's nobody left playing golf in the old Scottish manner: fast and unschooled. Not that long ago, Scottish golf had a style all its own—low, running hooks into the wind; quick, flat, handsy swings; wristy putting; bunker play where you nipped the ball cleanly; putting from twenty yards off the green; bump-and-run shots from anywhere. It was great fun, great sport, to play that way, but it wasn't very efficient. You could be impressive, but it didn't necessarily result in low scores. Of course, for a very long time we didn't care much about scores.

"That is another American thing, this fascination with score, always keeping track with pencil and scorecard. In the Scottish game, the only thing that mattered was your match, and you knew how you stood intuitively. Now you have all these endless first-tee discussions about handicaps and what type of wager to make and where the strokes are to be allocated. Too much."

The telephone rang, and Stark made arrangements for a fishing trip.

"You showed us that there's money in golf. That had never occurred to us. The money has corrupted us, all of us, myself included. Once you start making it, it's a damn cancer, the money is. You start thinking, 'What can I do to make more money?' In my generation, we went into golf with no expectation of wealth. The golf alone sustained us. For years, we resisted thinking of golf as a business. Right through the Second World War, we had clubs with one full-time employee: He gave lessons, made clubs and sold 'em, kept the caddies in line, and mixed the drinks. The game was cheap then: You might have paid five quid for a year's worth of golf, and you got your money's worth. You played after work, until you could see the ball no more. You played every day, except Sunday; the Presbyterians wouldn't hear of golf on Sunday. But you played the six other days, and you hoped for wind to make your game interesting. Scotland was poor, and there was nothing else to do, except the pubs. Golf was the national sport. Everybody played. Your mother played. Golf was the game."

He took a long sip of coffee and stared me down, not a hint of smile on his face. He was sizing me up, trying to figure out if I knew what he was talking about. I was transfixed.

"In 1953, Scottish golf took a mortal blow, when Hogan came to Carnoustie to play in the Open. He had already won the Masters. He had won your Open. If I hadn't witnessed what he did at Carnoustie, I would not have believed it. I was playing in the championship, but I felt we were playing in different tournaments altogether. I remember how he played the sixth hole, a par-5. I was a reasonably long hitter, but I never regarded the hole as reachable in two, because of the fairway bunkers that came into play if you hit a big driver off the tee. I thought you had to play short of the bunkers. We all did. But Hogan showed us we were wrong. He found this little strip of fairway, between the rough and the bunkers, maybe ten yards wide, and he landed his drives on that strip every time, and from there the green could be fetched. Nobody else would have dared such a tee shot. We were amazed. They started calling that little landing zone Hogan's Alley. I had never seen a technique like that before, a technique that could produce long shots that went so straight. None of us had. That was the beginning of the end of Scottish golf, in the classical sense. Hogan was playing a different game. Everybody was fascinated. Everybody became keen to study it. Everybody started thinking about method. What was Hogan's method? How could we achieve the ideal method?

"After Hogan's triumph at Carnoustie—and that is what it was—the shutterbug descended upon golf. Suddenly, there was this fascination with high-speed photography that enabled you to break down the swing into hundreds of stop-action photos. It all seemed so obvious: There was a correct position for everything, at all points in the swing. You just had to match yourself up with the pictures, make sure your angles, or your student's angles, matched the angles in the pictures. The swing, as a whole, was subverted. The important thing was all the hundreds of little movements. Every frame of Hogan showed the perfect position, for that split second."

At this point, Stark produced a pad from a desk drawer and found a pen with the top chewed off and started drawing lines and curves with much more care than the sputtering pen could convey. While he drew, he talked.

"You know that a line, in mathematics, is in fact a series of points? Most people see only the line, but the mathematician can see the points. That's what happened with the golf swing. We teachers became mathematicians, seeing all these bloody points, but we lost track of the line. I was as guilty as anyone. I turned my back on the Scottish game, the game of my youth. A year after Hogan won at Carnoustie, I went to Sweden to teach golf there, and for my seven years there I taught a very technical game. Used photographs all the time. It made great sense to me then, made sense to me for years afterwards. Now I'm not so sure. With all this technical instruction, I don't see people playing better, and I certainly don't see them enjoying their golf more, not at any level. I see them enjoying it less.

I see more frustration and less pleasure. That's what saddens me. If I stand for anything at this point in my life, it's to turn back the hands of time, to see if I can help people to treat golf as a game.

"You come to me and say you want to get better, that you want to take lessons from me, but I wonder if you really need them. You have been doing just the right thing, haven't you: working as a caddie, seeing up close world-class players, the Henry Cottons of your day. This is a very good thing. Think of the players you really admire. Right now, go on and think of them. Think of what makes them special to you. Adopt from them what is useful to yourself."

We again sat in silence for a moment. I thought of Teravainen, how his face got all scrunched up when he was trying to figure out the line of a putt, how hard he would try. I thought of the rhythmic pounding of Ballesteros's swing, a swing that reminded me of the crashing of a mighty Pacific roller.

"Who've you got in mind?" Stark asked.

"Peter Teravainen and Seve," I said.

"Interesting," Stark said. He relit his cigar. "And why do you particularly admire them?" I wanted to answer well; I felt that if I could somehow show Stark that I was a student of the game, that the game was as important to me as it was to him, that I was worthy of his time, that maybe he would take me on. I knew that he would be unlike any other teacher I would find. When he spoke of the mortal blow Hogan had dealt old-school Scottish golf, it was without cynicism or despair. It was with reverence and fascination. It was with the tone Cronkite once reserved for the *Apollo* liftoffs. Through Stark, I felt, I could reincarnate myself as a Scottish golfer. I could have a fresh start.

I struggled to put together the words of my answer. What is it that I particularly admire about Teravainen?

Finally, I answered. "Everything Teravainen has accomplished in the game has come by way of physical effort."

"Yes, that's right, isn't it?" Stark said. "You can see that in his scores. I've followed Teravainen for years—his Finnish name has always interested me—and I see that he is an exceptional par shooter, regardless of the course, regardless of the weather. That tells you that he may lack brilliance, but that he is tough, that he knows how to make par hole after hole, round after round, week after week, year after year. Yes, Teravainen—interesting. And why Ballesteros—what do you particularly admire about him?"

"Ballesteros's game seems to come from inside him," I said. "He seems to produce shots by subconscious force, by will. Seve doesn't seem to be aware of what he is doing, he just does it. He is the opposite of Peter in that."

"Ah, very good, Michael. Yes, will is the thing with Seve. There is no player in his class today. Nick Faldo may be a better player, but Ballesteros is a better golfer. He may be the last of the Scottish players. I could watch him all day. He came here a few days ago to put on an exhibition for the kids. They were fascinated by him, as if he were a magician, which of course he is. He said to one boy, 'I don't like your swing, but I like how your ball goes.' In style he is completely different, but Ballesteros is the first player since Hogan that I have found totally mesmerizing. Good choices, those two. Now what have you learned from Teravainen that you can apply to your game?"

It dawned on me that Stark was giving me a lesson. We were sitting in his office, surrounded by clubs. Though we had none in hand, he was giving me a lesson.

"Peter understands the value of every shot, he understands that all shots count equally," I said. "He never lets up, because he knows that one slipup will fast lead to another. He has this idea, which I think he got from Nicklaus, that when he stands over a shot, he knows it will be the only time in his entire life that he is able to play that shot. After the shot is played, the moment is lost forever. So every shot is important, every shot is once in a lifetime. He feels an obligation to make something of it. At the root of all this effort is great concentration. I very seldom can focus intensely on each shot through eighteen holes."

"Now there's your first mistake, Michael. Don't tell me what you can't do. What's past is prologue. Tell me what you want to do." I nodded; I understood. "You want to do like Teravainen and concentrate on each shot. A worthy goal."

Stark clasped his thick hands behind his head. He was enjoying this discourse, I felt. "Now what about Ballesteros, what did you learn from him that you can apply to your own game?"

"Seve makes the most beautiful swings," I said, "so graceful and powerful. He's fluid, uncluttered. I would love to make swings like that. On the practice tee, you can see he thinks about a lot of technical things, but you don't see that on the course. He seems to be thinking only about the ball and the hole. I would hope someday to have a fluid swing like that."

"You will, when you come to trust yourself," Stark said. "Seve looks uncluttered because he trusts his mechanics. He trusts his mechanics because he knows they're good. He knows they're good because he's had successful results with them in the past." He paused. "Sometimes the game seems so simple."

Stark stood up and walked awkwardly to a window—a damaged and arthritic hip and spine had robbed him of mobility, made sitting in one place for long periods painful, and ended his days of walking eighteen holes. He stayed with the game through teaching, reading, thinking, and talking. He leaned against a window and watched a cold early July rain fall, watched the trees shake. People were playing.

"This rain keeps up, our greens will look like bloody gargoyles," Stark said. He pulled and pressed on different parts of his face to show the softness of the greens and to imitate a gargoyle. In the shop, two or three people were waiting to see him.

"For how long will you be in Scotland?" he asked.

"Through the end of summer," I said.

"That's good, you've given yourself enough time to discover some of our secrets."

My time with Stark was drawing to a close. I gathered my things, happy for our excellent conversation, disappointed that he seemed unwilling to take me on as a pupil.

I was standing in the doorway of his office when he said, "Do you know what I mean when I say *linksland? Linksland* is the old Scottish word for the earth at the end of the sea—tumbling, duney, sandy, covered by beach grasses. When the light hits it, and the breeze sweeps over it, you get every shade of green and brown, and always, in the distance, is the water. The land was long considered worthless, except to the shepherds and their sheep and the rabbits, and to the early golfers. You see, the game comes out of the ocean, just like man himself. Investigate our linksland, Michael, get to know it. I think you'll find it worthwhile. Drop in on your travels. I'll be curious to know what you learn."

We had several more visits in the summer of '91. During one of them, Stark decided to give me something like a conventional lesson. We worked our way from his office to the practice field of the Crieff course, where he was professional emeritus. He handed me an old club, with a brown wooden shaft and a thin grip wrapped with a strip of thin, hardened black leather. The head of the club was shiny and forged, with worn scoring lines. The back of it was stamped with the name and residence of its maker, R. Forgan, St. Andrews. Stark reached into the pocket of his windbreaker and dropped a golf ball at my feet. I picked it up. It was gray, mealy, and small. The dimples were shallow. I could just make out the brand name: Price's Everlasting.

"Here is some equipment from long before your time, long before my own," Stark said. "I want you to see how difficult the game used to be."

The day was gray and cold and blowy, and the practice grounds, off in a field far from the clubhouse, were empty and dark. I took some practice swings with the old R. Forgan mashie Stark had handed to me, but the grip was slippery and I felt myself holding on hard, to prevent the club from flying away.

"Gentle, Michael, gentle. In golf you must always be gentle. Give a good spit into your hands, 'twas the early golf glove," Stark said.

I spat and rubbed my hands until they were sticky.

"Now swing the club, feel the weight of the clubhead, up through the soft wood of the shaft, through the grip, into your hands, and throughout your body. Be aware of the feel of the clubhead. You can feel it more with that old hickory-shafted mashie than with your modern clubs."

I continued taking practice swings, and I started to feel the clubhead and also the softness of the shaft. It was more malleable than any club I had ever swung. I could sense the care and skill that went into the making of the club. I was aware of the club's life. I could feel the mass of the clubhead causing the shaft to bend, and that was a unique sensation for me. My own clubs had stiff shafts, and my unfortunate, largely uncontrollable, lifelong tendency has been to try to swing with all my available might. People have been telling me forever to slow down, but knowing what you need to do and doing it are wholly different things, right?

I made some practice swings that felt good, but I did not delude myself. Swinging at daisies is like playing electric guitar with a tennis racket; if it were that easy, we could all be Jerry Garcia. The ball changes everything. When Stark told me to give the Price's Everlasting a try, I felt myself grow tight. It was time to plug in.

I took a deep breath—an anxiety antidote that John Sifaneck used to prescribe—and I swung fluidly and caught the ball cleanly and well. The mealy ball did not come off the mashie clubface with the zip or pep that it would have off a modern five-iron. Its flight had a floating quality, and the ball landed only 125 yards away.

"Not bad," Stark said. "Try it again." He put another old ball in front of me. "On you go."

An ugly impulse inside me took over. In trying to hit the second ball farther than the first, I swung harder. I hit it the same distance, but thirty yards to the left of the other ball. Stark said nothing, but I knew what he was thinking: I had missed the whole point. With the soft-shafted mashie and the old, soft ball, there was no need for forcefulness. The combination of ball and club were incapable of producing big hits, anyway. Stark just dropped another ball and said, "On you go." I pulled another shot. He dropped another, I pulled another. He dropped yet another, I pulled yet another. This went on for a while.

The setting was out of a dream. I was swinging a beautiful hand-crafted mashie and launching shots into the Scottish wind under the careful eye of a master teacher and to the accompaniment of his pleasing burr. But in golf the pull of one's old habits is terribly strong, and every time I completed a backswing I became overwhelmed with my usual irresistible urge, to hit the ball hard. We switched to a modern five-iron and modern balls, and the results were the same: basically good contact but shots that sailed far off the intended line, most often to the left, occasionally to the right.

"There's nothing terribly wrong with your mechanics," Stark said finally. "But your swing is horrendous." I felt as if I were standing before a judge, and in a sense I was. "Your problems are all about tempo, about timing. In order to feel the proper tempo of a swing, you have to hear the swing. You have to make the sounds that accompany a good shot in order to make a good shot." Stark took the mashie and hit a ball. He had a small hip turn, and, despite a big shoulder turn, he didn't take the club back far at all. He gripped the club as if he were holding the mushy arm of a tiny infant. There was nothing fast about his swing; the clubhead was never a blur. On his downswing, all the moving parts came together at once, not in pieces. The first ball he hit, without a single practice swing, shot off like a rocket, curving gently from right to left and landing ten feet to the right of the stake for which he was aiming.

"Hear the sound the shaft makes as it comes through the air, listen to how rhythmic and sweet that sound is. Hear the sound of the clubhead making good contact with the ball, and then, right afterward, the ground. These are the lovely sounds of good golf.

"Listen to these three swings," Stark said. He made a slow rhythmic swing, and the shaft made a soft, low, schwoo sound as it resisted the air. "That was Sandy Lyle," he said. He made a second, slightly faster swing, which produced a slightly higher-pitched schwoo. "That was Faldo." Then he made a fast, energetic swing that produced an even higher-pitched schwoo. "That was Olazábal," he said.

"There's no one proper sound. The only requirement is that the sound be pleasing."

He made another swing, and I closed my eyes and listened for the sounds of good golf. I heard them. They were lovely sounds. When I opened my eyes, I looked out to the stake and saw his ball fall right near it again. He handed the club back to me. "Try to make nice sounds," he said. "On you go."

Some weeks later, Stark gave me a final lesson. It took the form of a field trip. I put my clubs in the back of his silver Volvo station wagon, and we drove out of the Crieff Golf Club parking lot and onto winding narrow roads and into lush green Scottish summer. Stark didn't tell me where we were headed, and I didn't ask. His demeanor was solemn, though his clothes were not. He wore his white loafers, a white golf shirt, and fire-engine red pants, held up, in a manner of speaking, by a white belt. I had never before seen red pants that bright, and I thought about Teravainen's belief that red is a dangerous and powerful color. Embroidered on the right front pocket of Stark's trousers was the shield of the town of St. Andrews, depicting a robed Saint Andrew, the patron saint of Scotland, carrying the X-shaped cross on which he was crucified.

We drove for a few miles on the main road to Perth and then turned onto a smaller, rougher road. The countryside was undeveloped and magnificent.

"Where we're going, there's magic," Stark said.

I tried to keep up a calm appearance. "Are we going to a golf course?" I asked slowly.

"Yes," Stark said.

I paused, in the manner of Stark. "Have I heard of it?"

"No."

I wondered if he would take one more question.

"What's it called?" I asked.

Stark paused. "Auchnafree," he said. He pronounced the *ch* in the Scots manner, as a soft guttural sound, pushing air from his lungs to the top of his throat and trapping it there for a split second by momentarily lodging the tip of his tongue below his lower teeth. I had been traveling for so long that I had lost the sensation of being abroad, but at that moment I felt keenly aware of being in a foreign land.

We pulled off the secondary road and onto a dirt road, and we drove on for many miles. The land was inhabited only by sheep and rabbits, the air by birds. A river ran parallel to the road. Except for the road, there was no evidence of human life. "This road is an ancient way," Stark said. He pointed with his thick fingers. "That is the River Almond. Years ago, you would have found the wee little houses of the shepherds here. They lived up and down this glen. Before the days of electricity here, if you lived on the banks of the Almond, you were rich. Nobody wants that life today. That life is considered too hard now. Scotland's become civilized." His tone suggested he did not view this development favorably.

Stark pulled off the road and got out. The land was vast and treeless, like a plain. It was covered with vegetation like an English heathland, but there wasn't enough peat or shrubbery on it to be true heathland. For the most part, the land was covered with grass. It was the rich grass of suburban dreams, not the kind of grass you would expect to see in so rugged a setting. If you had grass like that in your backyard, or on the fairways of your home course, you'd be thrilled. With little movements of his big head, Stark looked approvingly at the hills, the sky, the river, the grass. He smiled.

The land, Stark explained, was owned by a man named Sir James Whitaker, who maintained an estate deep in its hills. For many years, the estate had had a shepherd named John Pollock, who had been a close friend of Stark's. Stark pointed to a boulder, onto which a plaque had been bolted. It read:

JOHN POLLOCK
SHEPHERD
1940–1990

"John Pollock was a member of Crieff, but this is where he lived and this was his true home course, in this glen called Auchnafree,"

Stark said. "John was a good player, and he loved the game. Dead only a year now. He had tried to save one of his sheep from drowning in the river, and he drowned himself. He was a strong man, but he didn't know how to swim. I remember at the funeral, his mother did not cry. I won't forget that. She was weeping inside, I'm sure, but she did not cry, the old Scot." For a moment, Stark silently remembered that day, and his friend.

"John Pollock laid out a six-hole course in this glen. He picked a superb spot. This is the finest turf on which I have ever struck a golf ball. We played two tournaments here each year: the Auchnafree Open and the Auchnafree–St. Davids match. I'd captain St. Davids; that's my village. John captained Auchnafree. You'd play the course three times, and between each six you'd go to the river and get out your flask and fix yourself up a wee drink."

The river babbled and sparrows sang. I thought of the sparrows as gulls and the river as a sea, and in that light the geological identity of the land was plain: It was linksland, no question about it. I'm certain Stark saw it that way, too. As he looked about the glen, his pleasure was irrepressible. "I'd like you to play the course," Stark said to me. "It'll be a little rough now, I'm sure; it hasn't been played since John's death.

"We plan to play the Auchnafree Open in the fall. We'll have to cut the greens, but this course needs little from the hand of man. Just some tin cans for holes, and flagsticks. It rains daily in this glen, so the grass is always green. The sheep cut and fertilize the fairways, and they build the bunkers. Natural bunkers, you know? All the sheep want to do is protect themselves from the wind and the cold, and in the process make our game bloody more difficult and bloody more interesting."

The bunkers on Scottish golf courses do not look like the bunkers on American courses, where they are typically shallow depressions filled with fluffy sand. In Scotland, the bunkers have walls and the sand is often coarse. That is how they were at Auchnafree.

I walked past the John Pollock memorial boulder and to the first tee. The tee markers were small rocks, painted white. The flagsticks were not even a yard high and their flags were tattered from years of flapping in the breeze. In their uncut state, the greens were barely distinguishable from the fairways—you had to chip your way to the hole. But it was unforgettable golf. You teed up among the dandelions and the boulder and the harmless piles of sheep dung. The ball flew fantastically well in the air of that glen and sat invitingly on its lively turf. Each hole had a natural design to it. Errant shots sent sheep scattering. The best hole was the last, the sixth, a par-4 of about 330 yards. From an elevated tee, you played for a narrow valley below, and there was little room for error: If you sliced the ball wildly, you'd be on the road or possibly in the river; if you hooked the ball, you'd be on a hill too steep for the sheep, where the grass was unplayable.

Stark had not planned to play; his arthritic hip had been acting up, and he was uncomfortable. But once I began, he joined right in. I felt I should tee the ball for him, as Old Tom Morris had done for the captains of the Royal and Ancient. Stark would have none of that. He grunted and put his peg in the ground, and grunted on his backswing. He was in pain.

My modern clubs seemed ill suited to the setting, but Stark swung them without comment or complaint, and swung them well. His shots made the same pleasing sounds they did when we had our first practice session together. His ball flight had a gentle draw, what he called his Scottish hook. When he hit a poor shot off the third tee, he said, "Another ball, please." He got off his next one beautifully, launching one of Teravainen's old balls into the sweet Auchnafree air.

We barely talked and we didn't keep score, but I know what I made on the last, and I know that Stark knows, too. I walloped a drive, pitched to fifteen feet, and holed my chip with a six-iron— the most satisfying birdie of my life. When the ball went in, Stark called out, "Master!"

I felt intoxicated. Not only because I had made a birdie, and not only because I had had the chance to show my teacher that all his good efforts were not in vain, but because I had come so far. I was thirty-one and newly married in the summer of '91, when I rekindled all the feelings for the game I had had as a boy in high

school. All the clutter that impedes the game in the United States—
the golf carts, the cost, the slow pace, the social trappings—vanished
from memory. Through Stark, I had discovered real golf, and I was
a happy man. Shepherd Pollock was the original golfer, and his
flock's grazing land, Auchnafree, the original links. Pollock was
the pathfinder, the original settler. I had followed in his footsteps.
Stark had taken me to a place where I could shed my former selves
and start anew. Auchnafree was an Eden, a six-hole Eden.

I saw Stark one last time, in our final week in Scotland, in the cathedral town of Dornoch, far to the north. It was September and
autumn was in the air. I had gone to Dornoch to play the ancient
links there, and because Stark was there for something called
Dornoch Golf Week. There was a banquet dinner to mark the conclusion of the week, and Stark was the after-dinner speaker. When
his lips finally stopped moving and he was out of words, he headed
out to his silver Volvo station wagon, wanting to get started on
his long drive home. I walked him to his car. This was my chance
to say thank you.

"You've improved, Michael. You've improved," Stark said. He
was wearing a navy blazer and the tie of the Scottish Golf Union.
"You're golfing within yourself now, and that's magical. But you've
got some Scot in you now, so you can no longer expect to measure
your improvement simply by numbers, aye?"

I can still see his face as he said that, his white hair, his gold
teeth, his blue eyes, ageless and wise.

"Why does the game grip us so, Michael, what do you think
it is?"

He paused. I knew that I was not expected to answer. Somebody walked by us. The crunching noise of gravel underneath
leather shoes built up and then faded away.

"Because it gives us energy, Michael, that's the single best thing
about the game. The better we play, the more energy we get. From
now on, ask yourself, after every round, if you have more energy

than before you began. 'Tis much more important than the score, Michael, much more important than the score."

And he was off.

The memory of that final conversation lingers for me still. I can close my eyes and see John Stark leaning against his Volvo under a fragrant evergreen that stood straight into the final moments of the blue-and-black Dornoch dusk, the wind passing haltingly through the brittle green needles. He had told me to come by his pro shop in Crieff when Christine and I made the drive from Dornoch to Heathrow Airport in London. He said he had a present for me—the old hickory-shafted mashie with which he gave me a lesson. I never made it to Crieff, and I'm glad I didn't. I like knowing there is an old iron, hand forged by a man in St. Andrews named R. Forgan, stuffed in a closet in the back of Stark's cluttered office, waiting for my return.

CHAPTER FIVE

DIGEST (1992–95, PART 1)

CHRISTINE AND I CAME HOME from Scotland and bought a house, in which I wrote a book about our European and Scottish travels called *To the Linksland.* Early in 1992, I went back to *The Inquirer.* I became the Sunday Outdoors columnist (I loved it) and a backup writer on golf and baseball, with a free hand to get other stuff into the paper. With our first child on the way (our second came soon after), I signed up with *Golf Digest* to do some writing on the side. You write for a lot of reasons, and one of them, of course, is to keep your family fed.

In 1994, the magazine sent me to see Michael Murphy, the author of *Golf in the Kingdom.* He had been a supporter of my second book. (The underlying similarities between his great fictional Scottish teaching pro, Shivas Irons, and my real-life John Stark were not totally coincidental. I was looking for my own Shivas Irons. But as personality types, Stark and Irons could not have been more different. Stark was a hyperrealist, and Irons was golf's ultimate dreamer.) I saw Murphy at a writer's confab in Carmel, California. He was at the center of the thing.

Murphy led a dual life. Many people knew him as the cofounder of the Esalen Institute in Big Sur, California, to which thousands journey annually to stir their spirits and stretch their brains. Many others knew him as the author of *Kingdom,* a book with incredible legs. Year after year, Murphy received hundreds of letters about the book. "It turns out," he said, "that golf is mystery school for Republicans."

For a long while, *Golf in the Kingdom* was a cult book among certain yoga practitioners and zen golfers. Bookstores carried the slim book on the philosophy shelf. In time, the book made its way to the sports shelf, and the congregation behind it was now too organized to be a true cult. There was a group called the Shivas Irons Society, "a nonprofit corporation to enhance golf's beauty and virtues," according to a line at the bottom of the official stationery (on recycled paper). The society's president was a spirited, bearded, recovering therapist named Stephen M. Cohen, who had taken his family and his New York brogue to Carmel, in the vicinity of Esalen. Cohen was signing his letters, "In true gravity," borrowing a phrase from Shivas Irons himself; Shivas says a golfer must discover his true gravity if he is to play to his capabilities. That was a life theme for Murphy. He had dedicated years of his life to exploring the limits of human potential.

On the strength of my two obscure golf books, Steve Cohen sent me an "In true gravity" letter and invited me to a society-sponsored three-day writers' confab devoted to "exploring the soul of golf through literature." To my thinking, the attempt to derive high meaning from sport is an excellent route to preciousness, but the itinerary did include golf, Murphy was to be there, I was flattered to be invited, and *Golf Digest* was paying. I went happily.

At the seminar, the subject of *Golf in the Kingdom* the potential movie came up frequently. Clint Eastwood was said to be on the threshold of directing the film version, and *Kingdom* buffs had already been debating for years the appropriate actor for the role of Shivas Irons. Usually, these conversations concluded that Sean Connery would be perfect. I warned Murphy that I had an inspired suggestion for the casting of Shivas. Murphy motioned me to sit, and his electric eyes widened. "Richard Harris," I said, citing the great Irish actor.

"Well, yes, that name's been mentioned often," Murphy said. Shivas was turning into a brand.

Late on the second night, a song called "Magnificence," about the opportunity for disaster or excellence to emerge while playing any shot, was played. As I watched Murphy close his eyes and smile at the earnest lyrics, tapping his fingers against his great forehead, my mind, inexplicably, flashed to certain colleagues of mine at the paper, men who wear T-shirts in the newsroom on hot summer days. The juxtaposition was more than I could take; my laughter came in uncontrollable bursts. Steve Cohen complimented me on my mirth; he said he wanted the conference to be about feelings. He said he wanted us to reveal ourselves.

And to a remarkable degree, we did. Murphy, in a confessional, talked about the twelve years in which he gave up both sex and golf, for religious reasons. (I realized you can tell a lot about a man not only by the way he plays golf, but by the way he talks about it, too.) A golf teacher named Larry Miller, the author of a book called *Holographic Golf,* said, "I propose that most people don't really enjoy the game," and talked about his struggles while playing the tour in the mid-1970s. More than once somebody said, "Good stuff."

The conference included two rounds of golf. Before playing Pebble Beach, we warmed up at the Monterey Peninsula Country Club, where we played the fifteenth hole, a par-3, in the manner of our forebears, with wooden-shafted clubs called barring spoons and ancient feathery balls. I played at Pebble Beach with Miller, and his round of 74 included some wayward shots that he handled with a serenity that must have been unknown to him in the days when he played here in the old Bing Crosby National Pro-Am. Maybe the whole thing was working. Our entire foursome found that all the intense golf talk had brought to the surface our deep feelings for the game. We holed our final putts in the dusk light.

Murphy came in behind us, finishing with a glow-in-the-dark ball. He plays only a few times a year, but I saw a swing that was long and fluid. You could believe that he had once been a four-handicapper. As he came off the green of the home hole of the links he had played all his life, somebody asked him about his round.

"Did I have any metanormal experiences? No," Murphy said. He was in his early sixties then, handsome and vital and energetic. "Did I have a good time? Definitely."

ↁ

I caught up with Sam Snead for a *Golf Digest* story one chilly West Virginia Saturday morning in the spring of 1994. He was wearing a lavender cashmere sweater, and he was weirdly limber, hitting crisp wedge shots on the practice tee of the Greenbrier, the famous golf resort. Several dozen guests, wearing locked grins, were watching the man carefully and silently. Somebody from the resort, introducing Snead, said, "People ask me, 'What does it mean to be golf professional emeritus?' And I tell them, 'It means you can do whatever you want.'"

Those words went under the brim of Snead's straw hat and reached his shaggy ears. Snead looked up and said, "That's not true." The words came out in the antique dialect of the Virginia hills, which turns *wash* into *warsh* and *banjo* into *ban-gee*. Snead's meaning was clear. He was eighty-two years old and twenty-five back-road miles from home. Of course he didn't want to be there, but there he was, the emeritus pro, still teaching. His classmate, Ben Hogan, retreated to the grill room back table early, but Snead never did. He looked like he'd die on a course.

"Eighty-five percent of all bad golfers have bad grips," Snead told the little group, of which I was part. He was holding his wedge in his thick hands, speckled with the purplish tattoos of age. "I don't have any calluses. Tension is the worst thing in golf. Grip the club like you've got a bird in your hands."

I wondered how many times in his life Snead had made that analogy with the bird. A thousand times? Ten thousand times? He came up with that classic grip thought in more agrarian times, when people knew the feel and worth of a bird in the hand. To hear it straight from his mouth, though, I felt as if I had never heard it before.

Snead hit a high, soft wedge shot. His swing was still fluid and rhythmic, the same essential swing, he said, that he used in winning the Bing Crosby Pro-Am in 1937 and the Greensboro Open in 1965 and 160-odd other victories, depending on who's doing the counting. He won everything sooner or later, except the U.S. Open. Then, calling his shot like a pool player lining up the eight ball, he hit a low, piercing wedge shot, the kind of under-the-wind, run-up shot that he must have found useful around the humps and hollows of the Old Course at St. Andrews, where he won the British Open over Bobby Locke and his close friend Johnny Bulla in 1946.

"Any questions?" Snead asked. We all chuckled, as if he had told a joke.

When a young, attractive woman—not dressed for golf, which is rare at the Greenbrier—approached him for an autograph for her father, Snead, a widower, signed with relish. He watched as she climbed uphill on the paved path back to the clubhouse in her short skirt and her tall cowboy boots and said, "I like them boots."

He packed up his clubs and his dog, Meister, a gentle golden retriever with his own seat on the cart Snead drives around the Greenbrier, floored the cart's pedal, and followed the young woman up the path, heading to the clubhouse to have an early lunch. I followed him, on foot. Snead walked down a carpeted hall in his shiny white golf shoes with bold red stripes, striding past pictures of himself: Snead with Arnold Palmer, his successor in many ways; Snead with Gene Tunney, the boxer, taken in 1937; Snead with Ike; Snead with movie stars whose obits ran years ago. He made his way to the dining room and was directed without fuss to a windowless table. A waiter arrived.

"I'll have a coffee," Snead said.

The waiter nodded. Snead winked.

"You know what I mean when I say coffee, Fat Boy, don't you?"

The waiter returned with a coffee in a glass topped by whipped cream, and Snead took a sip and said, "Good, Fat Boy." There was something in it, aside from the whipped cream, that pleased him.

His eyes were tearing in the indoor air. We ordered lunch, and while we waited for our soups and sandwiches, I asked if he enjoyed giving clinics.

"I'd like it more if they paid me more," he said.

I asked him some questions about the pro game. He kept up with it.

"There are a lot of nice young men out there," Snead said, "but they're not as good as they think they are."

I asked him what players he liked. He asked me to name names.

"John Daly."

"He can drive the ball, and he has a nice touch, but the way he brings the club so far back with the short irons, that's crazy. Nobody's ever won consistently doing that. Don't like his language around women, but he's a nice boy."

"Greg Norman."

"Doesn't have an ounce of fat on him."

"Nick Price."

"Can he stay good long with all that tension in his swing?"

"Nick Faldo."

"Overcoached."

"Corey Pavin."

"Now, there's a little bastard who's a good hands player. Doesn't look like much and I wouldn't want his swing, but he might be the best putter on the tour."

"Curtis Strange."

"Won two U.S. Opens moving off the ball on the backswing. Then he starts mucking with his swing. That's like a guy taking a pill having no idea what the pill does. I'd like to take him aside and say, 'Go back to what you were doing.'"

"Have you ever talked to Curtis about the swing?"

"No."

"Do any of the tour players come to see you, to pick your brain about the swing?"

"No," Snead said. "We used to do that all the time. Now they don't. I think they're too scared."

When the food and coffee settled in him, his answers started becoming longer. I was just a body on the other side of the table, another writer writing another profile, but he didn't mind talking. His references were to boxers, baseball players, entertainers, politicians, and capitalists that were yellowed around the edges:

Barney Ross and Joe Louis, Ted Williams and Babe Ruth, Bing Crosby and Jackie Gleason, Richard Nixon and Harry Truman, Malcolm Forbes and Howard Hughes. About the only woman he mentioned was his mother. I asked him to name his favorite course in the world.

"Used to be the Number Two Course at Pinehurst but not anymore," he said. "Not one of the changes they made there is worth a damn."

I asked him about the Masters, which he won three times. He was then the honorary starter, with Byron Nelson.

"I show up on the Monday, and I leave on the Thursday," he said. "I could get two thousand for my pass, if I wanted to."

I asked about Clifford Roberts, the cofounder of Augusta National, who died in 1977. The Augusta police have always said he was a suicide. Snead thought otherwise.

"Some of the colored boys down there," he said, "think he was killed."

Snead was born May 27, 1912, three months before Ben Hogan, three months after Byron Nelson, ten years after Gene Sarazen and Bobby Jones, and forty-nine years after the signing of the Emancipation Proclamation. He grew up in rural, segregated Virginia. He was the youngest of six children; his mother was forty-seven when he arrived.

The Sneads, Virginians of long standing, were poor but never hungry, not even at the height of the Depression, because they could kill or grow nearly anything they needed to eat. They lived in a tiny enclave a few miles up the road from Hot Springs, site of the Greenbrier's competing hotel, the Homestead, where Snead's father worked fixing boilers. Snead lived on a farm where his father and his father's father once lived, and it was on that farm that he first learned to play golf, with homemade clubs. En route to becoming Sam Snead, he traveled the world, but in a sense he never left Hot Springs and his nineteenth-century mother. Sophistication didn't interest him, not a bit. The old-time promoters and newspapermen had a field day painting him as a hillbilly, a backwoodsman, a caricature, and he played right along.

After lunch, Snead hit practice balls for an hour or so. He went through his entire bag twice. His eyesight was poor, and he had a dislocated shoulder—he invited me to touch the shoulder bone protruding through his sweater; it felt weird and pointy. When he stood over the ball, his hands shook. But his swing was amazing: elegant and precise, rhythmic, mesmerizing.

His irons shots didn't go far by his old standards—he was hitting five-irons about 160 yards—but he caught the ball right on the middle of the clubface. His good tee shots went 240 yards. There could not have been a better eighty-two-year-old golfer in the world.

"You still hit the driver pretty far," I said.

"Four years ago I was forty yards farther," he said.

"Did you ever feel it was important to get your left knee behind the ball at the top of the swing?" I asked him as he teed up a ball.

In old swing-sequence pictures of Snead, you can see how much of his power came from his legs. At his prime, he was hugely long. Now his left knee was barely going back at all.

"I've never thought about that," he said.

It was probably a truthful answer. One reason he never became a golfing mystic, like Hogan, was because his approach to the swing was so demystifying. To Snead, the golf swing had all the complexity of humming, and he felt there was a connection between musical talent and golf talent. His golf is earthy. "One of the reasons I like to play barefoot so much is that I feel like my toes are roots just digging down and holding the ground," he wrote in one of his books.

When he was finished with his practice session, he packed up his clubs and his dog, glanced over my way, and said, "You wanting to play tomorrow?" This was certainly no PR move—the story I was writing meant nothing to him. I think he was looking for easy pickings, or maybe just somebody to play with.

I spent the night mangling the sheets. What kind of wager do you make with a man who is one of golf's most legendary gamblers? I wasn't worried about how many strokes he would give me. I figured whether he was generous or frugal with the shots, I'd lose.

My quandary was to determine the maximum amount I'd feel comfortable forking over, knowing I had to offer enough to keep him interested in the match.

"What's your handicap?" he asked me on the first tee. We were playing the Greenbrier's Old White Course, a lovely C. B. Macdonald and Seth Raynor, par-70 design with fast greens and cleverly placed bunkers.

"Twelve," I said.

"I can hardly play to four, the way I'm playing. I'll give you three a side."

I knew six strokes wasn't enough. It didn't matter. I asked him what he wanted to play for.

"What suits you?" he asked, with some kindness, actually.

"How about a straight match for a hundred dollars?" I figured I could put a hundred-dollar loss on my expense account. I worried it would be too low for him, though. But all he said was, "That's fine."

We played from the middle tees. Despite my nerves, I managed to be three up by the time we arrived at the fifth tee, with three pars and a bogey. Snead looked down the fairway and said, in twanged disbelief, "You a *twelve?*" I then sliced my tee shot into the woods, chunked my second out, topped my third, and three putts later he was down by only two, with thirteen holes to go. My true game had found me. After he won the seventh, to go one down, he looked at me earnestly and said, "You trying, boy?"

I despise carts and started the round with a caddie—Snead shared his cart with Meister—but he told me that walking would not do, and I was moved into a cart. We sailed. The other players on Old White simply cleared a path for the pro emeritus. On a somewhat busy Sunday, we got around in well under three hours and played through about a dozen groups.

"Better than a police escort," Snead called out to me as we barreled down another fairway, leaving another foursome in our wake.

Snead drove the ball beautifully—he missed only one fairway— and his approach shots were either on the green or near, although seldom close. We both went out in 40, and I remained one up through fourteen. Then came the fifteenth, a par-3 that played two hundred yards, where Snead, putting sidesaddle, holed a ten-footer for par to level the match. His putt was smack-dab in the center of the cup; he had the chance to seize the game, and he took it. I was a gnat in his ear, and he'd had about enough of me. I felt the leading curve of the Snead steamroller hit me in the back of the legs.

On the sixteenth, a longish par-4 with a pond down the right side, he hit his only truly bad shot of the day, a pushed drive into the water. He played another drive, then an approach shot, then an exquisite chip with a hooded pitching wedge over a bunker off a hardpan lie that nearly went in for a bogey. I felt his heat again. I took two putts for a bogey and was one hole up with two holes to play.

On the seventeenth, a 520-yard par-5, he did it again. He smashed his drive and his second shot and was in front of the green in two. The hole was in the back, and his fifty-yard pitch shot hit a hard spot, skidded over the green, and came to a halt in a lousy, grassy lie. His chip left him with a fifteen-footer for par, which he willed right in.

For fourteen holes, he had made no putts and had chipped indifferently. Now he had made two putts in three holes and had nearly holed a chip. He was showing far more than mere golfing skill. He was showing the toughness he had developed over seven decades of beating nearly every wallet-carrying clown who ever knocked on his door. He was all about winning. I had an uphill six-footer for par, and it was one of my stroke holes. I slipped it in, for five-net-four. "Good putt," Snead said. "That's it."

I had won two and one, two up with one hole to play. Snead had played about as poorly as he could play and shot 80. I had 82— about as well as I could play. We headed to the clubhouse and sat down for lunch. The pro emeritus was in a bad mood. The maitre d' put Snead in a seat with his back toward the dining room. Snead scolded him. "I gotta face out," he said, sneering. "I gotta see what's coming at me." When the waiter finally came, Snead ordered his rum and Coke without any mirth, without any fat-boy jokes. There wasn't much conversation as we waited for lunch. Then, without any warning, Snead slid two crisp fifty-dollar bills across the table. He looked ill.

"Thank you," I said.

"Most of the time I win," he said. "Sometimes you get a day like today."

I tried to thank him for letting me join him.

"I played like crap," he said.

A white-haired man, someone Snead had known for years, ambled up to the table and described laboriously items he wanted Snead to sign. Snead gave the man a hard time.

"He's always having me sign things, for this person and that person and this relative and that one, and I know what he does with it all—he sells it," Snead said when the guy left. "The autograph thing is way out of hand. People send me balls and clubs and pictures they want signed, and half the time they don't leave me any postage. You know how much I spent last year on postage? Six hundred dollars."

We ate quickly, waited a long time for the check. I offered my host a ride home. I'm sure he didn't like needing a chauffeur, but by then it was a fact of life for him. He played the tour when it was a road game; add up all the days, and he spent years behind the steering wheel. Driving to Augusta in 1992, he failed to stop at an intersection and collided with another car, and the driver, a black man of little means, was left a quadriplegic. The resulting lawsuit was settled out of court. Snead's insurers paid the man more than $2 million.

"They tell me that if he was wearing a seat belt, he would've been fine," Snead said. We were now in my rental car, with Meister in the back seat and Snead's clubs in the trunk. The back way from the Greenbrier to Hot Springs, which is the route Snead prefers, is filled with sharp turns and hidden intersections. "Now the poor man can only move his eyeballs," Snead said. "That accident took a lot out of the both of us." His face looked long and deeply sad.

We drove on, up and down the hills, past streams, little farms, tall trees, past kids playing ball in front yards. Snead talked about his family. He had two sons, Samuel Jackson Snead, Jr., then fifty, known as Jackie, and Terrance, then forty-two, who went by Terry.

Jackie was a good amateur golfer and was then a fledgling entrepreneur. He was working with the Greenbrier on the Sam Snead Museum and working on opening more Sam Snead's Taverns, maybe starting a Sam Snead clothing line. Terry had a mental disability. He was able to dress and feed himself but could not live on his own and had not been able to work steadily. He lived with a family near his father, and Snead saw him often. Snead's wife, Audrey, had died several years earlier. They had dated in high school, took their own routes after graduation, and were married in 1940 in a church ceremony witnessed by only two people. For their honeymoon, the newlyweds drove to Niagara Falls, a stop on the way to the Canadian Open, which Snead won.

We arrived at Snead's farm. His house was on a hill, surrounded by cleared land, with the occasional flagstick protruding from a hillside. There were bird feeders and work roads but no cattle nor live crops, not anymore. The house was not twenty years old but looked much older. It was a simple, traditional farmhouse with big windows and airy rooms, without a hint of pretension. Someone had real taste.

We went downstairs, where all of his golf stuff—and there was tons of it—was in a finished basement. There were nearly two dozen Wilson golf bags down there filled with clubs. The walls were lined with pictures, framed magazine covers, awards, and plaques. His hunting and fishing equipment and the trophies from a thousand expeditions were down there, too.

It would be hard to overstate how much Snead knows about the natural world. For years, his preferred method for catching trout was with his bare hands, and this is not lore. "You can catch 'em with your hands if you know how the fish thinks," he told me. It makes you think again about his tip for grip pressure, like there's a bird in your hands. He built his life with his hands. He whittled his early clubs out of tree limbs. When he needed twenty extra yards with a match on the line, he would relax his hands, lighten his grip, lengthen his backswing, and let it rip.

We headed back upstairs. He poured me a glass of Coke. "If you need ice, let me know, but it should be cold enough," he said.

I put down my glass on a coaster.

"This looks like Julius Boros," I said, noticing the face on the coaster.

"That *is* Julius Boros," Snead said.

I'm not sure why he was using Julius Boros coasters—this was shortly before Boros's death—but it was not because he was a sentimentalist. When I asked him about Arnold Palmer, he said, "Arnold's all right." When I asked him if Hogan liked Snead, he said, "Hogan didn't like anybody, except maybe his wife."

When Snead talked about the old days, the natural course of his conversation went not to the romantic wanderlust of the tour in its infancy but to the baby Snead himself, in his infancy. He spoke unabashedly about being nursed by his mother; he recalled nights sitting in with his father and his uncles with a banjo or a trumpet in hand, and his first loops as an eight-year-old caddie, coming home smelling of skunks. His memory was extraordinary. "If it really happened," he said, "I can remember it."

I asked him about his first trip to St. Andrews in 1946, coming in by train, when he looked at the famous links and said, according to the story told forever, "Hey, what's that? Looks like an old, abandoned golf course!"

"Is that really what you said?"

"That's what I said. And the man next to me says,"—for this next part Snead did a Scottish burr—"'Laddie, that 'tis the Auld Course, and that's where we're playin' the championship!'" Which Snead won. When he was asked if he'd return the next year to defend his British Open title, he said, "Hell, no." He figured he'd lost money for his week in St. Andrews. He played golf for money.

It was Sunday afternoon, and Snead turned on the TV to watch the last round of the Greater Greensboro Open. He rooted for every putt to go in, regardless of who was putting. He never commented on the commentator's comments. He never analyzed the swings. He just rooted for putts to go in. When the commercials came on, he wondered if any of them would feature him.

I asked how much he was playing the tour when he recorded his eighth win at Greensboro in '65, at age fifty-two.

"Hardly at all," he answered, reclining in his chair, sipping his Coke. "I hardly played the tour after 1950. I got so mad: I won eleven tournaments in 1950. Hogan won one, and they gave him the Player of the Year. After that, I just said to hell with it."

"I guess they gave it to him for winning the Open," I said. That was the year Hogan returned to golf from his near-fatal car crash and won the U.S. Open in a playoff at Merion.

"It's still just one tournament," Snead said. "If I had shot last-round 69s, I would've won the Open nine times!"

I had the feeling he was still mad at himself for shooting 80 earlier in the day, and maybe a little depressed, too. There's the siren of mortality in fading golf skills. "I've had a good life," he said. "The only thing I didn't do was win the Open."

I looked at his bald head, realizing that I'd never seen him before without a hat on. His eyes were fixed on a commercial. It was time for me to go. I bade Sam Snead goodbye, insisting that he not get up, but he did anyway.

On my way back, I dropped in at the Sam Snead's Tavern in town. The golf tournament was on at the TV bar. The winner had just received a big check, more money for a week than Snead won in his best four years combined. Nobody at the bar was watching. I imagined Snead as I had left him back at the house—the TV remote in one hand, petting his dog with the other, watching golf with a placid, enigmatic expression on his long face.

On the drive home, I remembered a conversation from earlier in the day. A man had wanted to know Meister's age.

"He's twelve," Snead said.

"That's 'bout seventy people-years," the man said. "Dog looks older than you, Sam."

"Yeah, well," the old pro said. "Don't know how he feels."

Snead's line about his Masters badge—that he could sell it for $2,000—was a telling thing. Every year, the demand for Masters badges went up, and in the Roaring Nineties, there was an out-

and-out frenzy for getting to play the Augusta National course. It was news when two longtime Augusta National members were forced to leave the club. One, Peter A. Franklin, Sr., the son of a founding member, was said to be hosting too many foreign clients with whom he had no natural social connection. The case of W. L. McCrary III, the grandson of a founding member, was more involved. It pleased me when in 1995 *Golf Digest* asked me to look into it. I love a good mystery.

The McCrary case began in the early 1990s, when a young Englishman named Marc C. Wilson arranged to attend the Masters. He was smitten. To Wilson, who described himself to me as a wheeler-dealer, the Augusta National Golf Club was heaven. He loved its commitment to perfection and its whiff of money. Before long, he was a regular in Augusta, an old Georgia city where the haves and have-nots are obvious.

Wilson was an outgoing and handsome man with shiny black hair. He spent his evenings in Augusta at a restaurant called the Word of Mouth Café. He joined an Augusta country club, West Lake, connected to a fancy development. He made friends, in golf and out of golf. He started an informal Augusta branch of his London travel and promotions business, capitalizing on his Augusta connections to bring groups of well-heeled tourists to the Masters, securing the elusive tournament badges for his clients and putting them up in a luxurious inn, the Perrin Guest House. Wilson, who was thirty-seven when I was dogging him, got to be on a first-name basis with many prominent Augustans. He befriended local Augusta National members and played the course more often than many out-of-town members. On May 16, 1993, he made a hole in one on the sixth, with a five-iron, from 170 yards. His only disappointment was that his host and friend, W. L. "Larry" McCrary III, momentarily distracted, didn't see the shot.

Over the years, McCrary had seen many moments of golfing excellence at Augusta National. He had been around the course for six decades, practically his entire life and the club's entire life. His maternal grandfather, Fielding Wallace, was a founding member of the club and, in 1948 and 1949, president of the USGA.

McCrary's father, an Augusta businessman named W. L. "Pete" McCrary, Jr., was a member of the club, too, joining in the days when Augusta National emphasized familial ties over corporate achievement. As a young man, Larry McCrary was invited to join. This was in the middle of Clifford Roberts's long reign as chairman.

For Roberts, choosing McCrary for membership was natural, because his bloodlines were excellent and so was his game. As a teenager, McCrary had been a leading junior golfer in Georgia, although not as good as his friend and contemporary Doug Sanders. When he was in his twenties and thirties, and even in his forties, McCrary represented Augusta National well in Georgia amateur events. He was also a member of the Augusta Country Club, the city's social center for his class of Augustans. He and his wife, a former president of the Augusta Junior League, were solid citizens. In time, McCrary took over the family concern, an oil-products distribution company based in Augusta called Phoenix Oil, from his father. But business was never Larry McCrary's abiding interest. His love was golf—and Augusta National.

Then Marc Wilson came into Larry McCrary's life. Wilson entered McCrary's closeted world at a time when the native Augustan, with the lilting accent and the easygoing demeanor, was sorting out his personal problems. He was still coming to terms with an operation he had had sixteen years earlier, to remove a benign cranial tumor. The successful surgery had not affected his ability to reason, but it had affected his coordination, and McCrary's handicap had climbed from scratch to nearly ten. Then, in 1989, his son Robert L. McCrary, a lawn maintenance man, died. In that same period, McCrary sold Phoenix Oil to a fellow Augusta National member. McCrary had always played often, but now he started playing nearly daily during the club's eight-month season.

At Augusta National, there were people who thought Larry McCrary was loud. There were people who found irritating his complaints about shots he once could make. There were people who felt he played too much golf, for part of the unwritten code of the club is that members will use their hallowed links with discretion. Despite these judgments, nobody looked upon Larry McCrary harshly, not when they took full measure of the man, for they knew there had been hardship in his life. In the main, people thought of him as a nice guy who liked people and wanted people to like him.

Marc Wilson, skillful at cultivating useful relationships, recognized these qualities in McCrary's personality, and their friendship quickly blossomed. "He treated me as a second son, or a third son," Wilson said. Wilson brought McCrary to the Word of Mouth Cafe, and McCrary brought Wilson to the National. Before long, McCrary was playing golf at Augusta National with Wilson's clients, and Wilson made McCrary an associate director of his company, a position Wilson described as honorary. Over the course of two years, Wilson said he arranged for about two dozen people to play Augusta National with McCrary, clients who were not strangers to McCrary by the time they reached the first tee, for they had always shared at least a meal together first. After the golf dates, McCrary would send a bill to Wilson, for the green fees and caddie fees and meals and drinks, and Wilson would reimburse McCrary by check.

In March of 1993, Wilson was flying from London to Atlanta in the first-class section of a Delta flight when he met Robin Montgomery, a flight attendant from Tallahassee, Florida, whom he later married. Wilson moved into Montgomery's elegant home in Tallahassee and began running his business, Marc Wilson International, from there. In January of 1994, he invited a group of prospective clients to the Golden Eagle Country Club, a Tallahassee club he had joined, to watch a videotape about the British Isles and to hear about his golf packages. Roughly a dozen people showed up. Kenny Knox, then a regular player on the PGA Tour and a Tallahassee resident, was there. So was Flecia Braswell, a social columnist for *The Tallahassee Democrat*.

At least five people there, including Knox and Braswell, told me they recalled hearing Wilson mention Augusta National as he discussed his golf packages. On that night, when the videotape was over and little cocktail-sipping groups had formed, Braswell approached Wilson, notebook in hand. She asked him, she told me, to clarify his reference to Augusta National, because she knew a day at Augusta was the ultimate prize for many golfers. Wilson, Braswell said, told her he could get people on the course.

Braswell mentioned Wilson's little midwinter get-together in her column for January 13, 1994. One sentence read, "Last week Wilson gave a small group of mostly Golden Eagle Country Club members a preview of his golfing packages, which include access to play at Augusta National." A woman in Tallahassee was surprised when her eyes rolled across the mention of Augusta in the "Around Town" column. The woman had grown up in Augusta, and her father, an Augusta National member, still lived there. She knew the club would be disturbed to learn that a nonmember was boasting about access to Augusta National, particularly since it seemed connected to the nonmember's business. The woman called her father and told him about Marc Wilson.

The father of the woman—she asked me not to identify her—called James Armstrong, Jr., the club's general manager, and an in-club investigation ensued. At one point, Wilson said, he received a telephone call he subsequently realized might have been part of the investigation. By his account, a caller asked if he could get a player on Augusta National, and Wilson "with a bit of British humor, said, 'Oh, sure, what do you want to pay, $10,000?'" Wilson said he was never paid to arrange for a person to play Augusta National. Others familiar with the interior politics of Augusta National said they believe he was paid in the vicinity of $5,000 per player, per day. When Wilson learned that Augusta officials were aware of the item in *The Democrat,* he called Braswell and demanded a retraction, maintaining that she got her facts wrong. Braswell went to an editor and said she was certain the item was correct. She cited her husband as a witness. No retraction was printed.

As the investigation continued, Larry McCrary told friends and club officials he had never been paid to sponsor guests. He was told in response that he had violated the spirit of the club's rules through his relationship with Wilson and Wilson's clients. By April of 1994, three months after the tiny newspaper item appeared, W. L. McCrary III, a grandson of a founder, was no longer a member of the Augusta National Golf Club. He was forced to resign.

When I asked McCrary to describe his situation at Augusta National, he said, "I'm not at liberty to discuss it." People who know McCrary said his ousting from the club devastated him. Wilson wrote a letter to Jackson T. Stephens, Augusta's chairman, stating that McCrary never accepted any money to bring Wilson's clients on the course. Wilson announced his availability to be interviewed by the club on the subject. He never received a response.

Wilson also wrote to Larry McCrary. "I said I hope some day in the future we can sit down and have a drink together," he told me. Why he spoke to me, I do not know. I guess he figured he could make a better case for himself than anybody else could. His letter to McCrary also went unanswered. "I am sure he has a tremendous amount of bitterness toward me because people point to me as the guy who got him kicked out of Augusta National," Wilson said. "I've lost a dear, dear friend. I have to live with it and don't like it."

Wilson had just returned home from a golf game. I had been waiting for him in a rented car in front of his house. As he entered his house, this is what he was wearing: a sweater with an Augusta National logo on top of a vest with an Augusta National logo on top of a shirt with an Augusta National logo. Right about then, that logo was all powerful, better even than the one with the polo player. It was all about class and associating yourself with class. I swore off shirts with logos and typed up my report.

CHAPTER SIX

SNAPPERS (1992–95, PART 2)

YOGI KEPT PEERING UNCOMFORTABLY into his golf bag, strapped to the back of a gas-powered cart. The bag was filled with woods, and the Hall of Fame catcher, with doubt.

The great Yogi Berra, who played in fourteen World Series, who brought both the Mets and the Yankees to the World Series as a manager—the man who added whole phrases to our lexicon—was having a lousy day on the links, and for good or for bad I was there to record what he did for *The Inquirer*. He was playing in something called the Mike Schmidt Pro-Celebrity Challenge, at a course called Commonwealth National Country Club, out in the far Philadelphia suburbs. It was a Special Olympics fundraiser, and it was all very fancy.

Through fifteen holes, he had made one par, on a little par-3, and two bogeys. The rest were Xs. By the time he was on the tee of the sixteenth hole, a longish par-4 requiring a 160-yard carry over buggy marshland to start, he had already been playing for five hours.

"How am I gonna get over this?" he asked his two playing partners, both young pros. He searched through his bag for a scuffed-up ball, one he could lose without remorse.

You can put a baseball man in golf duds, but you cannot take a half century of baseball out of his golf swing.

Berra—who broke into baseball with the New York Yankees in the baggy-flannel era, and who finished, as a coach, wearing the garish colors and synthetic jerseys of the Houston Astros—looked marvelous. He wore white-and-black saddle-style golf shoes, teal blue pants, a white shirt from the Lahinch Golf Club in Ireland, a thick gold necklace, shaded prescription glasses, and a woven white cowboy hat. His look said, "I'm a golfer, man." Mike Schmidt, Michael Jordan, Julius Erving, good golfers all, were dressed pretty much the same way.

Berra slipped a driver out of his bag (leaving behind five other woods), put his ball on the tee, and launched a swing. Immediately, you were reminded of baseball Yogi, the lefthanded-hitting low-ball-loving powerhouse. He drove as a righty and putted as a lefty and began his backswing by collapsing both elbows. (Snead did not teach such a move.) The deeper he got into his backswing, the more crouched his stance became. You could almost hear him thinking, "Gimme something I can pull." By the time he made contact with the ball, his left foot had moved about a half yard ahead of its original position, and his entire body was facing the target. In other words, he was a slicer.

He was poor with the irons, and his driving was worse. During his round, the course superintendent—in Scotland, they're called greenkeepers—went up to him and asked, "How are the fairways?" The guy was fishing for a compliment. The fairways were beautiful, emerald carpets.

"Tight," Berra said.

The man is a genius.

Every slicer knows that some slices are better than others, and his slice off the sixteenth was a relative beauty, 170 yards long and finishing in the fairway grass of the too-tight sixteenth fairway. His fans loved it.

"Go, Yog!"

"Yogmeister!"

"You got all of that one, Yo-gee!"

He smiled wryly, signed a dozen more autographs, and plopped down on the cushioned seat of his cart. Somebody handed him a baseball to sign, and he gripped it as if he had been born with a baseball in his hand.

"Good one, Yogi," a marshal said of the drive, his best of the day.

"For me, anyway," Berra said truthfully.

"Tough course, huh, Yogi?" a spectator said.

"For me it is."

"You enjoying yourself?"

This one he considered before responding.

"Thing is, it's for a good cause, so that makes it worthwhile," he said.

It was the same as Snead, standing up when I bade him goodbye: manners from another generation.

Yogi Berra pressed down on the cart's accelerator and rumbled off.

⚑

That same summer, I wrote about a young golf course architect, Tom Doak, for the paper. Even in the early 1990s, when he was in his early thirties, Doak was considered one of the leaders of the modern minimalist movement in his business. He was almost like a star academician. But I saw somebody else: a skinny guy stand-ing on a hill in the Pennsylvania countryside that would become a fairway, trying to build his first private course, to be called Stone-wall, trying to get out of theory and into practice. He could talk the whole course. It was clear that he saw it in his mind. The trick, of course, was to build it. He knew that if Stonewall turned out to be conventional or uninteresting, it would likely take years for his career to recover, no matter how much ink he got from national magazines about being the father of the modern course-design minimalist movement.

Doak came to the Stonewall landowners at the suggestion of Ben Crenshaw, who had written an introduction for Doak's first book, a treatise called *The Anatomy of a Golf Course.* Doak was an egghead architect. But now he had a plum assignment, even if it did turn his life upside down. He had moved, with his wife and infant son, from their home in Traverse City, Michigan, to a rented townhouse near the course. On days off, he would travel all over Philadelphia to look at classic golf courses, or he would drive to Long Island or fly to North Carolina to consult on other projects.

Doak motioned for the bulldozer operator to come over. He was not pleased with the contour of a particular tee and fairway; from the tee, he could not see the bottom of the flagstick. "You can do it that way, but it ain't ideal," he said, trying to sound working class.

He was fooling nobody. After his freshman year at MIT, Doak transferred to Cornell (the alma mater of Robert Trent Jones) to enroll in its landscape architecture program. He became interested in golf course architecture when he was fifteen, during a trip with his father to Cypress Point, the celebrated Alister Mackenzie course on the Monterey Peninsula in northern California.

"What I realized was that you could take a beautiful piece of land, put a golf course on it, and make the land be more beautiful," Doak told me. Mackenzie, a Scottish-born physician who gave up medicine for course design, became a hero to Doak, as did other great architects, most notably Charles Blair Macdonald, A. W. Tillinghast, and George Thomas, all long dead.

During his Cornell years, Doak spent a year in the British Isles, working as a caddie at the Old Course in St. Andrews. "One day I was caddying at the Old Course for young girls, sisters, both beginning golfers," he said. "They were good athletes, and their parents had showed them something about the game, but they were beginners. They could get around the Old Course. They could play it. They could enjoy it. That left a lasting impression on me."

He practiced what he preached, and over time, year by year, course by course, he became a big-name architect. But when I first met him, there was no way to know which way his career would go. What you could tell was that he was iconoclastic, that he had a vision, and that while he needed to pay his bills, he wasn't pursuing golf course design as some sort of get-rich scheme. He was the work and the work was him.

⚑

I'm pretty sure Doak never made it to one of my favorite little golf courses. The course is off a country lane in a little Pennsylvania hamlet called Birdsboro, midway between Pottstown and Reading, an old and peculiar nine-hole public golf course called Green Hills. The course was commissioned by a Latvian-born, Prohibition-era beer brewer, had the kind of classical Scottish-inspired design lines that Doak would have appreciated, and was maintained nearly in the manner of a nineteenth-century links. You could travel far and wide and not find a more distinctive golfing environment.

Even in the early 1990s, the all-day green fee was eleven dollars. The maintenance crew consisted of two middle-aged men who watered the beautiful bent-grass greens and hoped for rain for everything else. The course was seldom crowded, and play was fast. Shirts were not required, at least not for male golfers. An odd local rule allowed for relief from . . . trees. If a tree was in your way, you could move your ball.

"We're pretty much lenient with the rules here," said Fred Nonnemaker, who ran the course with a partner, Hughie McCullough. (They were also the maintenance crew.) "We want people to have a good time. Nobody here's going to make it to the tour. What would you rather tell your friend, that you shot 88—or 78?"

The course record was set by a Green Hills regular, Herman Fry, a paint-plant worker who was the 1974 Philadelphia Amateur champion. Since the course record is 60, you might have the idea that par for the course is 65, or that it measures only 5,500 yards. Not so. Playing each hole twice, and using a different set of tees for each nine, the course measures 6,355 yards, and par was

72. In his historic round, Fry went out in 27 and came back in 33. He had an eight-foot birdie putt on the eighteenth for a 59, but the putt lipped out.

The home hole, Fry's nemesis, was pretty good, a 425-yard par-4, with a downhill tee shot and an uphill second shot to a putting lawn that was carved into the face of a hill, a little shelf of green, protected by bunkers and mounds and rough. An old-fashioned, rugged hole, the type of hole, I knew from my linksland travels, you find commonly in Scotland but seldom on public courses in the United States.

Green Hills was designed by Robert White, who was born in St. Andrews in 1874 and came to the United States twenty years later, a member of the first generation of Scots who helped spread word of the game in this country. He was the first president of the PGA of America, and he designed courses for, among many others, the Skytop Club in the Poconos, the Manasquan River Golf & Country Club in New Jersey, and the Berkleigh Country Club in Reading.

It was through Berkleigh that White came to the attention of the Hassel brothers, Max, Morris, and Calvin. The Hassels escaped from the pogroms in Latvia around 1903 and thirty years later were rich enough to build a country estate in Birdsboro: a big house, surrounded by riding stables, a trout pond, a tennis court, and a swimming pool. They were the Roaring Twenties. Max, according to family members, was the leading Prohibition beer brewer in the country; Morris was a real estate mogul; and Calvin was keeper of the estate. The brothers figured that a private nine-hole course, for use just by family and friends, would make the retreat complete. The Hassels—the name has remained prominent in Reading philanthropic circles, particularly at Kesher Zion Synagogue—prized privacy. "Old-timers used to say that the caddies carried a bag over one shoulder and a machine gun over the other," Herman Fry, the course record holder, told me.

In 1933, Max Hassel was killed, reportedly by Prohibition-era enemies, and about five years later, the surviving brothers began leasing the course to operators and opening it to the public, while maintaining the rest of the estate for themselves. Today the course is owned by Hassel family heirs, but otherwise the setup is the same.

"Our position is just to maintain it," Sarle Cohen, an internist and a Hassel heir, told me. She owned the course, with two cousins. "We're not interested in developing it," she said, referring to both housing developments and the occasional query about expanding the course to eighteen holes. "The whole property has some emotional value to me."

Except for the greens, the course has been in poor condition when I've been there. "It's really pretty close to a dump now," one golfer there, a retired accountant who had caddied at Green Hills in the late 1930s, told me. "It's obvious from the way the greens are positioned that there was some thought behind the design. And through 1960 it was pretty well maintained. But when the carts came, on that sandy soil, the course couldn't take it."

Herman Fry said he plays the course mostly in the spring, before it gets baked out. He often imagines the changes he would make at Green Hills if money were no obstacle. "You have to use your imagination when you look at Green Hills," he said. "You use your imagination, you could have a great course." Doak would get that, completely. Given the chance to rework the course, he might do something about the free drops from the trees. In the meantime, the club has its own style. Years after I first played it, the outgoing message on the club's voice mail said, "If you want to come out, that's fine." They had a special deal going: ten dollars, all day, walking.

⚑

One spring day in 1993, I covered ethnic conflict for the paper, out in the suburbs. Forty-five male golfers of Irish descent were playing forty-five male golfers of Italian descent at the Rolling Green Golf Club.

Before the competition began, the Italians received a mock papal blessing and were revved up by the chants of ten cheerleaders. It was not enough. The Irish beat the Italians, 78–63, to win the Joseph Caruso Memorial Trophy and a free dinner. That made the tally Irish 11, Italians 6, with one tie.

The opening fire came at high noon. Each member of the Italian team was issued a shirt with a depiction of the *Nina*, the *Pinta*, and the *Santa Maria* emblazoned on its chest. Then came the cheerleaders, employees of Tony Iacobucci, captain of the Italian team and co-owner of a large construction company. "The Irish got the muscle," went one cheer, "the Italians got the brains." Next, a jeep chugged up the club's driveway. Standing in its back was Joe Syernick—a man of Polish descent but with longtime links to the Italian team—dressed in a papal gown, carrying pink carnations and a container of holy water. "All right, team," he said, sprinkling water on his listeners. "Go out there and rock 'n' roll. Win for the Pope!"

Jack McGuinn, captain of the Irish team, stood beside the scoreboard, where the names of Irish players appeared in green marker and the names of the Italians in red. His lips were pursed and his arms were folded over his chest, which was covered by a green sweater from Ballybunion, the sublime Irish links. McGuinn saved his energy for the course, one of the best and most difficult in the Philadelphia district. He defeated his opponent, Amadeo Mascitti. His partner, Fran Dunphy, the Penn basketball coach, halved his opponent, Frank Sbandi.

The Irish-Italian golf competition was started by McGuinn and Iacobucci to encourage ethnic social intercourse at the club. Rolling Green was founded by Philadelphia Quakers in 1926, but over the years it had become, as far as I could tell, the most socially, economically, and ethnically diverse private club in the Philadelphia suburbs, at least of the clubs with really good courses.

When the golf was over and the Irish had won again, the players sat together for dinner in the clubhouse dining room. You could see maps of Europe in their eyes and in the shapes of their noses and the slopes of their foreheads, in their demeanor and in their language. These sons of West Philadelphia and South Philadelphia, these grandsons of Europe, sang "Danny Boy" and "O Sole Mio," emptied their beer bottles and their wine glasses, shook hands, and went home.

Y

One of the great oddities of the Philadelphia golf scene is the love of snapper soup. You see it on nearly every clubhouse menu in Philadelphia and at some of the old-timey restaurants in Center City, but that's really it. I used to enjoy it, when I thought it came from snapper, the fish. Then I learned more. I hung out with a snapper trapper for a day and saw how the turtles live and what they live on. "They're nasty animals, but they make a great soup," Tommy Zander, my snapper trapper source, told me. They've been known to bite off fingers.

Each May, young Zander's thoughts turned to snappers. (The rest of the year, his thoughts went to muskrats, crabs, clams, and bluefish.) I watched him set his snapper nets at high tide in a New Jersey creek. He placed pieces of oily fish—carp and mackerel— and also sardine cans punched with nail holes, in each trap. Snappers love oil. Zander was averaging one turtle per trap each day. His turtles averaged about ten pounds each, little shrimps compared to the sixty-pounders you could find in Maine, but they were considered sweet. The Philadelphia country club chefs wanted the little ones for their soup eaters.

I couldn't find anyone who could tell me why Philadelphia golfers were so enamored of snapper soup. Richard Bookbinder, a famous Philadelphia restaurateur, told me that snapper soup had been considered a local specialty for at least a century, but why he did not know. He also told me that I was not alone, that he knew of many people who did not realize they were eating turtle, and not fish, for their soup course until it was too late.

The whole world knows about New England clam chowder but not snapper soup. The peculiar Philadelphia golf scene, which became only more intriguing for me as time passed, had that market, and that dish, cornered and covered.

In 1990—nineteen-*ninety*!—there was an uproar in golf because of integration issues. Several months before the PGA Championship was to be held at the Shoal Creek Country Club, in Birmingham, Alabama, the man who owned the course said that while his club had ethnic members of nearly every kind, it didn't have any black members because "that's just not done in Birmingham." That comment—and everything it implied—set off a maelstrom. People were tempted to say the comment was just a vestige of the old Deep South, like Sam Snead's use of the word *coloreds*. But if your eyes and ears were open, you knew it was much more than that. Private-club golf across the country was all but closed to blacks. The game, at that level, was a bastion of institutional racism. The United States Golf Association, the Professional Golfers Association of America, and the PGA Tour were shamed into creating bylaws that required clubs that wanted to host events to demonstrate open admission policies. The Aronimink Golf Club, outside Philadelphia, was scheduled to have the 1993 PGA Championship, but the club refused to be pressured by the new rules into accepting its first black member. The word from the club was that a black member would be accepted when a black candidate for admission went through the same vetting process as any other candidate. The club lost the tournament.

Later, when the spotlight was off, the club took its first black member, a man named Ken Hill. He was the first black member of any of the prominent Philadelphia-area clubs. In the early 1990s, my club, Philadelphia Cricket, had a superb course, a beautiful pool, grass tennis courts—and, as far as I could tell, no black members, no Asian members, and a handful of Jewish members. The reason for this, some people said, was not racism, but something even harder to get your hands around: how people socialize. In truth, the two are intertwined, racism and how we socialize.

Two years into his Aronimink membership, I looked up Ken Hill. He told me over a lunch that his fellow members were exceedingly courteous, but he looked forward to the day he was not the club's lone black member.

"It'd be naive to say the club doesn't have a history of prejudice," Hill said. "But all I can go on is how people there treat me, and I've been treated very nicely."

So Kenneth D. Hill, vice president for community relations at Sun, the oil company, was making a little social history in Philadelphia. He was put up for membership by his boss, the chairman and chief executive officer of Sun, Robert Campbell.

"I wasn't pushing the club," Campbell told me. "I didn't perceive it as any sort of test. I proposed Ken for membership because he enjoys golf, because it would be useful to him in a business context, and because he's a very nice man with a very nice family. I put his name forward the way I have other Sun executives over the years."

The only thing that made his candidacy extraordinary was that he was black, the son of a chauffeur and a maid. Hill felt that had he been a white man with his career, club memberships would have been suggested to him decades earlier.

"At a certain point in corporate life, it's an expected privilege," he said. "I've had positions where I've had subordinates who have had club memberships, paid for by the company, as perks of their positions when I didn't have one." Of course, the whole Shoal Creek brouhaha—which started as a quote in a newspaper—had something to do with why Campbell put Hill up for membership, and something to do with why he took it.

"I like golf, I play at it, but I'm not a dyed-in-the-wool golfer," Hill said. He was a large man, overwhelming the small chair in which he sat. He already had places to play tennis, his main sport, and he belonged to a black ski club, the Blazers. He was busy without a country club in his life. Still, he went through with his application.

"I knew I'd be known as the club's first black member," he said. "You have to have a first before you can get to the point where people make no fuss over black members."

Ken Hill said he knew plenty of black executives who had a keen interest in golf, had six-figure incomes, and wanted to join a golf club, regardless of its history. But they don't, he said, know how the cryptic membership game is played. They don't know, he said, that to join a club you can never appear too eager, especially when being casually interviewed by admissions committee members over cocktails, and that the unspoken code of conduct of country club life is never to say anything too personal.

"The country club is not part of real life," Hill said. "For somebody who's the first in his family with a college education or the first in his family to get beyond working class, the country club is totally foreign. It can be very intimidating."

He told me about the day when he was a guest at a club, and a member said to him, "My shoes are over by my locker." To which Hill responded, "I'll do your shoes if you'll do mine."

"Racism is at the core of our essence," he said. "It's in everything that we do, but it's in degrees. We have to start from where we are today and move on. The real test will be what happens in the years to come. Will there be more black members? Will I be able to go to the club and be myself? "Once, I was at Merion," Hill said, referring to the elite Main Line course I love. "I was sipping a gin and tonic, wearing my blue blazer, sitting on the veranda, and I thought of the times my father made deliveries to the various exclusive Main Line clubs, and I was thinking, 'If he could see me now, he'd be doing cartwheels.'

"It was a courageous move on their part," he said of his acceptance. "I'm sure there are people there who are glad I'm in, and I'm sure that there are people who say, 'What's he doing here?' The only thing you can really judge people on is their behavior, and everybody's been very nice. I wouldn't have a family reunion dinner there. I don't think I'd be comfortable bringing out an all-black foursome. Not yet, anyway. But I think that day is coming."

Maybe the most peculiar person I know in all of golf—I mean that as high praise—is Howdy Giles, a dentist in Wilmington, Delaware. He's no ordinary dentist. He was a USGA committee-man, a position normally reserved for lawyers and bankers and the scions of old-line families, and he is a member of two of the great golf clubs in the world, Pine Valley, in New Jersey, and the Royal and Ancient Golf Club, in St. Andrews. Golf has taken him to cocktail parties with Bob Hope and to dinners with Jack Lemmon. He's had many visits with Jack Nicklaus. On one oc-casion, he walked eighteen holes with George H. W. Bush, when he was president, and documented the day with 220 photographs. Howdy likes to credit one of his patients, Arnold Palmer, with all his golfing riches. But really, it's all Giles. He just makes it look like it's all Palmer.

Howdy has a ball marker made from one of Palmer's old gold fillings—because he asked for it. Behind the bar in his finished basement is a life-size cardboard cutout of Palmer—because he made it. Most of the flat surfaces of his house are dedicated to Palmer memorabilia—Palmer visors, clubs, photos, golf gloves, magazine covers, books, golf balls, letters, scorecards—because he collects them. "His house is done in Early, Middle, and Late Palmer," Doc Griffin, Palmer's longtime aide-de-camp, once told me.

When I first met Giles around 1987, he was not yet fifty, with beautiful teeth and a buoyant manner. He was a member of three golf clubs owned by Palmer—Bay Hill, Isleworth, and Latrobe. He bought his Cadillacs from car dealerships owned by Palmer. His personal stationery had a faded image of Palmer in its center. There were giant photographs of Palmer on the walls of a Wilmington restaurant, Stanley's, of which Giles was an owner. When Giles's two daughters were looking at colleges, they visited many schools. "We never pushed them; we just hoped," Howdy said, speaking also for his wife, Carolyn. Both daughters went to Wake Forest, Palmer's alma mater.

His memory of the times his life has intersected with Palmer's is extraordinary. The first time he played golf with Palmer at Giles's home course, Wilmington Country Club, was on May 22, 1976. "Sixteenth hole, par 5, 603 yards," Howdy said, recreating the day in his mind. "The caddie bets Arnie that he can't get home in 2. The bet is for a beer. Arnie hits driver, driver, chips in with a sand wedge from fifteen yards off the green for a 3. Gets a six-pack for the caddie and signs the cans. Budweiser. Shoots 67. Amazing. My idol comes to Wilmington to play golf and have his teeth checked. He stays at our house, and I drive him to the airport. As he flew off in his jet, I had tears in my eyes."

Once, when Palmer played golf with the first President Bush, he made arrangements for Giles to accompany them. "Arnie said, 'Mr. President, I want you to meet Howdy Giles, my dentist, my photographer, and my good friend.' And the president said, 'Oh, sure, we were talking about you at dinner last night.'" Giles developed his manic interest in the golfing legend while going to dental school at Temple University, in the heart of black North Philadelphia, in the mid-1960s, when Palmer was at the height of his powers. Carolyn Boddorff, then Howdy's fiancée and now his wife, gave him a set of Arnold Palmer clubs. Soon after, he started buying all his clothes from the Arnold Palmer line at the famous Philadelphia department store Wanamakers. Some of his fellow students had a field day with him.

"They'd say, 'Hey, what's with all the Palmer gear?'" Giles recalled. "But who has the last laugh now?"

Exactly.

I asked Howdy what was so appealing about Palmer to him. He struggled to answer but then came up with this: "Somebody once told me that they thought Arnold Palmer had grace, and I think that's an excellent word."

Giles first met Palmer when he attended the Masters each April in the late 1960s. In the mid-1970s, when he joined Bay Hill, Giles got to know not only Palmer but also Palmer's longtime dentist, Ben Tacke. "One day, I happened to mention to him that it would be a dream come true for me to be Arnie's dentist. And he says to me, 'Arnie's a lousy patient. When I die, you can have him.' Two years later, Benny Tacke died." Giles had nothing to do with it.

Thumbing through his collection of Palmer magazine covers, Giles came across a *Golf Digest* from 1957 that showed Palmer with a toothy grin. "I shaved this tooth down a little bit," Howdy said, pointing to Palmer's mouth. "It had a little bit of a fang to it." The cover shot on an issue of *Senior Golfer* magazine pleased Giles greatly. It showed Palmer smiling, with teeth—white and tiny and looking strong and straight—much in evidence.

Giles gave me an extensive tour one night of the Palmer museum in his basement, including a mock locker room that had Palmer in locker No. 1 and Giles in locker No. 2. He stopped at one point and summarized his life philosophy. He said: "I keep telling my kids that life is doing neat things with neat people. And there's nobody neater than Arnold Palmer."

Naturally, Howdy Giles was there, the June day in 1994, at Oakmont, outside Pittsburgh, when Arnold Palmer played his last round in a U.S. Open. I was there, as well. It was the first time I ever felt the whole Palmer thing, and it was powerful. Palmer was trudging up the hill to Oakmont's eighteenth green, a slow march on a hot day, and the applause for him was thundering. For the final time, Palmer was coming home.

He had made his U.S. Open debut at Oakmont, in 1953, playing two rounds as an amateur with a game too raw for such a testy course, just a few hills from his lifelong western Pennsylvania home, in Latrobe. He lost in a playoff at Oakmont in the 1962 U.S. Open, when Jack Nicklaus announced his professional arrival. Palmer also played in the 1973 and 1983 U.S. Opens at Oakmont.

On this day in June, he took 81 shots, more than half of them putts, and, with an opening 77, missed the two-day cut by a mile. He joined the field through a special invitation. He was sixty-four, and everybody knew that he was done, that he would never play again, not in a U.S. Open. When it was over, Palmer cried. He cried, he said, for everything the game had given him over the decades.

"I wish that everyone who has played the game could have the experience that I've had," he said.

He won the Open only once, in 1960, at Cherry Hills in Denver, when he drove the first green in the last round with a wallop of 346 yards. With a single swing he helped move golf from pastime to sport. In his brief prime, the Open was always his tournament. Three times he was defeated in playoffs.

When his final putt found the bottom of the hole—a tap-in after a missed three-footer—Palmer went into the press tent with a towel draped over his shoulders, like a boxing champion. There was an air of formality and expectation. He took only a couple of questions. "I haven't won all that much," he said. His eyes started to well. He stopped talking, brought the towel to his eyes, then over his head. The flashbulbs stopped popping, out of deference to him. He removed the towel and tried to string some words together, but he could not. "I think I'm a little bit sun-whipped and tired, ready to take a rest," he said. "I think that's about all I have to say. Thank you very much."

Several hundred reporters rose to their feet and began applauding—I had never seen anything like that happening before, never even heard of it. Palmer found a side door, raised his right hand in farewell, and slipped out of the tent and into the heat of the late afternoon.

I was right on the green when he made his final half-foot putt. He was looking all around. He saw the old ladies on the clubhouse veranda, with their umbrellas. He saw the TV cameramen and the caddies. There were security guards chanting his name and clapping hard in the languid heat. He raised his hands, slowly—a kind of royal wave—and smiled and smiled, until the tears started to collect in his eyes and he could smile no more. When he came out of the scorer's trailer, a British radio man cornered him and asked him for his thoughts. "The game has been so good to me," Palmer said. It wasn't much of a thought, or a complete one, anyhow, but the expressed thought was never his specialty. With Palmer, it was about feelings, what he felt, how he made us feel. He was answering the question of a radio man he did not know, and his whole body was trembling. Standing there, you knew what the game meant to him—the same thing it means to us.

⚑

I love Martha's Vineyard, from my time on the *Vineyard Gazette,* and Christine and our kids and I go back to the island when we can. In the summer of '94, our Vineyard vacation coincided with one of Bill Clinton's holidays there, and I took the opportunity to do a little spying on his golf game. He played three of his first four days there, reporting scores in the 80s.

With sixteen clubs in his bag. (Two more than the rules allow.) And the Floating Mulligan Rule in effect. (A useful invention.) Improving his ball position in the fairways. (Not kosher.) And giving himself putts within a yard of the hole. (Common but frowned upon by golf traditionalists and other defenders of the moral code.)

Clinton was forty-eight then, and his announced golfing goal was to break 80 before he turned fifty. He made it sound as if he were close. One day, he reported a front-nine 39. Coming home, no doubt weighed down by the pressure of a looming sub-80 score, he shot 43 for a five-hour 82. "I didn't make a single putt," he said post-round, sounding like a frustrated tour player in a U.S. Open press tent.

That round was played at a wonderful public course on the Vineyard, Farm Neck. I knew the course well, from the two years I lived on the island. It is an expensive, manicured, and demanding course, where golf balls are easily lost in the groves of scrub oaks that line the fairways and in the ponds that guard some of the greens. The president's Secret Service agents would not permit Clinton to search for balls he sent into the woods—where there might have been disease-carrying ticks and other threats to national security—which made the Floating Mulligan so useful.

Thwack!

"Aw, dang, in the woods?"

Do over.

Reporters could not know Clinton's precise scores because they were not allowed to follow him through his rounds. His regular partner, Vernon Jordan, the Washington lawyer and a Vineyard summer resident, was not helpful in this regard, maybe because he had golfing problems of his own. The national press corps was dubious about Clinton's 39, but didn't have a way to report the story. I had an advantage, a back way on to the golf course that let me see a lot of Clinton's big, messy, curve-ball golf game, sadly reminiscent of my own. I could feel his pain. I know how hard it is to admit to shooting 96. By my figuring, that's about what he was shooting.

I asked Dee Dee Myers, then Clinton's press secretary, if the president was fastidious or casual about playing golf by the official rules. I thought her answer was brilliant: "I don't know."

Clinton clearly had golf skill. I saw a long, loose swing and a huge hip turn, and he could give the ball a hefty whack. He played right-handed and kept score with his left. His better drives went 260 yards, using a graphite-shafted Japanese-made driver that, it was reported to the press, was a gift from the emperor of Japan. He had four other woods in his bag, including a seven-wood and a nine-wood, suggesting he was a golfer more interested in results than in impressing others.

He was nothing like a stoic. He greeted one wayward tee shot with, "Oh, no!" After stroking a putt anemically, he admonished himself with, "Hit it, hit it, hit it." He gave a big hearty wave to my son and me when he went whizzing by us in a golf cart, a big cigar in his mouth.

I asked Tim Spring, one of the local pros who played with Clinton when he shot 84, to gauge the authenticity of the score on a 1–10 scale, 10 being strictly by the rules, 1 being a total fiction. He gave Clinton an 8. "He could be an 80-shooter all the time—when he's not the president," Spring said. "If the president can break 80, he's playing too much. You don't want a president who can break 80."

By the summer of '95, Brad Faxon, my old boss-for-a-week, was in his twelfth year on the tour. Over the years, we had stayed in touch. From a distance, his career seemed fine. He kept his card year after year, won tournaments here and there. He was revered as a putter, and his deep feel for the game was well known. But there were dissatisfactions. He had never won a major; he had never made a Ryder Cup team. He was sort of a Ben Crenshaw, with less glitter and a lesser playing résumé. He was thirty-four. For 1995, he had one goal above all others: make the Ryder Cup team. The PGA Championship, held that year at Riviera, in Los Angeles, represented his last chance. In the final round, he needed to do something extraordinary to make it happen.

He had been playing well, with scores of 70, 67, and 71 in the first three rounds. He was not really in the hunt to win; there were twenty players ahead of him after three rounds, twelve tied with him, five one stroke behind him. But a top-five finish would likely give him enough Ryder Cup points to make the team. Golf, the pro game, is always about the numbers.

He woke up at 2:14 a.m., in the glow of his digital clock. He stared at the ceiling for four hours and slipped out of bed. This is the part they never show you on TV. In the darkness, he put on the clothes he had already laid out: sheer green socks, green and white seersucker pants, a yellow shirt. Pro golfers, in my experience, control the things they can control, because there are so many things they know they cannot.

His start on the par-5 first was perfect: killed a drive, nutted a five-iron, nailed the putt for an eagle. He then went par, birdie, par, birdie, birdie, birdie, par, birdie. He went out in 28 strokes, 7 under par, on an extremely demanding course. These were the numbers on his card: 3-4-3, 3-3-2, 3-4-3. I ran out of the press tent to catch up with him. There were spectators yelling, "Shoot 59!" And, "Make the Ryder Cup team!" And, "Win the tournament!" Faxon was trying, to use a phrase of his psychologist (Bob Rotella), to stay in the moment.

After a par on ten and a simple two-putt birdie on the eleventh, the air around Faxon seemed to become incredibly still. Anything was possible now. I kept my distance, like the ballplayers do when their pitcher is throwing a perfect game. Suddenly, the magic disappeared. His birdie putts on the twelfth, thirteenth, and fourteenth holes did not fall. On the fifteenth, his first hiccup: He missed a sidehill, downhill three-footer for par. He would not shoot 59. He would not win the tournament.

Now the question was about the hardest one any golfer faces anywhere: Could he regroup? A top-five finish, a spot on the Ryder Cup team, a career with more shine, it was all still feasible. All he could think about was making shots. The TV interviewers go crazy when the players say they're just trying to play one shot at a time, but that's what they really try to do.

The eighteenth at Riviera is a brute, uphill and nasty, a par-4. Faxon asked a marshal to remove a can of soda on the tee—a brand called Slice, it was—and proceeded to hit a weak pop-up drive. Sundays had been his nemesis as a professional, but this Sunday was not, not so far. He had 205 yards, uphill, for his second. He hit a five-iron a yard short of the green, and his chip was poor, finishing fifteen feet past the hole. His playing partner, the great José María Olazábal, the European Ryder Cup star, putted from twenty-five feet to a yard, then quickly finished so Faxon could have his moment without distraction. This was an act of courtesy by Olazábal, to finish rather than mark. Faxon learned something from the Spaniard's putt, that his own putt was straighter than it looked. He knocked it in, and, when all the scores were in, he had made the team. Steve Elkington, another boss-for-a-week of mine, won the tournament. Steve was a purebred. He was bound to win a major. I could relate more to Brad's struggles. I knew a Ryder Cupper.

In the locker room, players and reporters were shaking his hand, one after another. Brad has always been a well-liked player, and they were happy for him. They knew what making the Ryder Cup team meant to him. On the Sunday when he most wanted it, Brad got his golf out of his body and onto his scorecard. He had closed with a 63. Nobody had ever shot lower in a major championship. My old boss was in the books now.

ľ

A few weeks later, I saw, for the first time in the flesh, the amateur golfer then listed as Eldrick "Tiger" Woods, who was a freshman at Stanford at the time. I drove up from Philadelphia to the Newport Country Club to watch him play Buddy Marucci, Philadelphia's best amateur golfer then, a high-end car salesman who was forty-three. They were in the final of the centennial U.S. Amateur. Their match mixed precision and craftiness in incredible ways. Marucci hung with Woods until the thirty-sixth and final hole.

Woods played with such poise, elegance, and sophistication he seemed to be not a college golfer, but in the same league as Greg Norman, Nick Faldo, and Ernie Els, which made Marucci's accomplishment even more extraordinary. He couldn't do the things with his golf ball that Woods could do with his, so all that was left were his guts and his ability to figure a bewitching course that would have been at home on the west coast of Scotland. When the day was over, Marucci said, "I feel more involved in the game now."

A small crowd gathered around the eighteenth green for speeches. "He is a wonderful young man," Marucci said of the victor. "And I'm not talking about his golf game."

Marucci's father was beaming. What father wouldn't be? The senior Marucci was fit and silver-haired and proud, and he had walked with his son all the way around, all thirty-six holes. Woods's father, in poor health, was in the shadows, in a cart. When it was over, Woods hugged his father, long and hard, his face in his father's massive chest, cameras swarming them. Off on the side, where nobody much was looking, the Maruccis were doing the same exact thing. Sometimes, not often, two people get in a final and they both win.

CHAPTER SEVEN

BUGS (1995)

AS A KID, all I wanted to be was a newspaper reporter, like Red Smith, or Bobby Kennedy in that famous photograph of him in front of the King David Hotel in Jerusalem in 1948 (it appears in the Arthur Schlesinger biography), snapped during his stint as a foreign correspondent for *The Boston Post*. I was happy at *The Inquirer*. When I got a call, out of the blue in the summer of '95, to come to *Sports Illustrated* for an interview, my act of protest was not to put on a tie. The managing editor then—the boss—was a brilliant talkaholic named Mark Mulvoy. The joke about him was that even dental hygienists with their fingers in his mouth would quickly find out that he was a member of Ballybunion and Pine Valley and that Dan Quayle was one of his golf buddies. He had started a golf section for home subscribers called "Golf Plus," and he needed one more writer. I told him I wasn't interested in a job where I was writing golf full-time—I never wanted the game to feel like work to me. He said that if I were a writer for *Sports Illustrated*, my children would have high status on their playgrounds. Nothing could have made me less interested in taking the job than that, but Mulvoy had plenty of other moves, an endless supply, really. He said it would be golf among other things and then talked some more about the state of his putting game. Golf permeated everything he said and did. We talked golfer to golfer. There was no way I was not taking the job.

The golf editor, Jim Herre, lived on news and knew I loved to report it. Right at the start, he assigned me to two newsy stories. He wanted to know what really happened when Greg Norman accused Mark McCumber of cheating at the 1995 World Series of Golf, and he wanted to know what really happened between Ben Wright, the CBS broadcaster, and Valerie Helmbreck, a newspaper reporter from Delaware who quoted him saying inane homophobic things about women's professional golf. (Wright had tried to squash her reputation to save his job.) These were my first two "Golf Plus" stories. I knew that reporting the CBS story could be awkward because of my friendship with Chuck Will, the CBS golf director from Philadelphia, and that professional reputations would be at stake in the McCumber-Norman story. Gathering news can be a messy business. Sometimes—often, really—you have to report what you know and let the chips fall wherever.

On a warm Monday night in late August of 1995, Mark McCumber, a highly accomplished golfer who always struck me as perpetually and excessively cheerful, flew into Akron, Ohio, on a private plane. Maybe it was just that he had much to be cheerful about. Nearly forty-four years old then, McCumber was in his eighteenth year on the PGA Tour, and his golf game was about as good as it had ever been. His side business, designing golf courses, was thriving, and his family was, too. He was about to play in one of his favorite tournaments, the NEC World Series of Golf, on a track he liked, the South Course of the Firestone Country Club. His life was, to use one of his favorite words, blessed.

Tuesday of World Series week was uneventful, Wednesday's pro-am was pleasant, and Thursday, the first round of the tournament, started nicely. McCumber was paired with Greg Norman, and he was nervous about that because the two Floridians—

McCumber has spent most of his life in Jacksonville, and Norman, a transplanted Australian, lives in Hobe Sound—had not played together since McCumber spoke critically and publicly about Norman's proposal for an international, stars-only golf tour. But McCumber plays his best when he's nervous—he's a fidgety man who talks quickly and endlessly when he's not whistling—and through the first six holes of the round, he was one under par and playing solidly. Norman, then the game's dominant figure and arguably its best player, was level par.

Then came the seventh hole, a par-3 of 220 yards. McCumber took three putts for a bogey, and his life was never again the same. It was on that green, according to Norman, that McCumber cheated by plucking a tiny clump of grass from the green and smoothing the turf with his thumb. McCumber refuted the charge. He said Norman was mistaken about what he thought he saw. But for a long time after that day—Thursday, August 24, 1995—McCumber's nights were interrupted by bouts of sleeplessness. Norman told me his sleeping had been fine.

In a world of rampant lawlessness, the fuss over a few blades of grass (if that's what it was) may seem quaint, but golf is a universe unto itself. The professional golfer's society is one of laws, and the touring pro would rather be convicted of tax evasion than charged with cheating. Norman said that while McCumber prepared to putt an eight-footer for par, he bent down, brought his right hand to a spot three feet in front of his ball and picked up with his thumb and index finger grass loosened by another player's cleat but still attached to the green. Norman says McCumber then fixed the wounded spot with his thumb and tossed away the grass, creating a smooth putting surface. In Norman's telling, McCumber violated the rule of golf that prohibits a player from touching the line of his putt, except when fixing a ball mark or removing a loose impediment, such as a twig or a bug.

That's what McCumber said he was doing. He said he squatted like a catcher, picked up a small black insect with a hard shell with his forefinger and thumb, dropped the insect, and picked it up again and tossed it aside, all within the rules of golf.

Norman, livid, summoned a PGA Tour rules official, and Mike Shea arrived as the players were walking up the ninth fairway. Shea, a highly regarded veteran official, heard Norman's charges and McCumber's defense and decided, as the rules of golf dictate, that in the absence of other evidence the benefit of the doubt had to go to the accused. In the scorer's tent after the round—McCumber had shot 68 and Norman 73—Norman's fury persisted. By way of protest he refused to sign McCumber's scorecard, so Shea signed it for McCumber instead, as the rules allow. Norman said loudly, "I'm out of here." Over the next two hours, Shea, among others, prevailed on Norman to finish the tournament. In the end he did. In fact, he won.

Tim Finchem, the PGA Tour commissioner and a skillful politician, somehow found a way to believe both men. "I think Greg sincerely believes he saw a violation, but I also believe Mark McCumber did not fix a spike mark," he told me, deputies at his side for a fifteen-minute interview. Norman had no use for such evenhandedness. He told me he was "110 percent sure" that McCumber cheated, then lied about it. "I'm five paces away," Norman said, speaking of the incident in the present tense weeks after it happened. "And I'm watching." As he, and others, framed the issue, either McCumber cheated or Norman tarnished a man's reputation with a false charge.

When McCumber spoke to me about his accuser and the accusation, it was not with anger. "This is his deal, not mine," he said, avoiding using Norman's name. "I don't want to get into a fight with him. I have a feeling of unsettledness at a time of the year when I want to feel relaxed. I never expected something like this to happen. But I have to ask myself, What is a tragedy? This is not a tragedy. This has been hurtful."

Norman received calls supporting his actions from several prominent people in the golf community. But nobody came forth to corroborate his charge. Nor did anyone come forward in support of McCumber's claim. After the conclusion of play that Thursday, McCumber and Shea scoured the seventh green looking for a discarded, dead insect but found nothing. Finchem said he had no interest in pursuing the matter. His stance was that the rules of golf had spoken, equitably and with finality. But others felt there was too much at stake to let the matter go unresolved. Sometimes with facts, often without, they assigned a reputation to McCumber and a motive to Norman and continued to debate the fine points of the case. For instance they asked, is it believable that McCumber would pick up an insect with the tips of his fingers? Why wouldn't he just flick it away? On the other hand, if he did pluck grass, would he be so bold as to throw the damning evidence into the air?

After the tournament McCumber went to Finchem and asked, "Have I ever done anything that would suggest I don't respect the rules?" The two men concluded that he had not. But in actual fact McCumber had a reputation among some of his touring brethren as somebody who was loose with the rules. It was a reputation he has been saddled with since his rookie year.

McCumber joined the tour in the summer of 1978, at the age of twenty-six, and his route there was wholly his own. As a teenager he was one of the best junior players in the country, but he turned down all the college scholarships offered him and moved instead to Brooklyn, where, as a Jehovah's Witness, he worked as a missionary. In his late teens and twenties, from 1969 through 1973, he played virtually no golf. But after getting married in 1974, he concluded that golf would be the best way to support his family. He started playing in the rough-and-tumble Florida minitours in the mid-1970s, then finally qualified for the tour on his sixth visit to Q School, the PGA Tour qualifying tournament.

In July of 1978, McCumber arrived at the Greater Milwaukee Open, the second event of his PGA Tour career. He was skilled but raw, and practically nobody knew him. Carrying his golf bag that week was a tour caddie named Bill Hubbard. On the tenth hole of the second round, McCumber drove his ball under a small tree, and what happened next caused a disagreement that stuck to him for years. Hubbard said McCumber swung and missed and failed to count the stroke. McCumber said he was taking a practice swing. After the round McCumber and Hubbard went to see Jack Tuthill, then the tour's director of tournament golf, to settle the dispute.

Tuthill asked McCumber if his intention was to hit the ball during the swing in question. McCumber said no. Hubbard disagreed. Hubbard said he could not work for McCumber and quit.

Success came quickly for McCumber. He won the twelfth tournament in which he played, in 1979 at Doral, in Miami. He came to the final event of the '79 season, the Pensacola Open, needing to make a check to secure sixtieth place on the money list. In those days, only the top sixty players retained their playing privileges for the following year. Bill Kratzert said he saw McCumber move his ball noticeably in front of his marker on a two-foot putt on the twelfth green in the second round. McCumber made the putt and the cut—and finished sixtieth on the money list, forty-eight dollars ahead of No. 61, Miller Barber.

Kratzert went to the late Dan Sikes, who, like McCumber, was from Jacksonville. "I said, 'Dan, somebody's got to show him how to mark his ball because it's only going to get worse,'" Kratzert told me. Kratzert also told McCumber that he was not marking his ball properly. McCumber recalled Kratzert advising him on the proper way to mark a ball and said the only advice he received from Sikes was, "If somebody's standing on top of you when you mark your ball, you go right back and stare at him when he's marking."

In 1980, again at Pensacola, McCumber was paired with Hubert Green for the first two rounds. After the first round, Green told me, he reported to an official that McCumber had repeatedly failed to properly mark his ball. McCumber did not remember Green calling for an official but did remember Green giving him "fatherly advice" about how to mark his ball. Told of McCumber's recollection of the day, Green said, "Would you call in a police officer to give some fatherly advice?" Green was not surprised when the tour official took no action. "He said what they all say: 'It's your word against his.'"

In 1983, at the Anheuser-Busch Classic, on the fifteenth green of the third round, McCumber chipped a ball that finished on the green in a small depression, according to his playing partner, Mark Lye. But by the time McCumber was through marking his ball and preparing to putt, Lye said, the ball was no longer in the depression. Lye called in a rules official, and McCumber agreed to move the ball back into the depression. "After the round, Mark's wife came up to me and said, 'How dare you even think that my husband would cheat,'" Lye told me. "And I said to her, 'Paddy, I like Mark, but I don't *think* he was going to cheat, he *was* going to cheat.'" McCumber said he did not intentionally move the ball out of the depression.

"The most peculiar thing about it," McCumber said, "is that later Mark said to me, 'I knew you were going to do that.' And I said, 'For heaven's sake, if you knew I was going to do it, why didn't you say something before I did it?'"

Reviewing these three ball-marking disputes from the early part of his career, McCumber said, "Things get more microscopic when you're on tour. I think it would be fair to say that over the course of a career you learn to be more precise in every aspect of the game, including your understanding of the rules."

But by 1983, McCumber's reputation among certain players and golf observers was sealed: He was a player you had to watch. In 1985 at Doral, he was leading by two strokes over Tom Kite by the time he reached the eighteenth tee on Sunday. He hit his drive way to the right, and Ken Venturi of CBS, basing his comments on a report from an on-course cameraman, said on the air that the ball had become lodged in a palm tree. During the chaotic search for the ball, McCumber was urged to climb the tree to search for the ball. He refused, saying the ball was hit far right of the tree.

A ball bearing McCumber's mark was found by a marshal forty yards right of the tree, sitting down in heavy rough, and McCumber went on to win. Still, throughout golf, there are people who believe that an outrageous act of cheating occurred on that hole, even though there was no evidence of it. Later, somebody went up in the palm tree and recovered several balls, none of them McCumber's. McCumber said of the incident, "CBS wouldn't give me the benefit of the doubt." Without a direct word being said, his reputation had reached the airwaves and the public.

In more than thirty interviews with tour officials, caddies, tournament workers, television executives and commentators, golf writers, and touring professionals other than Norman, I found only one other incident in which McCumber was suspected of violating a rule of golf. That came in 1990, in the third and final round of the rain-shortened Byron Nelson Classic, on the twelfth green. Davis Love III, McCumber's playing partner, thought McCumber repaired something on the line of his putt that was not a ball mark. Love called in a rules official. While the official was responding to Love's call, McCumber's ball, set down for him to putt, was moved by the wind and the green's slope, and the repair in question was no longer on the line of the putt. Love decided not to pursue the matter, although he believed McCumber had broken a rule.

But Love did not consider McCumber a cheater. "You can examine just about any player out here, and if you look hard enough, you're going to find guys who once didn't like a drop the player took, or how he marked his ball, or something," Love said.

Some touring pros and golf observers have been critical of Norman, saying that it was impossible for him to be certain of what he saw in Akron. More pointedly, they say his dispute with McCumber should have been handled more discreetly. Others have said that his actions at Firestone were rooted in McCumber's rejection of the world golf tour. McCumber was widely quoted as saying, "Who does Norman think he is, God?"

"What happened at Firestone has nothing to do with the world tour," Norman said. "My job is to protect the game of golf. I can't stand by and watch somebody not play by the rules of golf."

"If Greg Norman saw cheating and didn't say anything, he'd be cheating himself," Hubert Green said.

For as long as he has been on tour, Norman has been aware of McCumber's reputation for not being fastidious about the rules. However, he never saw any violation until he played with McCumber in the fourth round of the '92 Buick Open. There he saw McCumber illegally improve his lie but said nothing to McCumber or tournament officials. Asked why, he said, "Sometimes you don't want to believe what you saw." Although McCumber has no recollection of the incident, it was then that Norman began to watch him closely.

No one on tour purports to know Mark McCumber that well. He's merry on the golf course almost to the point of incredibility, and most nights he takes dinner alone in his room. In a three-hour interview, he raised the names of his family members constantly, a reminder that anything that is critical of him will hurt his family, as well. He sent his best to my wife and children, although he had never met them. He quoted the Bible frequently. Those who know him know he would not cheat, he said. His Creator knows, he said, that he would not cheat. In the meantime, there was Norman's serious accusation, McCumber's denial, and the testimony of experts.

"In late August we get this black insect, *Ataenius spretulus*, beetle family," Brian Mabie, the course superintendent at Firestone, told me. "It's about the size of a pencil eraser, and it hangs out near the putting cups, where it's cool and dark. If you had one in your line, you'd pick it up with your fingers. As soon as McCumber said he picked up a bug, I knew what he was talking about."

Greg Norman never saw a black bug on the seventh green of the South Course of the Firestone Country Club in the first round of the 1995 World Series of Golf. He saw a tiny, flying tuft of grass. He saw an incident of cheating; he's certain of it. To hell with damaged reputations. Norman said he could not stand idly by and watch his game, the game of golf, be defaced.

⚑

Knowing Ben Wright only from TV, I had always liked him. In the community of golf, Ben Wright, a CBS golf broadcaster and long-time golf writer, had always been invited to the best parties. He was an amiable, well-spoken man bursting with opinions and stories, delivered in a lovely British accent that wasn't quite Oxbridge, although it was close. He would describe his mother as a "minor Scottish aristocrat," and he prepared for London University at an all-boys English public school, Felsted. By 1995 he had already spent four decades in golf's elite circles. He had a veneer of refinement. His boss's boss, David Kenin, the president of CBS Sports, thought of him as "a complex, sophisticated guy." John Bentley Wright, corpulent and jolly, highly compensated and often smelling very good, called himself "a ham." Every so often he would slip up, and a coarser element of his personality, a Fleet Street side, would emerge. In an interview with me, he described a former editor of his at the *Financial Times* as "a raging fag." (His quick follow-up was unintentionally hilarious: "I have nothing against homosexuals.") In 1992, writing in an American golf magazine called *Southern Links*, Wright alleged that Muirfield's club secretary demanded "girlie pictures" in exchange for press credentials for the 1959 Walker Cup, which Wright was to cover for *The London Daily Mirror*. "I pleaded that I had no access to the newspaper's pin-up photographs, which were in any case nothing like as daring as the bare-breasted lovelies daily exposed nowadays in the British tabloids," he wrote. Later, to settle a libel suit, he dispatched a letter of apology and a $1,000 check to the secretary, the late Paddy Hanmer. "Seldom right but never in doubt"—that's what they often said about Wright, good-naturedly, in the CBS trailers.

It was in a CBS trailer—on the second Thursday of May in 1995, shortly before noon, on the grounds of the DuPont Country Club, in Wilmington, Delaware, site of the '95 McDonald's LPGA Championship—that Wright was interviewed by Valerie Helmbreck, a reporter on the *News Journal,* the most prominent newspaper in Delaware. They spent a half hour together, and after it their lives were never the same.

Helmbreck began her story on Wright, which ran on the front page of the *News Journal* on Friday, May 12, with a quote from him: "Let's face facts here. Lesbians in the sport hurt women's golf." He was also quoted as saying, "They're going to a butch game and that furthers the bad image of the game." He was quoted as saying that homosexuality on the women's tour "is not reticent. It's paraded. There's a defiance in them in the last decade." And, "Women are handicapped by having boobs. It's not easy for them to keep their left arm straight, and that's one of the tenets of the game. Their boobs get in the way."

Wright, Helmbreck's story said, believed that the LPGA's homosexual image hinders corporate support; that the tour's leading players, including Michelle McGann and Laura Davies, lacked charisma; and that modern women pros were wrong to emphasize power over finesse.

It wasn't much, really. It was crass, but much of it was true. Still, given the tenor of the times, it was enough. All hell broke loose.

Before the story was published, word of the interview reached Wright's boss, Frank Chirkinian, who was in Wilmington, and he called Helmbreck at the *News Journal* and told her that they needed to meet. I knew enough about the male-dominated culture of golf at CBS to have a good guess as to what his tone might have been like. Helmbreck provided the rest. She did not know Chirkinian, so she asked him to spell his name and reveal his title. He ignored her request, and the terse conversation ended when she hung up on him.

The story had been out only a few hours on Friday morning when Wright, who was sixty-three then, was urged to leave Wilmington and go to CBS headquarters, in New York. There, for six hours, Wright and Kenin, the CBS Sports president, discussed the interview and the story it produced. Both men were accompanied by a lawyer. At the *News Journal* on Friday, Helmbreck and her editors received scores of calls, some from readers but many more from newspapers, magazines, radio stations, and television programs, seeking comment. Helmbreck wouldn't talk, and the newspaper's editor said the paper stood by the accuracy of its story.

Late on Friday, Kenin released his findings: "I am convinced that the offensive statements attributed to Mr. Wright were not made." He also said that both Wright and CBS Sports had "been done a grave injustice in this matter."

Wright offered two releases of his own. In a statement for reporters, he said he never used the words "boobs" or "butch" with Helmbreck. He maintained that he never said lesbianism on the women's tour was "paraded" or that lesbians were bad for the image of the game. He wrote that he would "not discuss lesbianism with a stranger, just as I would not discuss my three divorces with a stranger." In a statement for the players, posted in the DuPont Country Club locker room Friday morning, Wright wrote, "I am disgusted at the pack of lies and distortion that was attributed to me." He said the same thing on CBS's Saturday coverage of the tournament. Looking directly into the camera and perspiring, he called Helmbreck's story "not only totally inaccurate but extremely distasteful."

Helmbreck's piece, an 1,100-word story in a cautious, responsible, small-state daily, had all the elements needed to ignite a modern press brushfire: gay sex, male chauvinism, political incorrectness, sports, network television, and a faintly famous figure— a TV personality—to wrap the whole thing around. *The New York Post* captured the moment in a five-word headline for its Saturday paper: "The Boob on the Tube."

The story had a short shelf life. It was a national story for a day or two, then interest sagged. Ultimately, the Wright-Helmbreck escapade proved to be an unsatisfying little saga, lacking a clear resolution. The interview wasn't tape recorded. CBS put its word up against Helmbreck's and created reasonable doubt. "They could easily stomp on her," Richard Sandomir, who covered the story for *The New York Times,* told me, "so they did. Had it been a reporter they knew, Ben would have been gone."

In 1988, CBS fired Jimmy "the Greek" Snyder when he said on TV that blacks were physically better suited for sports than whites. In 1990, CBS suspended Andy Rooney of 60 *Minutes* for three months for making remarks that some gays and blacks found offensive. CBS was pressured into pulling the announcer Gary McCord from its Masters coverage because the Augusta czars didn't like his idea of humor. But Ben Wright stayed on board. He didn't have to defend the reported opinions and quotations, which many people viewed as defensible, because, he said, they weren't his. LPGA officials gave him the benefit of the doubt. When gay-rights groups called for his head, or at least an apology, he ignored them; in his view, there was nothing to apologize for. He said the story was a "pack of lies"; his network supported him; and the duo of Bentley and McCord, a team valued by CBS, was saved. Wright later received a four-year contract extension. The only victim was Helmbreck and her reputation as a reporter, and no one at the network seemed to care about that. "The woman has disappeared, as far as I know," Wright said to me in a telephone interview. (I had reached him in a California hotel room, a call I made at 8:36 p.m. West Coast time. I saved the record. Wright, in a book of his own, later maintained that I called him at an "unearthly hour" after "an evening of drinking" when he was "nearly asleep.")

Then Ben did a silly thing. The great raconteur didn't stick to his story. On June 13, a month after the incident, at the summer home of Nancy and Jack Whitaker in Bridgehampton, New York, during the week of the U.S. Open at Shinnecock Hills, he attended an elegant dinner party. Barbara and Jack Nicklaus were there. So was Dan Jenkins, the *Golf Digest* columnist and novelist who helped Wright get his start with CBS in 1973. "I asked him, 'Did you say it?'" Jenkins, the legendary former *SI* writer told me. "And he said, 'Of course I said it. But I was granted complete anonymity.' What I don't know is if he was joking. He'd had about two bottles of wine."

Details of the interview emerged in other places. Ken Doig, a veteran tour caddie and a part-time CBS employee, said he eavesdropped on the interview because he couldn't believe what Wright was saying to Helmbreck. Doig, the oldest son of a well-regarded Canadian golfing family, said he likes Wright but that Wright's response to Helmbreck's story was disingenuous. "Her story was accurate," said Doig, who worked occasionally for *SI* as a photographer's assistant. "I heard Ben say boobs. I heard him say lesbianism hurts in getting sponsorships." Doig has worked odd jobs for CBS at the Masters and at other tournaments since 1977. Listening to him recreate the conversation, it was as if he had had the room bugged. I asked him why he wanted to come forward in the matter of Wright versus Helmbreck and jeopardize his employment with CBS. He said, "I'm a golfer, and golf is a game of integrity. I believe in telling the truth."

When I first reached Wright, an incorrigible talker, in his hotel room, he said he could not discuss the Helmbreck story without permission from Kenin, and permission had not been granted. ("I'm not going to give him the opportunity to talk and get himself in trouble again," Kenin had said.) But then he couldn't help himself. In a matter of minutes, Wright characterized Helmbreck as divorced, involved in a custody battle, possibly a lesbian. It was, he said, his bad luck to run into her around Mother's Day, when she was upset because she wouldn't be able to see her children. He described her as having a feminist, gay-rights agenda. "I was totally misquoted. She put into my mouth words she told me," he said. "She granted me anonymity. She chose to nail me. It's hurt me terribly. It's aged me ten years. She's a very unhappy woman."

Nothing Wright said checked out. Helmbreck was married— "happily married for fifteen years," she told me—to an assistant city editor at the *News Journal*. They were raising their three children. She had been a reporter on the paper for twelve years and had lived in Delaware most of her forty-three years. She was a features writer and a former TV critic, which is why she was assigned to write about the television coverage of the LPGA Championship.

Helmbreck then was often writing about food and had recently written a light piece comparing herself with her mock heroine, Martha Stewart, whom she looked like. In her years on the paper, she had been charged with misquoting someone on only one other occasion. That was in 1990, when the actress Kathleen Turner was staying in Wilmington at the Hotel du Pont. Helmbreck quoted the hotel manager as saying that Turner was not as attractive in person as she was on the screen. The manager said he was misquoted; the *News Journal* backed Helmbreck. For her foray into golf, Helmbreck said her original plan was to write about the differences between women's and men's golf telecasts. Helmbreck said she took notes throughout the interview with Wright and that the entire session was on the record, except when Wright told her it was not. She declined to reveal what was not on the record. I was able to get an internal memo from the *News Journal* that described the part of the interview that was not on the record. According to the document, Wright said that Helmbreck could use, but not attribute to him, the "fingernail test." According to the memo, he said that players with short fingernails are gay, and players with long fingernails are not. Helmbreck made no reference to the fingernail test in her story.

It was easy to find Wright supporters, JoAnne Carner among them. The LPGA Hall of Famer said Wright's line about women golfers and their breasts was originally her own, a joking way to explain the differences between men's and women's golf. Dottie Pepper, an LPGA player, said she couldn't imagine Wright intending to say the things he was quoted as saying. Still, she was surprised by what he had said at the recent opening of a golf course, Cliffs Valley in Travelers Rest, South Carolina, designed by Wright. The ceremony, attended by 1,500 people, featured an exhibition by Pepper and Jay Haas, among others. During the introductions, Wright, in his role as professional Englishman, mocked Haas for his performance for the United States in the '95 Ryder Cup. When he was through, according to people present, he said to the crowd, "This is payback because at dinner last night Jay asked me about lesbians." There was nervous laughter.

"I was a little disappointed that it was brought up again," Pepper told me. "I thought he could've been more sensitive."

When I was reporting the saga, six months after Helmbreck's initial interview, Chirkinian recognized that Helmbreck's story must have been at least partially true. "Something must have been said, for it to get into print," he told me. Kenin's view appeared to have evolved over that half year. "CBS never said it was a pack of lies," he told me. "There's a community element to it. She's outside the community. Ben didn't know that at the time. This was a case of one not understanding the other." Chirkinian said Helmbreck did not understand Wright's sense of humor. "[But] whether Ben Wright was serious or joking, if he admits to [the quotes], he's fired," Chirkinian said. "With our corporate lawyers? Ben would have walked the plank. And to walk the plank for that? I don't think so."

Helmbreck remained in Wilmington, a working reporter. She found that sometimes when she called people for a story, they recognized her name. They knew she was involved in some messy thing with a golf announcer for CBS. It was frustrating for her. Wright, she said, was a man of his generation, nothing more. She had to live with the consequences. "In this business," she said, "you can be a nut, you can be a drunk, but the one thing you can't be is dishonest." Helmbreck said she stood by her story, completely. Given the chance, she said, she would write it the same way again.

SI published my report, and CBS fired Ben Wright.

CHAPTER EIGHT

LOVE NOTES (1996)

FOR A WHILE, I referred to Davis Love as my close personal friend Davis M. Love III. It was just a little gag line, but for a while I did know him well, the only bona fide first-tier player I could say that about. Reporters have always been fond of him, because he's accessible and not bland, and his fellow tourists enjoy playing with him because his manners are exemplary. The general take on him, given his lavish talent and beautiful swing and tremendous length, is that he has underachieved in his career. Maybe that's true—through twenty full seasons he won a great big pile of money but only one major—but my take on him is different. I think he likes golf and being a professional golfer, but the terms by which success are measured by others mean less to him. We look at Davis and say what we would do if we had his swing. He looks at his calendar and sees that he's going snowboarding with his kids, Lexie and Dru, in Sun Valley, fly-fishing in Montana, to a Harley convention in Delray Beach, Florida—and to the Masters, the British Open, the Ryder Cup. Not a bad life. He'd change some things, of course, some putts in majors certainly, but only one significant thing: He wouldn't let his father board a small prop plane in bad weather to fly off to a golf school on the day that turned out to be his last.

One rainy week at Pebble Beach, staying at the home of his friend Jim Griggs, Davis found *To the Linksland* on Jim's shelves. He liked it. For years, Simon & Schuster had a brilliant editor named Jeff Neuman, with the face and manner of a Talmudic scholar but a keen understanding of the book tastes of your everyday *USA Today* reader. He was the editor of Harvey Penick's *Little Red Book* and all of its sequels. When Neuman heard that Davis's father, the teaching pro Davis Love, Jr., had been mentored by Penick, and that he had left behind boxes of notes about how golf is played, he approached Davis III and asked him if he wanted to write a book about his father. Kindly, Davis said that he would like to, if I would help him with it. I was flattered and enjoyed every minute of it.

The book is called *Every Shot I Take.* Only Davis's name is on the cover. He thought we should share that page, but I assured him the book was all his and his late father's. My role was more mechanical. On maybe fifteen or so days in 1996, Davis and I would sit in a breezy office in Sea Island, Georgia, and he'd tell me his stories, and later I'd write them in his voice. We'd play golf or go to the practice tee, and he would recall his father's various teachings. I was given boxes of his father's material and culled through it, looking for insights that would work in the book. The book won some kind of literary prize from the USGA, and Davis's joke was, "Think how much better it could have been had I stayed at North Carolina and gotten my English degree." He left school after three years to turn pro.

The most charming thing I dug out of the boxes was a letter to Davis from his father's old friend Paul Runyan. Runyan won the PGA Championship in 1934, and he taught for years with Davis Love, Jr., at *Golf Digest* schools. In 1986, when Davis III and his wife, Robin, headed out for their first year on tour, Runyan wrote a list of suggestions for them, by hand on stationery from the Holiday Inn in Augusta. He put this headline at the top: "Do's and Don'ts for a Husband and Wife on the Tour."

For Robin

1. Be sure not to surprise Davis with any errands you need him to do before he goes to play, as this may upset his practice schedule with serious consequences for the rest of the day.
2. Help Davis at day's end to get his mind off golf for the rest of the evening.
3. Suggest and prepare a proper diet and rest schedule for Davis as to give him the best possible mind and body for play.
4. Do anything you can to bolster Davis's confidence in himself.

For Davis

5. The best way to avoid bogeys is to play a course intelligently *and* aggressively.
6. Put in a good day's work every day, taking into consideration how much work you can do without becoming exhausted. You've done too much when you can't recover with a good meal and a good night of sleep.
7. Never forget what made you: your golfing skill. Don't take on too many other activities that may interfere with your pursuit of golfing excellence.

For Robin and Davis

8. If driving, try to relieve each other on an hourly basis.
9. Avoid any argument or unpleasantness before play. Settle any misunderstandings in the evening. If you can't, declare a moratorium before bedtime.
10. Be sure you young people work as a team. Anticipate and recognize each other's needs.

Another interesting thing in the boxes was the clips from magazines and newspapers the father kept, not about Davis's career, but about the game. One of the clips was a Charles Price column that ran in *Golf Digest* in 1986 about the seventeenth-century golf journals kept by a Scot named Thomas Kincaid. Price quoted from the Kincaid journals, and the parts that struck Davis Jr. were obvious to Davis III years later.

"You must hit through the ball, not at it, with the sensation that the clubhead is still accelerating after it has made contact," Kincaid wrote centuries ago. "This is the secret to distance. The way to perfect this sensation is to practice hitting the ball as easily as possible, then increase the force of the swing by degrees, practicing each degree until it becomes a habit. The time will not be wasted. Perfecting each degree will teach you to play half shots, pitches, and chips. The easiest degree will help your putting."

The writing is amazingly modern, right down to the use of *you* and *your*. The ideas, of course, are, too. Trip (the family name for Davis Love III) was amazed. "So many years later," Davis told me, "my father was saying the exact same things."

In 1987, in his second year on tour, Davis won his first tour event, at Hilton Head. Steve Jones, playing behind him in the last group of the day, needed a par to win on the final hole but drove it out of bounds and made six. Herman Mitchell, Lee Trevino's old caddie, was on Davis's bag, and earlier, when Davis unleashed a good one on the eighteenth tee, you could hear the gargantuan Mitchell say, "Thataway to drive it, babe." Davis's father was with his namesake son in the early part of the week but was teaching at a golf school on the Sunday when Davis won. In one of the boxes was a letter from father to son, sent in the days before e-mail and cell phones, when there was more time between the events of our lives and our reviews of them. Nothing Davis has from his father means more to him.

Dear Davis,

Our travel plans have kept us apart since your win, but I have thought often about it and wanted to talk with you, to tell you how proud I was of how you won, how you displayed maturity far beyond your age, how your conduct told

all of us who were watching that you felt sorry for Steve,
but that you were preparing to go extra holes if he made five.

Your golf shots showed me that there will be more wins,
that you wanted to hit those shots under pressure, that you
liked being in the hunt. Some don't. You belong there.
My hat is off to your courage—and to your composure.

Much love,
Dad

The father never got to see his son win again. In subsequent years,
Davis won four more times at Hilton Head, which is played the
week after the Masters. How, I could not say, but I think the letter, and Davis's first win there, must have something to do with
his success at Hilton Head. (That and the pressure of the Masters
being over.) Davis has also won the Players Championship twice;
it's played outside Jacksonville, Florida, where Davis Love, Jr., was
flying to when his plane went down fatally. In 1997, the year the
book came out, Davis won the PGA Championship at Winged Foot.
Davis Jr. revered Winged Foot, and he was a member of the Professional Golfers Association of America, so the win resonated
deeply for Davis and his brother, Mark, and his mother, Penta. You
could see that in the sobbing hug Davis gave his mother on the
eighteenth green. Behind them, a rainbow streaked the sky.

⛳

Penta—the fifth child in her North Carolina farming family—
gave me an envelope thick with letters the family received after
the death of her husband. One was from the ancient Harvey Penick,
written with great care and by hand, evidence of his age in every
penstroke.

Dear Penta:
    It was such a shock when we were called about Davis.
He was one of my favorites. Helen joins me in our prayers.
He will probably be teaching in Heaven.

I have not only had back problems, but I have shingles; my excuse for the poor handwriting.

Now, if I can ever help with either of the boys, please call on me.

Our deepest sympathy,
Helen and Harvey Penick

Here's the final paragraph of the book. The typing is mine, but the voice is Davis's:

In a day or two, I'll leave St. Simons and head out to California to begin a new year of golf, the 1997 season, my twelfth year on tour. If my father were alive today, he'd have already reviewed with me his notes for the new year. He'd have thumbed through his legal pads and made the lists of things I'd need to do to play better golf in 1997 than I did in 1996. I'd like to think at this point I'm pretty much taking stock of the inventory the way he would have done it himself. Dad would probably have two new files by this point, one for Lexie's golf, another for Dru's. He'd be sixty-one now. He never talked about becoming a grand old man of golf. I don't think he ever imagined himself retiring from teaching. He never met his namesake, Davis M. Love IV. He would have loved Dru, Dru's spirit, his buoyancy, his alertness. I thank God he was able to know Lexie, however briefly. I remember Dad cradling her, shortly before the accident, when Lexie was not even six months old. My father had never had a sister, he had never had a daughter, and now he had this tiny beautiful sleeping girl in his arms. He rocked her gently back and forth. He gave her rhythm before she could walk. And then he was gone.

CHAPTER NINE

ORIGINALS (1997–99)

ON THE SATURDAY NIGHT OF THE 1997 MASTERS, in the long Augusta twilight, there was one man on the practice tee and one man, really, in the tournament. The sight made me shiver. There was Tiger Woods, with a nine-shot lead with one round remaining. Who ever heard of a golfer having a nine-shot lead in a major? The other forty-five players in the field were playing in a different event, for a different prize. The inevitable was now only a day away. I was at my second Masters, and I could not believe what I was seeing. Nobody could.

Ben Crenshaw walked out of the Augusta National clubhouse on his way to dinner, wearing a tie, carrying a blazer. Crenshaw is old school. He grew up reading about Bobby Jones and hearing about Ben Hogan and watching Jack Nicklaus. The "real" athletes at his high school in Austin played football and baseball. Crenshaw had golf all to himself, and he liked it that way. Now he was feeling peculiar. "Something's changing. Something's about to pass," he said. There was a small group of writers around him—new friends of mine among them—as he talked about the change in the world golf order. Time seemed to stop. Crenshaw was in no rush, and none of us were, either. Everybody was trying to figure out what the whole thing meant.

The next day, it happened. The old order died. Dusk on Masters Sunday, 1997, was actually dawn. In 1965, Jones said of Nicklaus, "He plays a game with which I am not familiar," but the larger truth is that Nicklaus was Jones's heir. Charlie Nicklaus raised Jack to emulate Jones, and Jones lived on through Jack, through the Masters (which Jones started), and through the Augusta National club (which he cofounded). Over four days, Woods proved that Jones's course was obsolete—for him, at least. The four par-5s at Augusta National were not merely par-4s for Woods, they were short par-4s. When Jones was helping Alister Mackenzie design the course in the early thirties, he didn't imagine a player with Woods's length. Nicklaus had the idea that Woods could win as often as he lost at Augusta, the course was so well suited to him. Nobody had done anything like that before. Golf's like baseball— it's mostly about losing.

The core Augusta National members, old rich white men in green coats, were stewards of the game for decades, and they handled the responsibility ably, even if they were slow to invite a black man to play in their annual invitational or to join their club. Now there was a black man among them, age twenty-one, with his own green coat and an honorary membership, who with one Augusta victory had immediately become the most powerful force in the game. Upon winning, Woods said that kids—black kids, white kids, city kids, suburban kids—would take up the game in numbers never before seen. There was no reason to doubt his predictions, accurate assessments being one of his strong suits. You knew after the '97 Masters that the playing of the game at its most elite level would change quickly. Woods's game was about generating immense clubhead speed. Long, straight hitting has always been the surest way to golfing success—it was for Jones and Nicklaus, too—but it was not a requirement. Crenshaw and Larry Mize won at Augusta on touch and heart alone. But an otherworldly short game will never be as dependable as robotic repetition of full swing after full swing. In 1997, Woods, Ernie Els, Greg Norman, and Vijay Singh all had similar swings, upright and athletic. Then, such swings were considered exceptional for their athleticism. By 2017, you could imagine such swings becoming commonplace on the PGA Tour. And on that tour, courses would need to grow by a thousand yards if par was to remain, generally speaking, meaningful at 72. For the rest of us, the playing of the game will be the same. Breaking 100, breaking 90, breaking 80—those age-old goals will be no easier than they were before Tiger proved his supremacy. But the gap between us and them had been broadened again.

The transition of power went smoothly. Dan Forsman, a veteran touring pro who missed the cut in that historic '97 Masters, followed Woods up and down Augusta's hills on the final Sunday, just another spectator in the parade, traipsing after greatness. "I want to see what he's doing," Forsman said to me when we found each other hiking up a hill side by side. He knew me from my caddie days. "I want to see history. I really don't know if I can compete with him right now. But I want to try."

Woods's victory was bound to test our generosity. Our selfish goal was to keep the game to ourselves, the tee times, the pleasures of the purely struck shot, the language we knew that the guy in front of us on the Starbucks line did not. After Tiger's '97 Masters, we would never have the game all to ourselves again. It was obvious that Woods would be on magazine covers and cereal boxes and TV screens for the rest of his life. He was black, Thai, charismatic, and young, and he was bound to turn the game into something like our national suburban pastime. You knew he would bring millions of people into the game who had never heard of Bobby Jones or Ben Hogan or Jack Nicklaus. A new boatload was coming in.

⚑

At the 1997 U.S. Open, a familiar figure was in the field. That is to say, familiar to me and not many others: Peter Teravainen. He was forty-one, and I had not seen him in six years. His game was so strange. In the first half of the '95 season on the European tour, he was missing cuts left and right, eleven in a row during one stretch. Then, mysteriously, he won the Czech Open and $200,000 that August. In triumph he said, "Now I'm up to broke."

He was still an expatriate, an American in name only, and he found himself playing in the United States only because he had won the Japan Open in '94. He entered the Japan Open only because his wife, Veronica, a Singaporean of Chinese descent, agreed to fill out the necessary forty-two pages' worth of paperwork. He won the tournament because the course was extremely long, and Teravainen, in certain moods, was still extremely long. Winning the Japan Open earned him an invitation to Jack Nicklaus's tournament, the Memorial, in Dublin, Ohio. After the Memorial (where he missed the cut but made a double eagle), he stayed in the area for a U.S. Open sectional qualifier. He qualified, then played his Thursday and Friday rounds at Congressional in 144 strokes, which earned him the right to play the third round with another golfer who was at four over par, Jack Nicklaus himself.

Teravainen thinks the world of Nicklaus, but the pairing was not ideal for him. He was still walking as I had remembered him, fast, with his chest out and his shoulders back, always way ahead of his playing partners so he didn't have to talk to them. Nicklaus has always been a stroller, and he had become conversational in ways he never used to be. Teravainen was uncharacteristically accommodating.

Nicklaus: "How much time do you spend in Singapore, Peter?"

Teravainen: "Well, let's see. I play thirty weeks a year, so I'm home about twenty-two."

Nicklaus: "You sure you're home that much? Seems to me I see your name playing somewhere every week."

Teravainen: "You're probably right. I guess I play more like thirty-five."

Teravainen continued to have no interest in playing the PGA Tour. His game was still fueled by caffeine, and watery American coffee, he told me, was a problem for him. Same Peter. There seemed to be no passage of time. He was a little more lined, maybe a little more muscular, but otherwise the same. He talked to me as if I had been on his bag a week ago. Nothing was different. The visit with him was a reminder that it's not easy being Peter. Aside from the need for strong coffee, he still wouldn't play balls stamped with the number 4 (considered bad luck in many Asian cultures), still wouldn't change restaurants if he was playing well (no matter how bad the service), and still wouldn't wear red (unless he was willing to risk something powerful happening, for good or for bad). He continued to become agitated when people—certain people, anyway—talked to his airborne golf ball.

When Peter was finishing his second round, trying to make the cut, the little band following him was talking to his golf ball like crazy. ("Gentle, now, softly, gentle, gentle, GENTLE!") Not Veronica, not I—we knew better. But some relatives. Veronica, at one point, put an end to it. Speaking English with a Chinese accent—her "Peter" comes out PEE-ta—she said, "We are all talking to Peter's golf ball much much too much."

In July of 1995, when Peter was missing all those cuts, he called and asked me if I knew Wally Uihlein, the Titleist chairman. "I'm looking for a job," he said.

I was shocked because the only thing Teravainen had ever wanted to do—despite his economics degree and his analytic mind—was play tournament golf. Moreover, and he knows this, he is ill suited to working for anybody but himself. He is independently owned and operated. But a man has to make a living. "I can't play tournament golf anymore," he said.

He and Uihlein talked about a job at the 1995 British Open. At about the same time, Veronica encouraged Peter to wear special Chinese medicinal bandages, soaked in various herbal extracts, while he played. Immediately, his aching legs and feet—worn down by years of waiting for standby flights with a suitcase in each hand and a golf bag over his right shoulder (Teravainen was the ultimate bargain traveler)—felt youthful and alive again. Several weeks later, he won in Czechoslovakia. Aside from the bandages, his therapy included walking on rounded rocks (or golf balls when rounded rocks were unavailable) to massage his feet and wearing a necklace of magnets to cure him of other bodily pains. He got way ahead of broke. He earned $220,000 for winning the Japan Open and another $148,000 when he won another event in Japan. Things were going so well Colin Montgomerie asked him what he was thinking about down the stretch when he was trying to win for the first time on the European tour, in Czechoslovakia.

"I told him, 'I tried to pretend that it was Friday, and I was playing to make the cut,'" Teravainen recalled as we sat together at Congressional. "'Make a birdie coming in, you make the cut. Don't, no big deal, you've missed plenty of cuts.' He looked disappointed. It wasn't relevant to him, but he still listened to me."

Peter, with his brother Chuck silently on the bag, shot rounds of 71, 73, 74, and 75 for fifty-second place, earning $7,138 at the '97 U.S. Open. "The way Congressional is set up, this is what it's like every week in Japan, except in Japan the fairways are narrower," he said. He was grinning maniacally now, and I could see his little teeth again. His eyes, behind his glasses, were squinting, and the skin across his face was taut. By ancestry, Teravainen is Finnish and English. But to me, in some indeterminate way, he has always looked more Asian than anything else. "The USGA would love to do what the Japanese tour does, except the players here would scream," he said. "In Japan, the players don't scream. They respect authority."

He was on the veranda of the lush Congressional clubhouse, stretched out, taking in the sights and the smells like a traveler abroad. He had not read *To the Linksland* and told me he wouldn't, not until his playing days were over. "I feel good," he said. He threw back his shoulders and stuck out his chest and, in his chair, did an odd little dance. "I feel good and I feel young!"

⚑

In the late 1990s, the PGA Tour was becoming more and more international. Golfers would come from all over the world, often from hardscrabble backgrounds, and produce shots and scores virtually identical to what the kids who grew up playing American country club golf were doing. Jim Herre, the golf editor, was particularly interested to learn more about the background of one international player, Carlos Franco of Paraguay. In 1999, he sent me to Paraguay, with an excellent Spanish-speaking reporter named Luis Fernando Llosa, to learn more about Franco.

When I caught up with him, Carlos was in the middle of a three-week break after the Masters, in which he tied for sixth. He could not have been a better host.

"You like my country?" he asked. A barefoot boy was walking a cow along the side of the road. Two decades earlier, that boy could have been Franco, except that his family was too poor to own a cow. Now Franco was driving a big SUV, a Toyota.

"It's beautiful," I said.

"It is *very* beautiful," Franco said.

Nothing slowed him down. Not the cow, not the boy, not the oncoming traffic, not the many potholes. We were on the outskirts of Asunción, Paraguay's largest city. Carlos Franco was singing background vocals to a song playing in the car's tape deck. The song, recorded by a local band, was about the most famous golfer in Paraguay. (It was not a hit, except in the Franco home.) When he got to his name, he rapped me on the knee with the back of his fingers and laughed. "Carlos Franco!"

We stopped at an all-you-can-eat cafeteria. "Drink this tea, this special tea," he instructed me, handing me a cow's horn fashioned into a mug with a straw made of silver inserted through a layer of herbs. I started to ask him, "Is it good for your . . . ?" By Franco's judgment, there are stimulants for the male libido in just about every dish, fruit, dessert, and beverage in the Paraguayan diet. Amazingly, he has just two children.

My host cut me off, mid-question. "Si, my friend." He was grinning maniacally. "Si, si."

To be home! Or, as Franco would say in his native Spanish, "Estar en casa!" To ply his trade, he is required to leave not only his house but also his hemisphere. For five years, he played the Japanese tour and played it well, winning five times. In 1998, he was on the winning International Team in the Presidents Cup. He started playing the PGA Tour full-time in '99. At age thirty-three, he was a PGA Tour rookie.

He was born, literally, in a large shack near the fourth hole of the Asunción Golf Club. The house was built from mud bricks and had a thatched roof, a dirt floor, and a makeshift cardboard wall to separate the space where Carlitos, his five brothers, and one sister slept from the space where their parents slept. There was a crude outhouse, and water came from a well. If you wanted to wash with warm water, you heated up a pot over an open flame. When his mother was feeling flush enough to serve chicken, she went to the yard, grabbed a chicken, wrung its neck, cleaned it, and cooked it. Carlos's father, Francisco Javier Franco, worked on the golf course as a greenkeeper and as a caddie. He also made his boys their first clubs, carved by hand from tree branches. The boys played barefoot and for money they did not have. Carlitos, the second youngest, started playing when he was eight, imitating his older brothers. Later, he worked as a caddie. He never had a lesson and never saw an instruction book or a golf magazine. When he was fifteen, a member gave him a set of clubs, and he became a scratch golfer. At seventeen, he was named caddie master. Three years later he turned pro.

Golf is a fringe sport in Paraguay, a poor country of fewer than six million people, roughly six hundred of whom have somehow found their way to one of Paraguay's four courses. Many of those six hundred golfers are immigrant Korean businessmen and their wives. Another half dozen are the Franco boys, Carlitos and his brothers, all professionals. If you meet a pro golfer from Paraguay, chances are good his family name will be Franco.

In his country, his very beautiful country, Franco's golfing successes are a valuable distraction. Paraguay, experimenting with democracy, was in a jittery state when Luis and I were there. The vice president, Luis Maria Argaña, had recently been assassinated. Three nights later, a group of protesters was fired upon, and eight people were killed. The president, Raúl Cubas, resigned and fled to Brazil.

Driving along a narrow road in a residential area in Asunción, Franco said to us, "This is where the vice president was killed. He had a bodyguard and a driver. Two cars sandwiched him, and the firing started." He was speaking in Spanish. He also speaks fluent Guarani, a native Indian language. Both are official languages in

Paraguay. "I don't worry for myself. I worry about my kids, that they might be kidnapped. Everybody knows me. They respect me. They take care of me. I played golf once with the vice president, when he was on the supreme court. He was a duffer. I am not political."

He arrived at his destination, a television studio. He parked in its dirt lot, brushed his luxuriant hair in the rearview mirror, combed his mustache with the perfectly manicured fingernail of his right index finger.

In the studio, Franco appeared on a talk show. From behind the curtains came the man who allowed him to play the private Asunción Golf Club when nobody else would. He was followed by the man who gave young Carlitos his first set of irons, forged Hogan blades, their sweet spots now worn to the nub. He was followed by a Korean man who was one of Franco's early backers. On a TV monitor was Carlitos's elementary school teacher. His mother and sister were in the audience. He tried to hold back his tears—men in Paraguay don't cry in public—but he could not keep it all in. When he was done, he said to a producer, "Next time you invite me, bring tissues."

Later that night Franco spontaneously invited two dozen friends and visitors and family members to his home for dinner. The guests were served catfish soup and many, many pounds of grilled meats. They opened many beers. At one point, Carlos was talking about golf psychologists. "Anyone who needs a psychologist shouldn't be playing golf," he said. "Confidence comes from inside you, not from somebody else. My confidence is my game."

The house was beautiful, with many rooms, and you moved from inside to out without even knowing it. There were pictures of Severiano Ballesteros and Jesus of Nazareth on the walls. An armed guard was out in front.

The next day we went fishing, on a river deep in the jungle. It took hours on a dusty, bumpy road to get there. On a riverbank, I saw a naked native man fishing with a primitive rod. We passed him in our little skiff. Carlos managed the tiller in one hand and, literally, baited hooks with the other. His dexterity was incredible. The

PGA Tour seemed a million miles away and just about was. We caught one fish after another after another, grilled them when we got in, and ate dinner under the stars.

Ψ

Jeff Maggert was your standard-issue, anonymous, multimillionaire tour player, unremarkable and unknown. Jim Herre suspected there was more to him than met the eye.

Maggert grew up in the Woodlands, a massive planned community outside Houston, right on a golf course. He married his high school sweetheart, and they had two children. He liked golf but showed no particular passion for it. He was highly competent at it and nothing more. He didn't practice much. His career was uneventful. He joined the tour in 1991. The Jeff Maggert we thought we knew left us at the 1998 U.S. Open, at the Olympic Club in San Francisco. Over those nearly eight intervening years, he played in 202 events, won one of them and finished second in a dozen others. He was the poster boy for the anonymous, check-cashing touring pro, courteous but dour.

Then at Olympic, a new golfer named Jeff Maggert was born. He made a move, off the course, that nobody saw coming. He told his wife of twelve years, Kelli, the mother of his children, that he wanted a divorce. Kelli Maggert was one of the most popular wives on tour: cute, vivacious, outgoing. Everything the old Jeff Maggert was not. Everyone figured they were perfect together, another example in the long tradition of opposites attracting. Divorce? Kelli was shocked. Jeff's parents were shocked. The tour was shocked.

"You should go to Las Vegas and set up a tent and sell tickets," Steve Elkington, a fellow Houstonian, told Maggert. "You fooled all of us. You're better than Siegfried and Roy."

Jeff Maggert had been practicing not sleight of hand, but sleight of life. "There was this perception that everything was hunky-dory with us," he said. Talking to him, I had the feeling he had been waiting years for somebody to sit down and really interview him. "I took a certain pleasure in keeping part of my life private."

After Olympic, Maggert went public, and he has been doing unexpected things ever since. The first act in his new life was to start showing up at tournaments with his young new girlfriend, Michelle Austin of Greensboro, North Carolina. Then he won the '99 Andersen Consulting Match Play Championship—and its $1 million first prize—with Michelle and her young son in the gallery. Afterward, he went out and bought several shirts for himself. Just drove to the mall, took out his credit card, and bought them. Nobody could remember him ever doing anything like that.

One week, he had his girlfriend caddie for him. He spent the week making birdies and grinning like a schoolboy escorting a trophy prom date. He and Michelle had been dating only a few months when he asked her to marry him. All over the tour, players and wives and caddies began asking the same thing: What's Maggert going to do next? He was in love.

But this love story should not be confused with a happy story, not an entirely happy one, anyhow. Maggert said falling in love was bringing grief and confusion into his life, too.

Maggert's parents were married when they were eighteen, and they separated thirty years later. When he first learned that his parents were splitting up, he was angry with both of them. He wanted his parents' lives to be just like the lives of the parents he had seen on TV. Later, his thinking evolved. He saw his mother and father happier apart than they had been together. He began to wonder why they hadn't divorced much earlier. Then he realized that he and Kelli were repeating the pattern established by his parents. He and Kelli were teenagers when they started going out. They married when she was twenty-one and he was twenty-two.

"At sixteen, two young people can't look each other in the eye and say, 'Yeah, I want to spend the rest of my life with you,'" Maggert said. We sat in a deserted dining room and talked about his life for three and a half hours without a break. He didn't need one. "I had the fantasy of getting married, having kids, living happily ever after. My parents married when they were young. My brother, the same. I was just going with the flow. Kelli and I had dated for a long time. Getting married was what you did next."

The marriage had an underlying problem. They couldn't talk. Maggert was craving the opportunity to talk to somebody.

Then, on the Saturday night of the 1998 Greater Greensboro Classic, he met someone he could talk to. He was at a private party in a private house. There was a woman from a catering company tending bar. That was the first time he saw Michelle Austin. They talked that night, at length. Michelle returned home to her son and her diary and wrote in it, "He's the one. It's too bad he's married." The next day, she watched her first professional golf event. Maggert shot a final-round 72 to finish sixteenth. Too bad for Jeff, she thought, he won't get paid. Later, she learned that Maggert earned $30,863 that week.

Several weeks passed, with no communication between them. Maggert found himself thinking often of Michelle Austin. He admired what she was doing, raising a child as a single mother, attending college full-time, working on the side. He wanted to call her, and one night during the Byron Nelson Classic, he did. He picked up the phone in his room in the Four Seasons hotel in Irving, Texas, and reached Michelle in Greensboro. They spoke for nearly four hours. Soon after, they were e-mailing one another. He would return to his hotel room after a round, plug in his laptop, and see if he had mail from Michelle. He was saying things he had never said before, writing things he had never written before, feeling things he had never felt before. They almost never discussed golf. He said to Michelle, "You let me talk."

They met in person for the second time when she came up for the weekend of the Buick Classic in Rye, New York. Because it was often raining, and because she was spending the weekend with a well-known married man, Michelle seldom left the hotel. In a single weekend, the relationship was cemented. I was fearful that Maggert might start telling me what happened inside the walls of the hotel room, but he didn't.

Maggert emerged from the weekend with a new course in mind. The following week, at the U.S. Open in San Francisco, he told his wife that the marriage had to end. He told her she could have whatever she wanted when they divvied up their assets. His only concern was custody. He wanted to see his kids as much as he possibly could. The divorce went quickly. Before long, Maggert and Michelle were engaged. Then they were married. And then they had a child.

For a long while, Maggert's mother, Vicki Benzel of Houston, was upset, because she was close to Kelli. "I told him he might regret the divorce someday because of the children," said Benzel, who works for a conservative Christian political group. "I'm glad I stayed married for the sake of Jeff and his brother. I don't know Michelle very well. I'm hopeful she's going to free Jeff up, but Jeff has things locked in his head that no one will ever know. It has been a stumbling block for him in golf. He has a little hang-up somewhere on winning. He likes to blend into the woodwork."

Fifty-five thousand people live in the Woodlands. It has its own schools and hospitals and churches and movie theaters and malls. Soon after the breakup, Kelli Maggert began dating a doctor who lived in the Woodlands, and soon after that, Kelli and her doctor friend ran into Michelle and Jeff at a party. Kelli walked up to Michelle and introduced herself. The whole scene sounded oddly cozy, at least to me. Maybe it was a mammoth exercise in group passive-aggressive behavior. Nobody I talked to could make sense of the thing. The PGA Tour is normally such a well-ordered place, populated by predictable people. "That Jeff Maggert thing," one tour player said to me. "That's a weird deal." Everyone thought they knew the guy, but they didn't.

I asked Michelle if anybody knew her husband.

Oh, yes, she said. "He can't even go into the IHOP," she told me.

Yes, they recognized him. But did anybody *know* him?

"I do," she said. "I really think I do. My job is to let him be the person he wants to be. It's not hard. All you have to do is listen."

<hr />

In all of professional golf, the player I know best, and like most, is Mike Donald. He has a considerable following, mostly because of the way he handled himself in the '90 U.S. Open at Medinah.

That Open was an epic, decided in a playoff between Donald, the lunch-bucket pro playing on guts and near-perfect timing, and Hale Irwin, an aging icon seeking his third national championship. Both played the first four rounds in 280 strokes. Both shot 74 in the playoff. When Irwin's ten-foot birdie putt on the first hole of sudden death fell to the bottom of the cup, Irwin's hands went up in triumph while the loser's went down to retrieve Irwin's ball. "God bless Mike Donald," Irwin said. "I almost wish he had won." In '99, with the PGA Championship being played at Medinah, I revisited the '90 Open with Mike. He didn't need any Cliff Notes. The whole thing was right there in his head. Day after day, it was in his head.

"We should have flipped a coin for the honor," Donald told me. He sounded as if the playoff had been yesterday. He was referring to the order of play for the nineteenth hole.

After the eighteen-hole playoff, Donald and Irwin signed for their 74s and reconvened at the par-4 first hole for the first Open to be decided in sudden death. On the tee, P. J. Boatwright, the widely respected USGA official, awarded the honor to Irwin because Irwin had made par at eighteen and Donald had made bogey. "We should have flipped or picked numbers or something," Donald said. "We had finished a medal round, and now we were starting over."

He was not saying he would have won the Open if he had had the honor on the nineteenth hole. He was saying there was no way to know what would have happened.

The years after the Open were not kind to Donald. His mother died in '91, his father five years later, his swing coach, Gardner Dickinson, two years after that. For a while, he was as close to marriage as he had ever been, but her life was rooted in the rural Northwest, and the only life he has ever known is amid the suburban sprawl of South Florida. In the end, they decided that they were geographically incompatible.

Donald joined the tour in 1980 and spent most of a decade palling around with four other guys, but then the other four went their own ways. Jim Booros left the tour to run a golf-teaching center in Allentown, Pennsylvania. Our mutual friend Bill Britton worked as a club pro in New Jersey. Fred Couples became a star and once sent a Christmas card to "Mr. and Mrs. Mike Donald." Lance Ten Broeck became a tour caddie, most notably for the Swedish golfer Jesper Parnevik. In Mike's memory, the early years, when they were roaming the country and watching their savings accounts and sharing cheap rooms, were the best. He remembers pulling up to a Motel 6—or maybe it was a Hampton Inn—after a long drive with Fred and hearing him say, half asleep, "Check in as a single." A room for a single was thirty dollars, and a room for two was thirty-five. Five bucks was five bucks.

Donald realizes that Booros and Britton and Couples and Ten Broeck have interests, encumbrances, and complications in their lives that he does not. "I don't know anybody like me," he said. "I've got no boss, no job, no wife, no children, no girlfriend. My parents are dead. I've got a two-bedroom apartment. No lawn to mow. I've got no responsibilities."

Once a day, at least, somebody or something will remind Donald of his day in the sun at the '90 U.S. Open. "If I had won, my life would be the same as now," he said. "The only thing that would be different is that I'd have my name on the Open trophy." Maybe he'd have more money, but he has plenty of money.

One Wednesday night, Donald and I were talking on the phone—I was in Philadelphia, and he was at home in Florida—and as we were hanging up, he said, "I think I'll fly to Milwaukee today. I'm first alternate for the Greater Milwaukee Open and have a shot at getting in." The next day I called the press tent at Brown Deer Park and learned that he had teed off in the first round at 7:39 a.m. and shot 67, four under. From Milwaukee he came to Philadelphia, and we played a couple of days of golf together.

One afternoon we played at Merion. "Now, who won Opens here?" he asked. "Hogan in a playoff. Trevino in the playoff against Nicklaus. David Graham in '81. I wonder how many people remember that? Seems like nobody."

The night before his U.S. Open playoff, Donald was in his hotel room, which he was sharing with his younger brother, Pete, who was caddying for him. The phone rang. On the other end was a prominent agent. Mike had never had an agent.

The agent said, "I'm going to fly in tomorrow. If you win tomorrow, you're going to need me."

Donald said, "If I win, the only thing I'm going to need is a limo and a map."

But after the Open, Mike hired the man as his agent. "He got me a deal to play in Sweden for a $35,000 appearance fee and all expenses paid and for my parents to join me," Donald said. "They had a great time, but I played horribly. I felt the whole time that I shouldn't have been there. I should have been playing the Memphis tournament, on a course I played well. I should have been getting ready for the PGA Championship. To be honest, I felt like a whore. I never played good golf again." He's always been a little hard on himself.

When we were at Merion, Mike met a woman who remembered the playoff at Medinah but not the details. He reminded her of the outcome. "Well," the woman said, "it's nice to have been there."

He looked at her as if he were hearing something brand new. "You know what?" he said. "You're right."

⚑

I don't know what it says about me, but I'd rather write about losers than winners. Mike Donald is a loser only in the most narrow of definitions. The same could be said for Jean Van de Velde, who played the final hole of the '99 British Open at Carnoustie in seven strokes when he needed six to win, with the oddest mixture of panache and horrid luck the old Scots game has ever witnessed. He grew up in a converted thick-walled fourteenth-century church in a small town in southwestern France, and when I caught up with him a few weeks after he lost that British Open, he was examining the marvelous thick-walled clubhouse at Medinah. He's interested in architecture, and wine, skiing, soccer, bullfighting, bicycling, rugby, skin diving, and music. (I could go on.) He was late for something but in no particular rush. He placed his delicate hand on an interior wall.

"Iz theese fa-breek or pent?" he wondered aloud. Fabric or paint. His accented English invariably brings smiles (his imitation of Inspector Clouseau is effortless), but he can express intricate thoughts in English far better than most native-born Americans. He ran his thin fingers over the wall. "Ah, pent. Supairb."

He went off to do an interview with Jim Nantz from CBS. Van de Velde was in the midst of a long, hectic day, but he still looked like a million francs. He was wearing brown-and-white saddle shoes, sheer socks, lime-green pants with an extra heavy hem, so that they would hang just so, and a white Lacoste shirt. He did not wear a hat. (Try to find an American pro who doesn't wear his sponsor's hat during an indoor interview.) He declined makeup. His cheeks are perpetually pink. His upper lip is as thin as a Patek Philippe watch. His nose is considerable. His eyebrows are thick and dark and so is his hair, which he parts in the middle. Ladies and gentlemen, your Continental golfer.

Nantz asked Van de Velde if he had seen *Tin Cup*, the movie in which Kevin Costner plays Roy McAvoy, a journeyman pro who dunks one ball after another in the water on the last hole of the U.S. Open, blowing his chance for victory by prizing pride over prudence. Van de Velde had seen it. He sees all the popular American movies. He said you could not compare Roy McAvoy to him. "He went for the dream, the perfect shot," Van de Velde said. "I was just playing my game." I understood completely what he was saying. I know nobody who agrees with this, except for Van de Velde, but he did not misplay a single shot en route to his seven on the last hole of the British Open at Carnoustie, not mentally. When things go wrong mechanically, what can you do? But if a person is trying his best, there's not much to criticize, although Lord knows people make a nice living doing so anyhow.

Analyzing Van de Velde's triple bogey finish brings out a person's deepest feelings about winning and losing. Golf people— tour pros, tour caddies, reporters, officials, fans—responded to Van de Velde's collapse with a mixture of disbelief, sadness, pity, disgust, even anger. Van de Velde's own response was far more interesting. At a press conference before the PGA Championship, Van de Velde and a reporter had this exchange:

Reporter: "Jean, you say that golf is not a big deal. What is a big deal in your life?"

Van de Velde: "My family is a big deal in my life. Health is a big deal in my life. Having people feeling good around me is a big deal. The rest is a bonus."

The French have a word for this attitude, and so, actually, do we: *perspective.*

Standing on the eighteenth tee on the Sunday of the British Open—last pairing, three-shot lead—Van de Velde was having the time of his life. The home hole at Carnoustie is 487 yards, with a stream, the Barry Burn, that comes into play twice, numerous bunkers, nasty rough, and out-of-bounds left and over the green. It is a par-4 in name only. Van de Velde hit a driver off the tee because, as he told me, "I always hit a driver, whenever I can." Many have been critical of that decision. They don't recall that when Tom Kite came to the final hole of the 1992 U.S. Open at Pebble Beach with a two-shot lead, he hit a downwind driver, despite the ocean that lines the left side of the hole and the out-of-bounds on the right. He won with a par.

There was nothing wrong with the tee shot, even though Van de Velde pushed it wildly to the right. It carried the burn and finished in the rough, where he drew a perfect lie. The golfing gods had been smiling on him all week, and they continued to. For his second shot, he had 189 yards to clear the burn in front of the green. "I am a professional golfer. I miss my two-iron, it still goes 200 yards." Easily. He pulled his two-iron from the bag and pushed the shot. He carried the burn, easily. The ball was sailing into the grandstand. No big deal, he thought, that's a free drop.

And that's when the golfing gods stopped smiling on him. The ball ricocheted off a grandstand handrail, bounced off a stone wall that lines the Barry Burn, and careened backward into a patch of untamed grass. From there, he had no shot. There was nowhere for him to drop. "I thought about going sideways, back to the fairway, but I didn't think I could necessarily get it out, and if I did, I thought I might hit it through the fairway to the rough on the other side and draw another bad lie," he said. He was thinking clearly. He was not going berserk under the pressure. He could not go back and take a drop from where he played his second shot; the rough there was too unpredictable. Given that there was no safe shot, he tried to play a heroic shot, but the grass was too thick to get the club face on the ball, and his third shot finished in the middle of the burn. That's the shot he regrets, not the driver, not the two-iron. If he could live his life over again, he would try to pitch out and onto the fairway. It might not have worked, either, but that's what he would have tried. But what did him in was the handrail.

He cited other regrets. He wished he had jumped into the burn immediately after his ball did, because when his ball first hit the water, only about a third of it was submerged. There was a half minute or so when he could have played it, he said. But the tide was coming in, and by the time he removed his shoes and socks and waded to his ball, it was unplayable.

He took a drop from the burn, for his fourth shot; then, for his fifth, he hacked a shot out of the rough and into a greenside bunker. His playing partner, Craig Parry, had beaten him there. "He says to me, 'Let me get out of your way,'" Van de Velde recalled. "Then he holes the shot. I say to myself, 'The chances of that shot being holed are a thousand to one, and he does it. Now the chances for me are two thousand to one.'" The bunker shot that Van de Velde played and the eight-footer for triple bogey he made to get himself into the playoff with Justin Leonard and Paul Lawrie should be regarded as one of the all-time clutch up-and-downs. Instead, it has become a footnote. His play in the four-hole playoff was mostly poor, and Paul Lawrie, a Scotsman, was the last man standing. Peter Alliss, commentating for the BBC, said of Van de Velde's play on the seventy-second hole, "It's beyond a joke. He's gone gaga." Jean Van de Velde shrugged when he heard that. We were driving from the suburbs to downtown Chicago, because he wanted to go out for dinner at a good Japanese restaurant and the restaurants near the golf course and his hotel were substandard. The drive was an hour. He did not care. He ordered expertly.

Immediately after the Open, Van de Velde started receiving calls and letters and e-mails. In his graceful and lusty play, most of the correspondents saw something they liked. "Theese one was zee best," Van de Velde said. "A man wrote, 'The next time someone says, "Even I could have made a six on eighteen to win," tell them, "Here's ten pence. Give me a call when you get a chance in your next major."'"

It was the same exact point the lady at Merion made to Mike Donald, that Mike was lucky to have had the chance to win a U.S. Open. It took Mike nearly a decade to get it. Jean Van de Velde got it before Paul Lawrie even hoisted the old claret jug.

CHAPTER TEN

CLUBMAKERS

(2000, PART 1)

THE END HAD BEEN COMING FOR A LONG WHILE, and finally it
arrived, on the Sunday before the 2000 PGA Championship, at
Valhalla, in Louisville, Kentucky. I was playing in my regular game,
at the Philadelphia Cricket Club. I used my $400 Titleist 975D
titanium driver twelve times. Didn't hit a single fairway. Given
the places I was driving the ball, my round of 86 was no small feat.
(I had an 11 handicap then.) The next morning I was in the factory
of the Louisville Golf Club Company, down the road from Valhalla.
Louisville Golf is the last large-scale manufacturer of persimmon
drivers in the United States. I was looking to go back to wood. Right
about then, it seemed like most everybody was.

Well, okay, that might be a slight exaggeration. But that's what
Elmore Just, the president of Louisville Golf believed. I was sit-
ting with him in his office, and he was citing all sorts of evidence.
For instance, he had heard that Bob Estes, the winner of the 1994
Texas Open, was thinking about going back to a wooden driver.
He had also heard that Bobby Nichols, the '64 PGA champ and a
native son of Louisville, had sent a nephew to the factory to pick

up one of Elmore's new Smart drivers, with the idea that Nichols would consider using it at Valhalla. Then, most unfortunately, Nichols had to pull out of the tournament. Still, he had been thinking about going wood. He was part of the trend.

Wood, he said, had enjoyed a good past. "No reason it can't have a good future," he said. "We're just trying to keep our dog in the fight." He was like every other golfer I've ever known. Player, caddie, spectator, architect, manufacturer—we're all optimists.

Louisville Golf was founded in 1974, in the heyday of persimmon, an era when all golfers, but pros in particular, had a much more personal relationship with their headcovered clubs. After all, the wood with which they made their living had itself once been alive. On the practice tee at tour events, players would routinely use the words and manners of courting in regard to their wooden clubs. A tasseled sock would be pulled off triumphantly, and a neighboring player would grip the club loosely, waggle it a few times, and say, "She's a beaut."

Many of those beauts were made by Louisville Golf, by Elmore Just or one of his four brothers: Ron or Mike or Robert or Gerard, all of them in the early years of middle age. Mostly, the Just brothers made clubs for other companies. When Payne Stewart won the '91 U.S. Open, he was playing a laminated, big-headed Wilson Whale driver that was made in the back shop of Louisville Golf on Grassland Drive, in an industrial zone on the outskirts of the city. The Hogan Apex persimmon driver Tom Kite used in winning the '92 U.S. Open was made by Louisville. "I remember on the last hole," Ron Just told me, "the TV guy said, 'Looks like Kite's using a three-wood here to play safe,' and then they show the club up close and I say, 'That's no three-wood. That's our driver!'"

At its peak, Louisville Golf employed more than a hundred woodworkers and produced about eight hundred clubs per day. By the turn of the century, the company had eleven woodworkers and made maybe a hundred clubs a day, half of them fairway woods and drivers, the other half wooden-headed putters. The Just brothers watched as the tour, and the golfing world with it, went from all wood to nearly all metal.

The last holdout was my close personal friend Davis M. Love III, a superb driver, who used the same No. 1 wood—a pear-shaped Cleveland Classic—from his rookie year in 1986 through the middle of '97. That year, Love came out with his book, *Every Shot I Take,* which included this sentence: "Golf is somehow more pleasing to me when played with a driver made of wood." We were of like minds. I had enjoyed a long-term relationship with a MacGregor Eye-O-Matic driver from the '50s, a thing of beauty that I hit sort of short but mostly in play. Love was the hero of Elmore and the Elmores everywhere, wood men trying to hold on.

Then in August of 1997, Love won a major, the PGA, using a new driver, a Titleist 975D with a titanium head that had the loft of a putter and a shaft about as flexible as a wooden leg. A while later, he gave me one of his spare drivers and said, "If I switched, maybe you should, too." I spent three years trying every loft and every shaft flex. There were some good moments, and my best drives with those clubs were my best drives ever. That was the tantalizing thing. But there were more moments of misery than anything else. My heeled shots went dead left. They had no curve to them, tree bound from the get-go. Toed shots were the same, affording me a visit to the right woods on an equal-opportunity basis.

I wasn't telling Elmore Just anything he hadn't heard before. "That's why wooden clubs are better," he said. "The wood club has more curve to it, more bulge and more roll. Because of that curve, an off-center hit with a wood club imparts more spin on the ball. What people don't seem to realize is, that's good. You want your heeled shots to start down the left side and fade back into the fairway. You want your toed shots to start down the right side and draw back."

I had come to the right place. Just fitted me for one of his Smart drivers, a solid piece of persimmon—a hard and heavy wood—but with a somewhat bigger head than the classic shapes from the Eisenhower years. With hope in my heart, I plunked down $375 for the club. (About the only good thing the titanium clubs have done for him, Just said, is raise the bar on what golf nuts will spend for a driver.) My club was assembled to order. I asked for a heavy head with 10.5 degrees of loft, a D-5 swing weight, a 44-inch lightweight graphite shaft with a regular flex, and a Winn grip, one wrap oversized. My new wood would be ready the next day.

Louisville is a woodworking town. One of the biggest employers in the city is Hillerich & Bradsby, maker of the Louisville Slugger baseball bat—Powerized!—and PowerBilt golf clubs. Elmore Just, who was then in his early fifties, grew up in south Louisville, the working-class side of the city, and was the first Just to go to college, which he did at a small college called Bellarmine on a partial golf scholarship. After college and the army, Elmore came home to Louisville and took a job at H&B, and it was there, in the early '70s, that he got bit by the clubmaking bug. When a clubmaker, the late Earl Gordon, left H&B to go into business for himself, Elmore went to work for him and learned alongside him. "If you heard Earl Gordon talking about clubs, he sounded like a poet, but Lord was he mean," Elmore told me. "He'd say to his pregnant wife in the dead of winter, 'I got to take care of some things; go out and warm up the car for me.'"

Before long, Elmore left Gordon, too scared of the man to return for his Royal manual typewriter and big wooden desk. That's when he started Louisville Golf.

Elmore had been a tree buff and a persimmon head since he was fifteen, when he started playing golf at a public course that had a small stand of persimmon trees. In the fall, he would eat the sweet, ripe fruit in mid-round. The great places for persimmon in the United States are the bottomlands along rivers in Arkansas, Mississippi, and Louisiana, but a half dozen persimmon trees grow on Grassland Drive in Louisville, too. Elmore planted those trees in the mid-1980s, and now they're thriving. "Come fall I'll go out at lunchtime, gather a dozen or so persimmon fruits, and eat 'em at my desk," Elmore said. "I like to leave the fruit in my mouth till you've got nothing but seeds." He is the author of a self-published book titled *The Persimmon Story,* which concluded with a family recipe for persimmon pudding. As the book is not easy to find, I include the recipe for eight here:

Squeeze 1 quart of persimmons through a colander, producing about 2 cups of pulp.
  Beat in:
  3 eggs
  1¼ cups sugar
  1½ cups all-purpose flour
  1 teaspoon baking powder
  1 teaspoon soda
  ½ cup melted butter
  2½ cups rich milk
  2 teaspoons cinnamon
  1 teaspoon ginger
  ½ teaspoon freshly grated nutmeg
  1 cup raisins or nutmeats (optional)
  Place the pudding in a greased 9-by-9-inch dish and bake
at 325 degrees until the pudding is firm (about an hour).
Serve with cream or hard sauce.

Reading the recipe, I meant to ask Elmore what nutmeats are,
but I didn't, and then I lost the chance. Nine months after I met
him, he died suddenly of a heart attack after a round of golf. He
was a trim, gentle, nice man.

Also a zealot and a pamphleteer. One afternoon in his office
during the 2000 PGA Championship, he handed me a green piece
of paper with six of his own wood-club talking points on it. This
was the last of them: "Is there a conspiracy? In 1989 a leading golf
publication did a test comparing persimmon to steel heads. The
results showed persimmon actually outperformed metal. The test
was never printed." I took the green sheet and my persimmon seeds
and wished Elmore a good day.

He may well have been correct about the conspiracy theory. It
was certainly not in the interest of the golf magazines to promote
woods made out of wood—magazine ads are placed by manufac-
turers selling the newest and the latest. Metal woods, which are far
cheaper to produce than woods made of wood, benefited from a
marketing campaign the likes of which golf had never before seen.

One Tuesday morning at Valhalla, I asked Greg Norman, possibly the greatest driver of the ball in golf history, if he missed playing with wood and if wood could ever come back. "We were discussing that on the driving range the other day," he said, "wondering what would happen if players used their old wooden clubs. Quite honestly, they'd probably do just as well as they're doing now. As to wood coming back, I don't see that taking place. It's not a very forgiving material for all you guys." Elmore went to his grave believing the opposite. He believed that wood *was* more forgiving for all us guys.

At Valhalla, I went looking for Bob Estes and found him in the locker room, actually reading the news section of a newspaper. I asked him if he was considering a return to a wooden driver. "Considering?" he said. We left the locker room, found his caddie and his golf bag, and Estes pulled out his driver. It was gorgeous, a MacGregor Tommy Armour 945TW Tourney made in 1953, with a medium coffee finish and an X-100 True Temper steel shaft in it, 43½ inches long. He had bought it from a man in Mesquite, Texas, for $700. The Valhalla tournament was his first week with it.

"I've tried about every steel and titanium driver there is," Estes said. "I feel like I'm going to hit more fairways with this one. That's the main thing. I get more feedback with this club; I know where on the face I've hit the ball. The titanium drivers carry a little farther in the air, but on a dry fairway I don't feel as if I'm giving up any distance. At home I've got a bunch of wooden three-woods and four-woods and five-woods. They might be coming out soon, too."

He went off to practice, and all around the practice tee, thousands of people started to gather for the Champions Clinic, a PGA Championship tradition in which the golfing gods—former winners of the tournament—share their wisdom with the rest of us. The driving portion of the clinic was handled by Love, Jack Nicklaus, and, in his first Champions Clinic, Tiger Woods. Woods, using a Titleist 975D, was launching tee shots so far and so high that Lanny Wadkins, the emcee, said he could have two balls in the air at once. Now would be a good time to point out that I have never thought that my problems with my 975D could be laid at the head of the club. As Woods demonstrated, the club worked when swung properly.

At the clinic, Woods gave an excellent tip: If you feel as if your head is coming over the ball at impact—he was talking to me!—move your head back in the stance by moving your right foot back. I was eager to try it.

It was getting late. Elmore was at the Louisville Golf booth in the merchandise tent. He had my new Smart driver. I went over to pick it up. It was gorgeous, with a tan grip, a black shaft, a mahogany finish, his neat signature on the heel, my initials on the bottom, and a black insert and no scoring lines, just a circle of eight gold dots to indicate the sweet spot. (Just believed scoring lines did nothing for a driver.) I shook hands with my clubmaker and said goodbye, club in hand.

I was more than eager to try it. It was past seven p.m. Only a few players were on the practice tee at Valhalla, and not too many security people were on guard. I gathered a dozen balls out of a practice bunker and slipped onto the tee, next to Jesper Parnevik, who was wearing out his Callaway Great Big Bertha driver. The ting sound he made was so stinging it almost made my ears hurt. I made eye contact with no one, afraid of being thrown off the range. I thought about my new head position, about what Tiger had said, and made some swings. My shots off the heel were all in play, and I could feel where I was hitting them. My good shots sailed through the heavy, musky Louisville air. What a joy.

On my way back to my car, I walked through the players' valet area. Brent Geiberger was waiting for his car. I reintroduced myself to him and told him I had caddied some for his adoptive father, the gracious Al Geiberger, the '66 PGA champ, when he had a bright red Spalding golf bag made of kangaroo skin and a beautiful Spalding driver made of persimmon (and a beautiful swing to go with it). I triumphantly pulled the headcover off my new Smart driver and handed it to Brent. He waggled it a few times and placed it gently on a straight line on the concrete sidewalk to check if the face was square. He had grown up on wooden clubs. He knew the drill. He handed the club back to me and said, "Not bad looking. Not bad looking at all." With that, I proudly put my wooden Smart driver, personally made for me by Elmore Just, back in my bag. For several glorious weeks the club made the starting fourteen lineup. Then, sadly, the magic wore off, and the search was resumed. Steel, graphite, titanium, wood—I've dated them all. But when you go into an old-time golf shop, it's always the wood ones that catch your eye.

ᐟ

I was in the golf business myself right then. In the summer of 2000, all manner of cable outfits were running a thirty-minute infomercial for a club of my invention, the E-Club (for everybody, from everywhere). I have a U.S. patent on the club and USGA approval, too. It's a conforming club.

The infomercial was always the same, but I never got bored watching it. Here's Nick Price playing a beautiful bunker shot with my little invention. Here's Judy Rankin punching a lovely recovery shot from the rough. Here's a nine-handicapper called Doc holing out a forty-foot chip shot. The E-Club never fails—not in the infomercial, anyway.

I had no plan to become a golf entrepreneur. I sought only to fix my ailing chipping game. That thing about necessity being the mother of invention? It's true.

My earliest notion about the E-Club popped into my head during my first trip to Scotland, in 1985. I was playing the Old Course, thrown into a game with three locals. I was amazed by how often they used their putters off the green. They used their putters to hit sixty-foot chips and fifty-yard bump-and-runs, to run shots up the faces of bunkers and to extract themselves from the heather.

Back home, I tried to incorporate those shots into my semi-dufferish short game. The results were sometimes good and often not. American courses are too lush to make the putter the versatile club it is on Scottish linksland. I didn't know it, but my long search for the E-Club had begun.

Then came 1991, caddying for Peter Teravainen on the European tour. Peter would sometimes play practice rounds with the American golfer Glen Day, who was then a kid on the European tour. Glen liked to play a shot I had never before seen: He'd chip with a Ping metal three-wood. He played the shot beautifully, but when I tried, it was a disaster. The shaft was too long, the head too light, the lie angle too flat. Then a half decade later, in 1996, I was helping Davis Love III with his book. I asked Davis, "If the ordinary golfer could have only one chipping club, what should it be?" "The putter," he answered quickly. "My father was one of the guys who'd say, 'A bad putt is better than a bad chip.'" Around that time, Tiger Woods and his bag of tricks showed up on tour, bringing his three-wood chip shot into millions of homes. Evidently, he learned the shot from his longtime teacher, Butch Harmon, who learned it from his father, the Winged Foot professional Claude Harmon, who learned it from another legendary Winged Foot professional, Tommy Armour, who brought it over from Scotland. The shot was an old one. My innovation was a club designed to play it and other shots, as well.

My idea was a club that would combine the properties of a putter and a fairway wood, with the weight of a sand wedge—a utility club that would allow you to hit all sorts of greenside shots but also punch shots 150 yards or longer with nothing more taxing than an elongated putting stroke. I went to see George Izett, an old-line clubmaker in suburban Philadelphia. I brought him a five-wood and an offset putter and asked him if he could build me a club with a very heavy fairway-wood head, combined with the offset hosel, shaft length, and lie angle of my putter, with the head weight of a heavy sand wedge. George was the first person I had tried out my idea on, and he responded to it with a single word: "Interesting." I took that as encouragement. It would take him a while to get to it, he said. First he had to make a putter for a psychiatrist. Everybody's an inventor.

A month or so later, I telephoned George. He hadn't begun work on my club, but what he said next turned out to be my first break. In a golf catalogue, he had come across a driver with a peculiar hosel made by a company called Tegra, based in Florida. He gave me the toll-free number. I called and asked for the name of their chief designer. The designer's name was Art Chou and he worked, I was told, in King of Prussia, in, it so happens, suburban Philadelphia. Within a week, in December of 1997, I was sitting in Art's office, a five-wood and putter and sand wedge in my hands, telling him of my idea.

Before we started, Art, the son of an engineer and an engineer himself, said that he would have to cut me off if my idea sounded remotely like anything he was working on. He had worked as a designer for Titleist for a decade, helping to develop the DCI iron. He knew the terrain. When I was done, he said, "I've never heard of anything like it." I took that as encouragement, too. He became a consultant to the project, to use a term of business. What he really became was my club-design guru.

Art introduced me, over the telephone, to an engineer in Taiwan named Stanley Liu, who had a foundry there called Top Spin. For about $3,000, Stanley agreed to make a model, a master, a tool, and a dozen prototype clubs for me. We had many involved conversations about things like soleplate thickness, welding lines, face progressions, and USGA regulations.

In February of 1998, I met Stanley at the International Golf Trade Show in Orlando, and he showed me a wooden model. It was bulky looking, but it was a start. Four months and thirty or so telephone conversations later, a large box arrived at my house. The first prototypes! Within minutes, the kitchen floor was covered with crumpled Taiwanese newspapers used to pack the clubs.

I drove out to the Cricket Club. I should point out that with $3,000 worth of clubs in my trunk, the value of my ride, a tired '69 Type III VW Squareback, quadrupled. The club worked. It did everything I hoped it could do. You could chip with it, play bump-and-runs, hit greenside bunker shots with it, all with a putting stroke. You could play punch shots out of the woods and out of fairway bunkers. When I started playing with it, my regular partners called the club "the Bamburgler," and when I played the club from an unusual spot, say buried under a bunker lip, I'd warn them that I was "playing for science."

Through the summer of '98, I refined the club and thought about ways to turn it into a business. I experimented with different lofts, from sixteen to twenty-four degrees, different head weights, metals, shafts, grips. My phone bills to Taiwan were comically high, as were my Federal Express bills. I brought the club to Frank Thomas, then the technical director for the USGA, seeking official notification that the club conformed to USGA regulations. He experimented with it on his office rug and said, "We may have to make this club illegal. It makes the game too easy." He was joking. The USGA ruled that it conformed. I hired a patent lawyer and applied for a patent on my invention. That set me back another $5,000. I was now $10,000 in the hole.

My first thought was to sell the rights to my club to a real golf company. I wrote to John Solheim, president of the company that makes Ping golf clubs, to find out if he wanted to see the club. Received no answer. I brought the club to Dick Helmstetter, the chief of new golf club products at Callaway. He was intrigued. He brought me and the club to the company's Richard C. Helmstetter Testing Center, where two of his minions gave the club a workout. They played beautiful shots with it, but no offer was forthcoming. I brought the club to Davis Love, while he was playing a casual game at Winged Foot. He played incredible shots with it. At the end of the round, he said, "Just tell me what I can do to help. If you want me in an infomercial, let me know." An infomercial with Davis? I floated home.

The first thing people wanted to know was the club's name. Finding a good one was tormenting. One friend, working overtime and without pay, suggested the following: the Runner, the Wizard, Merlin, the Chipmunk, the Bailer, the Rescuer, the Hero, the Lifesaver. Another friend suggested Pudge, thinking the club combined the properties of a putter and a wedge. Several people, unconnected to one another, came up with Bamburgler. The club needed not only a name, but also a category. I didn't want people thinking of it as a chipper. I explained this problem to my friend Jim Finegan, who is truly learned in the game, and he reminded me that in his golf youth, in the 1930s, there was a rubric of club called jiggers, which were essentially short-shafted five-irons, utility clubs used for chipping, run-up shots, and recovery shots. That's what this club was, a modern jigger. Early on, I called the club the Jigger E, already on to the everyman part of it. With critical input from Art Chou, the name evolved to what it is now, the E-Club. By category, it's a Type II Jigger. It is a modern utility club. I borrowed Type II from my Type III Squareback, which died its final death practically at the Cricket Club parking lot on the day we were shooting the infomercial there.

That would never have come about without my second big break. I have a friend in Philadelphia named Amy Banse, an executive at Comcast, the cable company. Amy is not a golfer, but she was then on the board of the Golf Channel, which is owned by Comcast. I had been one of Amy's golf tutors. I told her about my club, and she showed me how to write a business plan, a tool to find investors for the infomercial I now dreamed of, starring Davis Love. She took the business plan and a club to our mutual friend, Brian Roberts, the president of Comcast. Brian sent both to a friend of his, Tim Neher. Tim was a good golfer, a member of Pine Valley and Seminole, a friend of Arnold Palmer, a successful cable television executive, a board member of the Golf Channel and its original financier. Tim went out for a game at his home club. His approach shot on the first hole came up a little short. He reached for the E-Club, in the name of science. He had never hit a shot with it. He holed the shot. Soon after, in November of 1998, we became partners. We formed a company, Bantam Golf. For a while, it had one $119 product.

Tim was a force of nature. A year after our first meeting, our infomercial was being tested on the Golf Channel. In that time, Tim had negotiated a deal with a California company called Script-to-Screen to produce the infomercial. He negotiated a deal with a Pennsylvania company called Q-Direct to take care of ordering, shipping, manufacturing, and media buying. He negotiated a deal with Nick Price to be our spokesperson (after Titleist would not al-low Davis to endorse it). He invested hundreds of thousands of his dollars and hundreds of hours of his time. We shot the infomercial in Los Angeles and South Florida and at the Cricket Club.

And then, in the spring of 2000, we went into rollout, airing our infomercial every other day or so on the Golf Channel, among other places. I didn't know the word *rollout,* just as I did not know the word *nutmeats,* but my new friends in manufacturing used the word, so I did, too. At first, I was getting rollout updates every time we aired the show. Even at five on a weekday morning, we had been able to sell sixty-four clubs in a single airing on the Golf Channel.

When I was researching how to become a golf manufacturer, I called another golf inventor, the man who designed the Alien sand wedge. He told me, "You'll sell 50,000 clubs. There are 50,000 golf kooks out there who buy one of everything, no matter what it is. You'll have a business if you can sell 50,001." We made 70,000 clubs.

For a while, it all looked very promising. Lee Trevino, with no commercial incentive to do so, put an E-Club in his bag when he played the British Open, his final one, at the Old Course in the summer of 2000. Fred Couples watched the first President Bush use one over the course of a weekend and later told me, "Every golfer over the age of sixty should have that thing in their bag." We sold the first 50,000 very quickly, within a year. And only a smatter-ing since then. When we went into liquidation, I personally bought hundreds and hundreds of E-Clubs. They remain available for a limited time only. At $59, I believe the club to be one of golf's best values.

Go to www.eclubgolf.com, if you care to.

CHAPTER ELEVEN

TEXAS (2000, PART 2)

IN THE SUMMER OF 2000, on the fiftieth anniversary of Ben Hogan's win in the 1950 U.S. Open at Merion, the members received a letter from Hogan, which was odd, because Hogan died in 1997. I will say that I know the typist.

To the Merion membership:

I won the National Open at your course in June 1950. Mid-year, mid-century, mid-career for me, it turned out. Everyone figured my career was over after the accident. Would have been over had I not won at Merion. I'd have been too tired to go on.

Sometimes I run into people up here—God's blimp, that's what Young Tom Morris calls it—and they were members of nice clubs down below, places I visited, places I won, places I didn't. They're never very direct about it, but they want to know what I think of their club and its course. Strange that people want to know such things, that people fuss over these lists that rank courses. If you enjoy your club and your course, what else matters? I'm no good at telling people what they want to hear, anyhow. I once heard Nicklaus say, "I love Pebble Beach." Baffles me. How can a professional golfer love a golf course? The golf course exists to humiliate you, to show you up, to reveal your frailties. I know at Merion you're all very fond of Bobby Jones. I've heard more than a few of you repeat that old Jones chestnut about beating "old man par." Pardon me, ladies: That's horseshit. Par is a contrivance. To the professional golfer, the only thing that matters is the number of strokes you take. The amateur game is meaningless to me. They tell me that Nicklaus won a National Amateur at Pebble, that Jones won one at your place. Very nice. I started playing professional golf at seventeen.

Anyway, about Merion and me. First played it in 1934, at the Open. Shot 79, twice. Needless to say, I didn't have to play the Saturday rounds. Merion Cricket, it was called then. I didn't hate it. I will say I found it confounding, couldn't figure out where to drive it. In those days, I hit a hot hook that rolled right off your fairways, which were firm and fast and brown, and into the nastiest rough I'd ever seen. In Texas, where I grew up, the rough was mostly burned out by June. Couldn't figure out your June wind. Number 4, the long par-5 with the downhill second shot, plays due north, correct? It was always into the breeze. Fair enough. Then the fifth, the par-4 with the hook fairway, plays in the exact opposite direction, due south, correct? It always played into the breeze, too. I don't know what you do with your wind there in Philadelphia, but it's a mystery to me. In Texas, the wind just blows.

When I came back in 1950, I wasn't a hooker anymore, so I thought I had a chance. I stayed at the Barclay Hotel, on Rittenhouse Square. That was the hotel at the time. Frank Sullivan, my lawyer, one of your members, set it up. He lived at the Barclay. The other players skimped on hotels. I never did, not at tournaments, anyway, not once I had a few dollars in my pocket. I needed a room with ceilings high enough to make a full swing, full-length mirrors so I could study what I was doing, carpets that putted at a realistic green speed, and a large man-sized bathtub with no shortage of hot water. I needed a long soak with Epsom salts, morning and night, to get the aches out of my bones, get my muscles moving again. That damn accident.

What I did at Merion in June of 1950 is meaningful only if you understand the accident, what happened to me on the first day of February, 1949. My dead father's birthday. I hate talking about the accident, but you've probably heard about it and you've probably heard it wrong. About the only guy to get it right was a Texan named Curt Sampson in his book about me, *Hogan.* In 1948, I had won ten tournaments. I'm not going to tell you how good that season was, how it compares to Byron Nelson in '45 or Nicklaus in '72 or Tiger Woods in '99. I will say the war was over, and everybody was playing: Nelson, Sam Snead, Gene Sarazen, Jimmy Demaret, Paul Runyan, Cary Middlecoff, Lloyd Mangrum. I was on the cover of *Time,* with a quote: "If you can't outplay them, outwork them." I'm glad they didn't write "them" as "'em." I hate that hillbilly Texas crap. I've always believed in doing a thing right. Anyway, on the West Coast swing, in the winter of '49, I played four times and won twice, at Bing Crosby's tournament and the Long Beach Open, where I beat Demaret in a playoff. Then he beat me in a playoff at the Phoenix Open, the last event on the West Coast swing. From Phoenix, everybody was driving to Texas for the Texas Open in San Antonio. My wife, Valerie, and I were driving to Texas too. Not for the tournament. I was taking the week off. We were driving home, in our black Cadillac, to Fort Worth. Every ex-caddie dreams of someday *driving* a Caddy. I had mine. It was paid for, cash.

We were driving on Highway 80, on a narrow bridge, on a foggy night, a half hour outside of Van Horn, a one-motel town in the heart of West Texas. A packed Greyhound bus, a thirty-seven seater—over ten tons, they tell me—was barreling down the road, right at us, going maybe fifty miles an hour. We were going half that. The bridge had concrete walls, and there was no place to bail out. Right before the crash, I dived onto to Valerie. By trying to save her life, I saved my own. First the steering column and then the engine came flying at us. I broke my left ankle, and the rest of that leg was mangled. I broke my pelvis and a rib. I bled, massively, internally and externally. Lost damn near all my eyesight in my left eye (and never got it back). Val, thank God, was unhurt. I was on death's door. When the ambulance finally came, I was fading in and out. They tell me that on the drive to the hospital, I gained consciousness for a moment and yelled, "Fore left!" Figures. My nightmares were always filled with hooks.

I spent two months in the hospital, did chin-ups on a bar over my bed to try to get my strength back. They put that in that movie about me, *Follow the Sun*. They didn't get too many details right, but they got that one. Anyway, the chin-ups didn't do much good. I left the hospital weighing 120 pounds.

Before the accident, I played thirty events a year. After the accident, I knew I'd be lucky to play a half dozen. I had to set my priorities. The U.S. Open was at the top of my list, because it was the most demanding. The higher the winning score, the better I felt my chances were. The '50 Open at Merion was the fiftieth Open. I had a whole lot vested in it.

I was always a slave to ritual, but after the accident more so than ever before. I needed four hours to prepare for a round, including a half hour or so to wrap my legs in bandages, from ankle to thigh, to reduce the swelling. I needed a minute to drink a glass of ginger ale before teeing off. I believed that helped reduce the swelling, too. In the Thursday round, I shot 72. Could have been worse. I had an awful cramp as I came off the eleventh green, a shooting pain through my legs and body. I had to lean on my caddie to stop from tipping over. Somehow, I made it up the hill to the twelfth tee.

I thought 72 was good, but one score I had to take notice of, much as I hate to do that. I was never one to spend

much time looking at the golf of others. There's an old story
about me playing the twelfth once at Augusta National, the
par-3 over Rae's Creek, with Claude Harmon. Claude's son
is Butch, the one who's on TV all the time, Tiger's teacher.
Anyway, Claude makes a hole in one. But coming off the
green, according to the story everyone tells, I say to him, "I
do believe that's the first two I've ever made on that hole."
The story makes the point well. In tournament golf, you've
got enough going on worrying about your own ball, let alone
somebody else's. Anyway, that Thursday round at Merion,
something exceptional did happen, and you had to pay attention to it. A score of 64 shot by a kid from Birmingham
name Lee Mackey. Lowest round ever shot in an Open. He
came home in 31, with a bogey on seventeen and a three on
the last, where he hit a three-wood to eight feet. The next
day, he shot 81.

I wasn't surprised. For one thing, I'm sure he woke up
that Friday morning and realized he wasn't playing in the
Birmingham Assistants Championship, but for the national
title. More to the point, the greens were too fast to go really
low on consecutive days. When your blade is red hot, it
doesn't stay that way for more than one day. I had never
putted faster greens than those at Merion that year. I'd guess
the greens were about the same as they are now on a typical
summer day, maybe a little faster. Merion's greens were like
no others. All the pros knew about Joe Valentine, your first
greenkeeper, and his secret methods and seed combinations.
These days, everybody talks about Augusta having the fast-
est greens. But in those days, the greens at Augusta were
still Bermuda, and you couldn't compare them to the speed
of the greens at any Open, the '50 Open at Merion in particular. The greens at Merion were so fast I changed my
putting routine, something I did with great reluctance. (I
changed any routine with great reluctance.) Before putting,
I did not rest the head of my putter on the green on downhill putts because I was afraid a wisp of wind would come

up and cause the ball to move. That happened during the Thursday round. As I stood over my ball, the ball started trickling toward the hole, must have moved four feet. A USGA official was there. I confirmed with him that I had not grounded my club, hadn't addressed it. Had I, it would have been a stroke. As it turned out, I needed every stroke I could get.

In the Friday round, I shot 69 and at the end of the day was in fifth place. One more day and two more rounds to go. Saturday was warm but not hot, breezy but not windy. I was feeling good about my golf if my legs could hold me up. In the morning I shot 72 and was, as the newspapermen liked to say then, still in black numbers, three over par. This is the thing that irritates me. I mean, everybody was in black numbers. I could have told you Thursday morning that nobody would be breaking 280 for four rounds at Merion, no matter what some kid shot in the first round.

Anyway, now there was just one more round. Middlecoff and Johnny Palmer were tied with me. The three of us were one behind Dutch Harrison, two behind Lloyd Mangrum. I vowed to give the final round everything I had. I always did. I knew time was running out for me. I didn't know how many more chances I'd have. To be totally candid, there were only a very few players still in the tournament. There would be no 64s shot in the last round. Seventy-four would be a good score. Last round, U.S. Open, playing for your country's most important title, your every muscle, your every bone, your every breath becomes tense, not natural. Not many can handle that. I could. How I did is part of my secret. I'll tell you this: It has something to do with preparation. I remember hearing Joe Paterno, before the Rose Bowl one year. He was all cranky because his team had practiced poorly. He said, "How can you expect to play well if you don't practice well?" Exactly.

And then came Saturday afternoon. I went out in 37, with a bogey on the third. That may not sound like much, but I was gaining on the field, even at four over through sixty-three holes. I made the turn, but making the turn at Merion doesn't give you the sense of relief you get at other courses. You don't feel like you're playing home. You feel like you're entering a manicured corner of golfing hell. By the time I got to the twelfth tee, I had a three-shot lead, but I knew it wasn't enough. On my tee shot there, my legs froze. I lost all feeling and nearly tumbled over again. This time I had to lean on a friend in the gallery, Harry Radix, to get my strength back. My caddie had to retrieve my ball out of the cup. In those days, at a USGA event, you could mark your ball only if it interfered with another player's line. You couldn't clean it. I was playing with Cary, Cary Middlecoff, and when my ball needed to be marked, he did it for me, which was both legal and gentlemanly. I played the twelfth in five, a three-putt bogey, crossed Ardmore Avenue to the little par-3 thirteenth, where I made three, made the walk past the flagpole to the fourteenth tee. The leader in the clubhouse at that point was one of your own, George Fazio, of Norristown and Pine Valley and Jupiter, Florida. Good golfing family. His brother's kid is Tom, the architect. George had shot 287, seven over par. I knew that score was damn good. I felt it had a good chance of holding up.

When the legs give out, the thing you can't do is putt. You need strong legs to putt well. Your legs have to ground you. I took three putts from eight feet on fifteen for a bogey, made a par 4 on the hole over the quarry, the sixteenth, then made a bogey 4 on seventeen, when I put my tee shot in a trap. Now I was seven over par, too. My legs were gone, and my cushion was, too.

People complain about the pace of play at the Open today. In 1950, it was worse. My afternoon round took six hours. I just wanted it to be over.

I hear some of these golfers—Lee Trevino, Peter Jacobsen, others—saying that professional golf is part of the entertainment business, that they play for the fans. More horseshit.

Professional golf is the most intense form of sporting competition known to mankind. The fact that others are willing to pay to be part of the heat, but at a safe distance, is nothing more than a happy accident for the players trying to make a living at the game. They tell me that as I played the eighteenth virtually all the spectators at Merion that day were congregated around the hole, maybe 13,000 people. They all knew about the accident, about what I had endured. They were involved in some drama. I was not. I can tell you I was aware of only one person in the gallery, my friend Fred Corcoran, the golf promoter, and that was only out of self-interest. I asked him what the low score was. He told me 287, seven over par. I needed a four on the last to get into a playoff. Old Man Par. Well, what the hell. Birdie to win was not something I was thinking about, not on that hole. You cannot imagine how long your eighteenth played in 1950, when the ball was practically dead, compared to today's ball, so peppy it's become a joke. From the back tee position—not your new back tee position, which I think restores the hole's mean dignity—every player in the field in the '50 Open needed a fairway wood or a long iron to get home, even the longest hitters. Try to find a par-4 today where Tiger Woods needs his best drive and a fairway wood or a long iron to get home. It doesn't exist, not in normal wind conditions.

The hole was in the back right of the green on eighteen. I needed a four-wood to get the ball all the way back to the hole, but if the ball took a big bounce, it would run forever and leave me with a difficult up and down. I knew I could reach the front part of the green with my one-iron. To play a one-iron would be to play for par and for a playoff, an eighteen-hole playoff. I hated the idea of a fifth round. But it was the only thing to do.

In those days, we carried sixteen clubs in tour events but fourteen clubs in USGA events, owing to the USGA's fourteen-club rule. I made room for the one-iron in my bag by not carrying a seven-iron. That might seem strange to you, to not carry a seven-iron, and it seemed odd to a lot of my fellow competitors. I said, "There are no seven-iron shots at Merion." I was not being arrogant. Just accurate.

I dragged on my cigarette, tossed it, pulled out the one-iron. I never had caddies draw clubs for me. I didn't want anyone touching my clubs. I waggled, I swung, the ball soared, I held my finish. Maybe you've seen the picture of that finish. It was taken by a *Life* photographer, Hy Peskin, one of the prominent sports photographers of the day. To me, what it captures is balance. Others see other things in it. They see the extra spike I put in the sole of my right golf shoe. They see eccentricity. They see a second chance, grace under pressure, whatever. All I see is a properly balanced finish, in black and white and gray. No logos on anything I'm wearing. My brand was me. I put the club back in the bag and lit up another stick.

I limped up the hill and to the green and surveyed my forty-footer. It was not a putt you could make. It was not one to three-putt. Frame of mind has everything to do with golf, and maybe in a more positive frame of mind I might have thought about holing that putt and winning with a birdie. But I was feeling despondent over wasting that three-shot lead.

I misread the putt. Try it sometime, from the front left of the green to the back right. The green hasn't changed any, thank goodness. Too many damn things change these days for no good reason. It looks like it should break to the right. Mine broke to the left, and I was left with a four-footer for par. I wasted no time over it. Made it. There was a three-way tie for first place, George Fazio, Lloyd Mangrum, me. One more round. Frank Sullivan drove me back to the Barclay. A bath, a good night's sleep, another bath, and I was good to go.

Some people say the playoff was anticlimactic. Not for me it wasn't. To me, that's where the drama was. Mangrum and I went out in 37, Fazio, hitting the ball the best of the three of us, in 38. Through fourteen, Fazio was just a shot behind me. Through fifteen, Mangrum was just a shot behind me. Then on sixteen, one of the most unfortunate rules infractions in the history of golf occurred.

Mangrum missed the green on his approach shot, made a poor chip to eight feet, and was standing over his putt for par when he noticed a bug crawling over his ball. He marked the ball with his putter head, which everybody did in those days in our tour events, and blew the bug off. He put the ball back down and holed the putt. But, as I said earlier, the USGA had its own rules, and we were playing by them. In those days, you could not mark a ball unless it was in another player's line. As Mangrum approached the seventeenth tee, a USGA official, Ike Grainger, told Mangrum that he did not have the honor, that he had made a six on sixteen, not a four. He had incurred a two-shot penalty for marking the ball when he shouldn't have. At the moment, I felt no emotion for Mangrum. I couldn't allow myself to. The rules are the rules. In retrospect, I feel very bad for him. But I still feel the rules are the rules, and the rules are sacred. The fact is, we played with an informality in those days that was different from today. I'd be more comfortable with the way touring pros go about their business now. Mangrum's response to Grainger sums up what it was like to be a touring pro in those days: "Well, I guess we'll all eat tomorrow." I won the playoff. I shot 69, Mangrum had 73, Fazio had 75. I won the Open because nobody needed to win it more than I and nobody wanted it more than I and nobody had prepared for it more than I. Call that arrogant, if you like. It's the damn truth. It was the biggest win of my golfing life. As I told Dan Jenkins once, "It proved I could still play."

I want to conclude with one other thought, about Merion, about what you have. What you have is the best parkland golf course in the United States. Is it suitable for a U.S. Open today? Of course, it is. Why? Because it demands a player to be in total control of his golf ball, from start to finish, and that's what U.S. Open golf is all about, controlling your golf ball, and controlling your emotions so that you can control your golf ball.

But there's more to Merion's excellence than that. It's the membership, your appreciation for the game. It's the flagsticks, with the red wicker baskets perched on top. It's the porch, tumbling out onto the first tee. It's the walk from thirteen green past the practice putting green to fourteen tee and how nobody would dare walk across that practice putting green because they have too much consideration for the course. I like to peek in at Merion in winter, when the course is quiet and the fireplace is going in the grill room and the members are carrying their own bags and playing fast and to their handicaps. That's golf. That's golf as much as anything I ever did in the game. It took me a lifetime and then some to realize that, but I finally got it. If I could love a course, I'd love Merion. The only thing I'd want is a practice field where I could hit full drivers. I've said this often, but only a few get it: The secret is in the dirt.

Sincerely,

Ben Hogan

Hogan's friend Claude Harmon, the head pro at Winged Foot in New York in the summer and Seminole in Florida in the winter, had four sons, all of whom became teaching pros. I knew the youngest of them, Billy, who caddied often for Jay Haas. The oldest of them, Claude "Butch" Harmon, was a golfing celebrity—at least by 2000 he was. His life looked glamorous. His kids were grown and he was single and he had lost a bunch of weight. He wore custom-made suits. He was building himself a sparkly new house on the outskirts of the new capital of the free world, Las Vegas. His postmodern academy there, the Butch Harmon School of Golf, was a sort of spectacle, nestled into the hillocks of the Rio Secco Golf Club, a course so shiny its fairways literally glimmered. Harmon's pupils—rich, white, middle-aged men, mostly—made the pilgrimage there to spend $500 for an hour with the man who taught Tiger Woods, and to spend much more at the Rio craps tables downtown. Harmon himself didn't go to those places. He gambled off the Strip, at the places known only to locals and insiders, Harmon being both.

Even then, when both were at the peak of their powers, Tiger didn't need that much from Butch. You could see the end coming, someday. But in 2000, Tiger was still jetting in for tutorials and anonymous gambling sessions. Other times, Harmon would go to the Woods bachelor crib at Isleworth, in Orlando. They'd hit balls, work out, play golf, watch basketball. In those days, Harmon was not only Tiger's teacher, but also one of his best friends. He was the ultimate insider in Tiger's insulated camp. And that raised his stock immeasurably. You want to see Butch? Take a number, pal. His hourly rate was scaring off nobody.

Twenty years earlier, in 1980, Butch was broke, living on his brother Dick's couch, drinking too much, acting surly, driving tractors on Texas golf courses under construction. He was a failure as a tour player and a dropout as a club pro. He was in a marriage headed for divorce, and his two children were being raised in a battleground. Through it all, Butch's three brothers told me, he never lost his cockiness. It was as if he could see the day coming when he'd be the king of the teachers.

When Tiger was at the height of his powers in 2000, Butch was everywhere. At the Masters, wherever Tiger was practicing, Butch was nearby, sanctum sanctorum, with several hundred people leaning over a green-and-white cord trying to hear a snippet of conversation between teacher and pupil. If you were at the hotel at the World Golf Hall of Fame in St. Augustine, Florida, Butch was on SpectraVision, his taped lessons available on command twenty-four hours a day. He was in every mall bookstore in the country, too, two Harmon titles sharing shelf space with the author's alphabetical neighbor, Ben Hogan. If you put on the Golf Channel, there was Harmon, on *Golf Academy Live*. Click over to Fox looking for a baseball score, and there was Harmon selling his

four-tape video series, immodestly titled *Conquering Golf.* He was
in the catalogue of a Canadian clothing manufacturer, Jack Victor.
He was a commentator for British television at ten tournaments a
year. He was at your dentist's office, playing one-handed bunker
shots on the cover of *Golf Digest.* You saw him more than you saw
Tiger, just about.

What a roll he was on. At a match-play tournament, Tiger was
playing one of Butch's former students, Davis Love. After Woods
nutted one of his 330-yard drives, a spectator called out to Harmon,
"What are you feeding him?"

"Davis, today," Harmon replied.

It was not a kind comment—particularly considering that Love
helped launch Harmon's career as a teacher of elite players—but
nobody went to Butch for kind. Through most of the '70s, Harmon
was a club pro at a rough-and-tumble Texas muni where he ran
the carts, worked the snack bar, sold golf balls, and did trick-shot
exhibitions. He was hard to begin with, and harder yet after some
years of that. At the end of the decade, he somehow became the
director of golf at Lochinvar, a swanky club in Houston. His first
world-class student was Love, with whom he started working in
1991. Greg Norman saw improvements in Love's swing and signed
on with Harmon late in 1991. In 1993, Woods, then seventeen
and inspired by Norman's progress, enrolled with Harmon, unable
to pay but more than willing to work and to learn.

The zing line was one of Butch's trademarks, just as it was for his
father, who won the Masters in '48, stopping at Augusta at Hogan's
insistence while making the drive from his winter job at Seminole
in Florida to his summer job at Winged Foot in New York. When
Butch was the club pro at the tough muni in Texas City, his father
had said to him, "All you need is a tattoo parlor in your pro shop,
and you'll be set for life." Butch had learned the art of the needle
from the best. Love and Butch parted ways, amicably, in 1996. Later
that year, at the PGA at Valhalla, Norman and Harmon got into a
dispute over Harmon's clothing contract, and Norman fired his
teacher in the middle of a practice round. Inevitably, Butch being
Butch and elite players sharing certain basic traits, the same thing

was bound to happen with Woods and Harmon, and eventually it did. Tiger grew tired of seeing Butch everywhere, and they broke up. For a long while, though, it was a perfect match. Both could give, and both could take. On the Sunday before the 2000 Masters, Harmon played thirty-six holes at Augusta, and he played the par-3 twelfth, where his father made the ace in the Hogan story, in five shots through two trips.

"I don't know why you guys are always bitching about twelve," Harmon told his star pupil. "I made a par and a birdie there when I played it on Sunday." Woods saw his opening. "Wrong Sunday," he said.

Woods was twenty-four then and Harmon fifty-six, but Tiger was the boss. He hadn't always been, but he became it. "Tiger is the show," Butch said to me when I went to see him in Las Vegas. "His caddie, Steve Williams, has one role. I have another. We're not the show. A lot of what I have in life is because I'm Tiger's teacher." Butch was saying all the right things. Woods was paying Harmon, people told me, $1 million a year. Harmon told me that Norman was the hardest worker he had ever seen, until Woods came along. Ultimately, they were both out of the Hogan school, finding the answers to golf's puzzles in the dirt. Butch was a worker, too. It was one of the things that bonded him to Tiger.

Tiger's father, Earl Woods, liked Harmon. Both had both been army men, veterans of the Vietnam War. Both believed the routines of war—preparation, discipline, loyalty, sacrifice—could be applied to civilian life. Both men were scarred by Vietnam. In the name of his country, Harmon descended into Asian jungles, where he killed men, stood next to friends as they were killed, had his foot on a land mine that should have killed him but for some reason did not detonate.

Bill Harmon, the kid brother, could be critical of his brother but also very generous. "With Butch, you always go back to that foxhole question," Bill said. "Who would you want in a foxhole with you with your life on the line? Nobody would be better than Butch. There's a lot of that in his relationship with Tiger. It's 'You and me against the world, Tiger.'"

That spirit was challenged in 1998, the year Woods won only once on tour, the year he and Harmon made subtle, important changes to his swing, the year Harmon and Earl Woods gave conflicting advice to Tiger on his putting. Harmon would not acknowledge this, but others did: During that year, despite Harmon's strutting cockiness, he was nervous about what he was doing. After all, the old Woods swing was good enough to produce a twelve-shot victory in the '97 Masters. But both believed the same thing: In golf, you're either getting better or you're getting worse. Sometimes you play worse while getting better. Even in his mid-twenties, Tiger had the kind of head where he could understand that.

Butch, when he was young, did not. He was a hothead and a rebel. As a kid he might play fifteen holes in a couple under par, make a snowman (eight) on sixteen, and walk off the course. At one point, his parents, not knowing what to do with their first child, enrolled their little sweetness in an Augustinian boarding school, Villanova, in Ojai, California. His stay was brief. One day one of the priests, upset with Butch, picked him up by the collar and threw him against a wall. Butch was a football player, wiry and muscular. He clocked the priest with a left hook. When his parents arrived to collect him, his father asked, "Why'd you punch a priest?"

"I don't know," Butch answered, "but I guarantee you that guy will think twice before he picks up another kid by the shirt and throws him against a wall."

Harmon played golf at Houston for part of a semester. He left for school with a set of clubs given to him by his father, clubs his father had used in finishing third in the '59 U.S. Open at Winged Foot. When Butch left Houston, the clubs were broken into so many pieces they could fit in a shoe box.

I had wondered what kind of teacher Harmon really was, not so much for Tiger, but for students with more ordinary golfing problems. Butch allowed me to sit in on some lessons. He was impressive. One student was a man in his early sixties, a corporate success, a golfing failure. Harmon sized up the man in three swings.

"You're a strong guy, in good shape, you're taking care of yourself," the teacher said. "You need to get more out of your swing. Sometimes we get so afraid of hitting bad shots, we don't let ourselves hit good ones."

The man looked at Harmon, nodded his head in long, sad strokes. He was standing before a master teacher, the man who taught Tiger Woods, and it was as if his whole life had been bared. Harmon spent an hour with the guy and moved on. Someday, he knew, he'd do the same thing with Tiger, and he'd survive it.

⛳

One crisp fall day in 2000, I went to visit Peter Lynch, the stock-picking guru with the Andy Warhol hair. Earlier, his secretary had told me that he didn't give interviews, but when I told her the subject was golf in general and what her boss had learned caddying as a kid in particular, I was able to get in quickly. He had a cramped office and an ignored sandwich on a cluttered desk. There was a blinking computer behind him. At one point, he closed his eyes and went into a mental drift. He was remembering his boyhood days as a caddie at Brae Burn Country Club, in the heart of Boston's well-hedged suburbs. He was an investing legend, credited with growing the Fidelity Magellan Fund 30 percent a year, on average, from mid-1977 to mid-1990, when he stopped managing it. His memory for numbers, particularly stock prices, is photographic. But just then he was trying to recall what he earned in 1955 as an eleven-year-old "C" caddie at Brae Burn, and for that faded number his memory was hazy.

He had a nutty-professor quality about him, or maybe it was just self-absorption. He didn't say thank you to the woman who brought him his sandwich. His handshake with me was four limp fingers. But he could go off wildly, amusingly, on conversational tangents. He was a self-made billionaire.

The number came to him. "I got maybe two dollars a loop, with tip, that first summer, but that was carrying a single," Lynch said. His mother would sew padding into his shirts, for protection. "By the time I was an 'A' caddie, in high school, I was carrying two bags, doing two rounds, making ten dollars a day. My friends who had newspaper routes couldn't make that in a week."

His experiences at Brae Burn shaped his life. He attended Boston College—where his father, who died the winter before Lynch became a caddie, had been a math professor—on a Francis Ouimet Caddie Scholarship. Tuition at BC in the mid-1960s was $1,000 a year. The caddie scholarship paid $300 of that, and Lynch earned the rest working at Brae Burn.

It was at Brae Burn that he learned about the stock market. Young Lynch would hear the men at the club—lawyers and doctors and businessmen—talk about their stock picks, and he was entranced. He began charting stocks.

One of his regulars was D. George Sullivan, the chief operating officer of Fidelity Investments. "Outstanding person, big tipper, bad golfer," Lynch said. Lynch carried for him, and others, for ten years. In the fall of 1965, Lynch applied for a position at Fidelity for the following summer. There were seventy-five applicants for three spots. Lynch secured one of them. Except for a stint in the army, he's never worked anyplace else.

All his success, he told me, was rooted in what he learned in golf. As a teenager he was giving golf advice to men four times his age, men who had fought in wars, made fortunes, been audited, raised families, men accustomed to professional counselors. Because the kid knew what he was talking about and wasn't afraid to express his opinion, they listened to him on the most sensitive subjects of all: Can I clear the water from here? In the years since then, the only thing that has changed for Lynch is what he is analyzing.

"Golf courses are dynamic places, and so are businesses, always changing," said Lynch, a sixteen-handicapper. "On different days you have different pin placements, different winds, different weather conditions; the golfer is different from day to day. You have these variables. You have to have concrete reasons to pick a stock, just as you have to have concrete reasons to pick a club. If a guy needs a three-iron to get over the water, but he can only hit his three-iron well enough to get over one time in four, it's not a good pick."

He learned disappointment as a caddie, too. In 1963 the U.S. Open was played at the Country Club, in Brookline, three bowls of chowder from Brae Burn. One hundred seventy-five local caddies entered a lottery to get bags in the Open. All but about twenty-five landed jobs, Lynch not among them. "That was crushing," he said. "But guess what? There are crushing things in life. I learned to move on."

One of his investment adages is, "Know what you own and why you own it." He believes stock tips lurk everywhere. He told me he didn't invest in golf companies because he didn't follow them. He wished he had bought Callaway stock when "you had to wait in a line to buy the club." He would have sold "when I saw the clubs being given away as raffle prizes." He must have been a good caddie, I'm guessing: good eyes and good ears, the things that made him in his other line of work.

In midsummer, *Sports Illustrated* has a special issue called "Where Are They Now?" For the writers, it's a treat, a way to get subjects into the magazine without much of a news hook. One year I wrote up Dom DiMaggio, Joe's kid brother. One year I wrote about Ted "Double Duty" Radcliffe, an old Negro league ballplayer who pitched and caught, sometimes in the same day. One year my subject was Mickey Wright, one of the great enigmatic figures in all of golf. She was another Hogan, really. She put everything she had into the shot before her and then moved on. When the football writers, stuck covering golf in their off-season, would ask her to go through her entire card—often a 69 or a 68 during her prime, on two occasions a 62—she hated it. She couldn't remember the shots, well played or not. They didn't matter. All that mattered to her was the next one.

Bad feet, a chronically injured wrist, eleven pairs of shoes, two dozen pairs of Bermuda shorts, seven cocktail dresses, the hopes of the sponsors, the demands of the writers, the anxiety before teeing off late on a Sunday afternoon—she hauled around a lot of stuff. But she coped. From 1955 to 1980, she won eighty-two times on the LPGA tour, thirteen of those in majors. No golfer, man or woman, has dominated a ten-year period the way Wright did from '56 to '66, not even Annika Sorenstam, not even Tiger Woods. No golfer ever swung a club the way she did, every part of her swing ideal, the sum of those parts perfection. Hogan himself, late in his life, said, "She had the finest golf swing I ever saw."

But while she was playing, she knew, as few do, that she was working her way toward a final swing—a final competitive swing, anyhow. She spent much of her career anticipating it and a smaller portion welcoming it. She was a realist. That final swing came in '95, and for that shot she has total recall.

"I was playing in the Sprint Senior Challenge at the LPGA headquarters in Daytona Beach, in 1995," she told me one summer morning in 2000. She was sixty-five. She'd already had her morning coffee, smoked several cigarettes, and read *The Wall Street Journal,* which arrived with the day's first light, when Wright would rise. "On the last hole, a par-5, I hit a pull-hook drive into the rough. The ball was way above my feet. There was water left of the green and traps on the right. I used a four-iron. I wanted to work the heel of the club through the ball and hit the inside part of the ball. The ball sailed, nice and high. I liked to hit the ball high. I two-putted for a birdie. It was a wonderful way to go out." She has not played a round of golf since.

She was on the phone. That was one of her ground rules. I could talk to her on the phone. I could write to her, and she'd write back. But I could not see her. She saw the people she wanted to see, and she didn't want to see anybody she didn't already know. She seldom left Port St. Lucie, Florida, where she was living in a modest white stucco house with a backyard that abutted the Club Med Sandpiper Sinners Golf Course.

In January of 2000, the LPGA celebrated its fiftieth anniversary with a glittering dinner at the Breakers, in Palm Beach, an hour south of Wright's home. Virtually every living LPGA star, past and present, was there. Mickey Wright was not. She does not do dinners, unless they are her own. Her routine was to eat breakfast at half past six, lunch at eleven a.m., and dinner at five. She had her habits and her routines, but she did not, she said amusingly, wash her hands "fifty times a day." Her life was as full as she wanted it, following the stock market, playing poker and canasta with her friends, and spending time with her longtime housemate and partner, Peggy Wilson, with whom she played the tour. The house in Port St. Lucie was their second together.

She still enjoyed watching golf on TV. Well, maybe *enjoy* is not the correct word. The U.S. tours—the men, the women, the old guys—frustrate her. She'll see a poorly played chip shot or a lapse in concentration and turn off the box. She prefers European tour golf, which she said was more varied, rugged, and creative. She can get it on the Golf Channel.

Wright herself shows up on the channel, but only—to the frustration of its producers—in clips from the game's past. "When we started in January 1995, we drew up a dream list of guests," Peter Kessler, the host of *Golf Talk Live,* told me. "There are only two people from that list we haven't had on: Ben Hogan—who even then was in poor health—and Mickey Wright. We've mailed her tapes of my work, had people call on our behalf. We've told her she could dictate all the terms. Nothing. I would love to ask her, 'What's the most important thing in the golf swing?' And then listen to her answer. That would mean everything to me."

When I asked her that question, she referred me to her book, *Play Golf the Wright Way,* a ninety-six-page classic published by Doubleday in 1962. The guts of the book are in two lines on page 92: "This is my anodyne for your future in golf. You will be better if you practice and you won't be if you don't." The last three lines of the book border on haiku:

I think and do everything just the way I have said.
It has helped me.
I hope it helps others.

If you want to know about her life, Wright refers you to another book, *The Illustrated History of Women's Golf*, by Rhonda Glenn. The part about Wright is fifteen pages and called "Golf's Golden Girl." One sentence, in particular, bears repeating: "She viewed golf as a form of self-expression rather than a contest between people." That pleased Wright, to be portrayed with such economy. She despised the limelight. The less time spent on her, the better. "You never hear her say 'my swing,'" Glenn, one of the few people to interview Wright extensively, told me. "She always referred to 'the swing.'"

When Charlie Mechem took over as LPGA commissioner in 1991, he made it a point to get to know Wright. "I just called her up and said, 'I'd like to see you,'" he recalled. "'I'm not coming to ask you to do a thing.'" He could not have chosen better words. Had he wanted something, he would never have seen the inside of her front door. They struck up a friendship. By 1993, Mechem wanted to have Wright play in the Sprint Senior Challenge, but he was too smart to ask. "She's a person who likes to lead her life her own way, and you have to respect that," he said. "The only thing I said to her is, 'It would be very, very meaningful to the LPGA if you played.'"

"That darned Charlie Mechem," Wright said, giving me her version of it. She was laughing. Her voice was low and had a slight Texas twang—she lived in Texas for a while as an adult, although she did all her growing up in San Diego. "I still don't know how he got me to do it."

Before that 1993 senior event, Wright had not played a competitive round in eight years. She got out her 1962 Wilson Staff irons, hit thousands of balls and played daily for months. On her first morning at the Sprint event, at the Killearn Country Club in Tallahassee, when she walked onto the practice tee, scores of LPGA players were on hand, eager to see the legendary swing and the woman who made it.

"Everybody knew Mickey didn't want pictures taken, so I just watched, by myself, trying to take it all in," said Patty Sheehan, the Hall of Famer who had never seen Wright in person before that day. "I had seen old film clips of her swing. It looked the same: very fluid, very powerful—flawless. You could see she was in love with golf and dedicated to hitting a golf ball purely. She had these old clubs, old as dirt, and it was clear they were her best friends. She had an inner confidence. I picked up on that very strongly. You knew that ultimately all those wins came from something deep inside."

Wright played in that event in '93, again the next year, then for a third time in '95. She hit that four-iron shot on the last hole, took her final two putts using the same Bulls Eye putter she had used in all eighty-two of her wins, and she was never seen again.

The truth is, Wright started to retire in 1965. One of her confidants then was Lenny Wirtz, the LPGA's tournament director. He told me that no golfer did more to contribute to the growth of the LPGA. "We were struggling to find thirty girls to play the tour because we weren't paying enough money to the lower spots," Wirtz said. "I said to Mickey, 'I want to reduce the winner's percentage of the purse from twenty to fifteen so we can pay more to the others.' The only player it was going to affect was Mickey, because she was winning everything. She said, 'If it's going to help the tour, I'm for it.' Nobody knows this stuff. She made sacrifices, put up with all sorts of crap: sponsors who threatened to cancel their tournaments if Mickey didn't play, writers who treated it like an insult if she didn't win their hometown event. She felt so much pressure to play, so much pressure to win. She'd say to me, 'I can't do it all.' She didn't have a life of her own. The people who don't know Mickey, those are the ones who say she's a recluse. She's not. Mickey's leading the life she wants to lead."

She gave me all the time I could want, on the phone, and she talked about personal things: her father's five marriages, her mother's three, her relationship with Peggy Wilson. She talked about her one year at Stanford, how she followed a San Diego boy there in pursuit of a romance that never worked out. "I thought that fellow hung the moon," Mickey said. She talked about her pain when that boy, Jerry Wood was his name, died in a military training exercise in the late '50s.

She enjoyed, particularly, talking about her late father, Arthur, a prominent lawyer in San Diego, a poker player, a fisherman, a weekend golfer, a smoker, an investor, a horse-track gambler. Her father was always doing something adventurous, and he allowed his only child to come along. Her father gave her $1,000 when she left Stanford in '54 with the goal of playing the tour, which had started four years before. She never needed to go back to him for more.

There's no one reason that she started curtailing her schedule in the late 1960s, no one reason that she didn't show up at the splashy fiftieth-anniversary LPGA dinner. "It's just like my fishing," she said. "Caught all the bass I wanted to, and now I don't want to catch any more. Been there, done that." She did the *Ed Sullivan Show* when the whole country watched Ed Sullivan. She got all the acclaim she needed.

I found her to be modest but not falsely so. "The greatest winners in golf—Hogan, Nicklaus, Jones, you might have to think about Tiger Woods—they were all great swingers, but their inner drive was off the charts, too," she said.

I asked, "Would you include yourself on that list?"

"Yes," she said, not hesitating. "Yes, I would."

She could not play casual golf. The game meant too much to her to play it casually but also too much to abandon it. She told me she hit balls almost every day, early in the morning, off a mat on her back patio and onto the neighboring course, forty or fifty balls, seven-irons that went 155 yards, fifteen yards longer than the seven-irons she hit when she joined the tour. One of the rangers from the course, a man named Harry Dobbs, would go by daily, to watch from a distance. Dobbs himself was a good player. His son, a club pro, was an excellent player.

Dobbs told me he could watch Wright make swings all day, but the sessions are brief. "She's beautiful to watch," he said. "Solid, even, fluid, smooth, round, not a wasted motion, no wasted energy. Her shots make a great sound, right on the sweet spot, shot after shot. She hits it high, with a little draw. It's a picture."

When Mickey Wright was done, she'd collect her balls, wave to the man, and get on with the rest of her day, and the rest of her life.

For 2000, Tiger Woods was *SI*'s Sportsman of the Year. Though he played only difficult courses, his stroke average was 68.17, breaking Byron Nelson's 1945 average of 68.33 strokes per round, a mark you might have guessed would never be broken. I wrote the Sportsman of the Year story and did it oral-history style, finding one witness for each of his ten wins, including the first three majors of the year, the Masters, the U.S. Open at Pebble Beach, and the British Open at St. Andrews. For his win at Pebble Beach, Trey Holland, a urologist and a former president of the USGA who was the rules official in Woods's group, offered this testimony:

On Saturday I was waiting on the first tee for the round to begin. Tiger comes up the steps that lead to the tee, and he's laughing and joking with his caddie, very loose, very relaxed. Then he gets on the tee, puts his right hand on the headcover of his driver, and starts staring down the fairway. The smile is gone. The eyes widen. Just staring, for a full two minutes. I had never seen that kind of concentration. People are yelling, "C'mon, Tiger! You can do it!" I don't think he heard a word of it.

Then on the third hole he hits his second shot short of the green, near a bunker. The ball sinks in the grass. He says to me, "I think my ball is embedded." If it's embedded, he gets a free drop. There's an intensity in his voice. He knows how he wants this to come out.

I say, "Mark your ball, lift it, and test the dirt with a finger. If the plane of the dirt—not the grass but the dirt— is broken, it's embedded."

He tests it. He says, "I think it is." I say, "Let me have a look." I put my finger down there. I say, "It's not." He doesn't say a word. Replaces his ball. Hacks it out. Makes a triple bogey.

On Sunday we're back on the first tee. He says hi. Doesn't say anything about the ruling. He does his two-minute stare again, plays his final round, wins the U.S. Open. I congratulate him, and he says, "Thanks, that means a lot. But I sure would have liked to have gotten that drop yesterday on three." Twenty-eight hours later and after winning the Open by fifteen shots, he was still thinking about it. I was under the clear impression that he wanted to win by eighteen.

CHAPTER TWELVE

DEATH (2001)

WHEN I JOINED THE PHILADELPHIA CRICKET CLUB, I enjoyed a small measure of status, because of my caddie roots, with the caddie master. The boss of the caddies was a gargantuan and frequently grumpy man, often cupping a cigarette, named Joe Smondrowski. Having some rapport with Joe was a good thing, because for years he was the most powerful and intimidating person at the club, and he could make or break your golfing day. He controlled the first tee and all the other places on the course where you thought you might be able to insert your fast-moving self. Everybody knew how they stood with Joe. If he didn't like you, he gave you a hard time. If he liked you, he gave you a harder time. How this made him endearing I'm still trying to figure out, but it did. His power came from his innate knack for making people, members and guests, think that they worked for him. Joe was a genius.

A visiting friend once showed up for the big July member-guest tournament hoping to make a trip to the practice tee for a preround warmup. Such a trip required the use of a golf cart, and the carts, of course, were the province of Joe. Joe could not stomach the idea of giving up any of his carts. "Where's your member?" Joe barked at my friend when he asked for a buggy. In his fantasy life, my friend placed his right palm under his genitalia, gave a northward yank, and said, "Right here, buddy!" In real life, of course, he said nothing. You didn't give Joe lip. My friend waited for his member in silence.

Joe had about a dozen regular caddies, double that in the summer months. The caddies were and are a central part of the golf experience at the Cricket Club and all the other good clubs in Philadelphia. I know the same is true at the top clubs in New York, Boston, Chicago, Los Angeles, and San Francisco, at least at the San Francisco Golf Club. At the Cricket Club, the caddies would wait in the sun by the door of an old garage, playing cards, reading newspapers, deconstructing Joe. They range in age considerably. In any year, some are in high school and college, others are in their sixties, having retired from the workaday world. Among the loopers there were golf bums, caddie lifers, and societal dropouts. Same as forever. Boxcar. Woody. Slider. A bunch of good guys. In the summer of 2000, in the good weather, they were making $80 a day, cash, $160 if they could carry two bags twice. There was a female caddie that summer, maybe twenty, a delightful blonde who played field hockey and lacrosse at a local college. Joe never put her on my bag.

Joe was a golf person. He once played the game well, and he had a son who became a club pro. He reserved his most enthusiastic caddies for me, in deference to my caddie past. The truth is, all I want from a caddie, in the way of refinements, is the ability to distinguish between uphill and downhill putts, a tricky business, but I'll take an overinvolved caddie over a moping one anytime. In my early days at the club, Joe used to give me a caddie called Cobra. Cobra was an overweight red-haired kid in his mid-twenties from a golfing family. He knew the game, and he was consumed with helping his man shoot better scores. He was also a recovering alcoholic, a fact he discussed openly with me. Sometimes when I'd come in from a round, Joe would say to me, "Cobra save you a shot today?" Joe liked Cobra, not that Cobra ever knew. All part of Joe's special charm.

When my wife and I moved into our first house, I hired Cobra for the day to help with the hauling. (I sought Joe's permission, of course. Joe was okay with it, as long as it wouldn't be on one of his busy days.) Cobra's work was excellent, and he put in a long day, with much grunting and sweating, interrupted only by a Burger King lunch. I wanted to pay Cobra generously for his work. This was in late 1991, when we had returned from our long linksland trip. In those days, the top caddies got $20 from most of the members, $22 from some of the men. I figured if Cobra had carried two bags in the morning and two bags in the afternoon, an excellent payday would have been $88. I gave him $100. He looked neither pleased nor disappointed. I've suffered with the idea that I underpaid him ever since.

A couple of years later, Joe had Cobra on my bag when we came to the eighth hole at our club, a par-3 playing 157 yards into the breeze on this particular day. The hole was cut in a tricky position, on the right side of the green, on a knoll. There was no debate for me: It was a six-iron shot. I hit my six-iron a little over 160 yards in still conditions. As I put my hand on the six, Cobra said, "No, no, no, not the six. It's a seven-iron." I knew I'd have to smash a seven to get the ball to the hole. It was not the right club, but I took it from Cobra anyhow, for two reasons. One, I still felt pangs of guilt that I might have underpaid him that day. Two, I didn't want to do anything to diminish his self-esteem as he continued his daily battle with sobriety. I distinctly remember taking the seven and saying to myself, "This one's for Cobra." The swing was solid and the contact was pure, and the ball went in the hole, the only ace I've ever made. The word was out before I made it back to the clubhouse. Joe said to me, "Heard Cobra pulled a good stick for you on eight."

I was one of the few members Joe could use caddie jargon with, a nice bond to have. He talked to me more as a caddie than as a member, which I appreciated. I was among the first Jewish members at the club, and when his daughter married a man with the same name as my father, Joseph Bamberger, I asked Joe if his future son-in-law was Jewish. Joe's exact answer was, "Do you think I'd let my daughter marry a goddamn Jew?" Joe was Catholic and Polish, went to Philadelphia's parochial schools in the '50s. He was a creature of his time and neighborhood and background. In its

candor and nakedness, his response was oddly comical to me. I knew
there was no hate in it. A few years later, a member, not realizing
I was Jewish, made a more bothersome anti-Semitic comment to
me. I didn't say anything and wondered if I should. I sought Joe's
advice. Joe said, "He can be a crude son of a bitch, but he's basically a good guy." Joe had the guy right. Saying something, I decided, would gain nothing.

The early months of 2001 were extremely snowy and icy in
Philadelphia. In mid-March, with mushy piles of gray snow still
standing in the corners of the parking lot, I went to the club, just
to check in. I hadn't been there for months, and the start of the
real golf season was still weeks away. Joe was in his little, smoky,
cluttered office. We talked about various shared interests: Davis
Love's tempo, the Phillies' rotation, the superiority (in our opinion) of our course to just about every other course in the area. We
talked about the winter whereabouts of his caddies. (Cobra had long
retired from caddying and was working as an alcohol counselor.)
Joe looked skinny, for him. He was uncharacteristically chatty. He
wasn't giving me any crap, about anything. He was just talking. I
asked him about Joseph Bamberger, his son-in-law.

"You heard about my daughter, didn't you?" Joe said.

I hadn't.

"She died three days before Thanksgiving." Tears were stream-
ing down his broad cheeks. The sight of Joe crying, the sight of
Joe helpless and alone, left me trembling.

Deborah Smondrowski Bamberger was thirty-seven, in good
health, with three daughters. The cause of death was a sudden coro-
nary aneurysm.

"She was one of the good ones," he said.

We stood there in silence for a moment or two, in his cold office, looking out at the wintry course. Nothing was green. Everything was gray and white.

"Month from now," Joe finally said, "this place will be hop-
ping again."

The season did start again, of course, but Joe was different. He
was subdued. In May, he made an announcement. He would be

leaving the club to move in with his son, the club pro, in Washington, D.C., and to become the caddie master at a high-roller men's club there, one where Michael Jordan was a member. But the main purpose of the move was to be near his late daughter's three girls. He worked our big July member-guest tournament, and he was gone.

ꝉ

Sports Illustrated and Arnold Palmer came up together. The magazine was founded in 1954, the year Palmer won the U.S. Amateur. In 1960, he was the magazine's Sportsman of the Year, and a wonderful, timeless watercolor of him ran on the cover. He epitomized the modern, masculine athlete to an incalculable number of *SI* readers, Joe Smondrowski among them. For his contracts, Palmer was represented by Mark McCormack, the founder of the International Management Group, who himself cultivated a close relationship with many editors and writers, at *SI* and elsewhere. The relationship between *Sports Illustrated* and Palmer flourished for years. And then, in October of 2000, Palmer endorsed a driver made by Callaway that was not approved for play by the USGA, although golf's other ruling body, the Royal and Ancient Golf Club of St. Andrews, did allow its use. The "Golf Plus" section of the magazine took a tough stance on Palmer, criticizing him for the endorsement in a brief story that ran with this headline: "When Arnold Palmer said it was O.K. to cheat, his reign as the King ended." The story was written by my friend Gary Van Sickle, both a good golfer and a funny person, a rare combination.

Palmer was furious. Some weeks later, Jim Herre assigned me to write a follow-up story. He wanted me to see Palmer and try to figure out how he got involved with the "nonconforming" Callaway driver in the first place. What he really wanted was for me to take Palmer's temperature. I got Palmer on the phone with surprising ease.

"Hi, Arnold," I began, "this is Michael Bamberger from *Sports Illustrated.*"

"I know who you are," Arnold said, "and evidently you don't give a shit who you write for these days."

All of Palmer's humor came out of saying true things. When he first bowed out of playing in the Masters, he said it was because he was "afraid [he] might get a letter," referring to the terse missives Hootie Johnson, the Augusta National chairman, sent out to certain former winners, urging them not to play in the tournament anymore.

Arnold had talked to me here and there over the years, me and a thousand others. Everyone in golf of a certain age, ultimately, is either a Palmer fan or a Nicklaus fan. I was a huge Nicklaus fan. Nicklaus was tremendous in the press tent, extremely knowledgeable, and the grace with which he accepted his runner-up finishes has everything to do with why the golfer's civil code from the 1920s continued to flourish eighty years later. Until his farewell U.S. Open at Oakmont in '94, I never felt the spark about Palmer that others did. Mostly, probably, because I was too young. When I came of golf age, Palmer was a decade past his prime. And then, only because of the Callaway flap, I got to spend several days with him, in the three states where he has homes, Florida and Pennsylvania and California. He flew himself around the country on his own jet, a Citation X.

When I asked him how he was doing, he said he was sleeping well but his days had been hell. There were people calling him a cheater, even in the pages of *SI.* Nothing like that had ever happened to him before. Nicklaus used to say of him, "Nobody could enjoy being Arnold Palmer more than Arnold Palmer enjoys being Arnold Palmer." But in the spring of 2001, there was little sign of that man. After nearly half a century in the public eye, the Callaway driver debacle was the most tumultuous event he had ever endured.

Early one morning, we were sitting in his small, stylish house in the California desert. Palmer had an unopened vitamin pack in one hand and a cell phone in the other. The walls of his casita were decorated with pictures and photographs of himself. In a room adjacent to the kitchen was a photo of him and his late wife, Winnie, standing in front of his jet. The colors in the photo were incredibly rich and vibrant, autumnal. Winnie Palmer had died fifteen months earlier, in November of 1999, of cancer, at sixty-five. They had been married for forty-five years, and she advised her husband on most everything. Her counseling method was to listen and listen while Palmer weighed the pros and cons of an issue, waiting for him to say, as he joked, something smart.

"If Winnie were alive, maybe I would have never gotten involved with the Callaway driver," Palmer said. He was referring to a $500 titanium driver called the ERC II. It did not conform to USGA regulations because its face, essentially, was too thin. (The ball would rebound off the face too quickly; there was too much "trampoline effect.") The club could not be used for USGA-sanctioned play, which meant all serious competitive golf, professional and amateur, and all by-the-book recreational golf in the United States and Mexico. The rest of the golfing world falls under the auspices of the Royal and Ancient Golf, and under R&A rules, the club was legal. Palmer, by contract a Callaway spokesman but also a longtime and highly visible unpaid advocate for the USGA, said publicly that if using a nonconforming, long-flying driver would help ordinary duffers enjoy recreational golf more, they should go ahead and use it, no matter where they lived and played. Expressing that seemingly innocent opinion turned his life inside out. "Maybe Winnie would have said, 'Don't do it,'" Palmer told me. "But I doubt it."

His eyes were damp. I had been told that he didn't like to talk about Winnie, but I found the opposite to be true. "I had finally gotten a clean bill of health on my prostate cancer when we got a call that now Winnie had cancer," he said. "That was in late October, in 1998. We always thought she was going to make it, right up to the end. She was so strong. She had so much faith. We set up a hospital room for her in our home in Latrobe. One of the last things she told me was, 'Get on with your life.' I couldn't talk at her funeral. Winnie had written out her own funeral service, what music she wanted played, what prayers read. Turns out, she had done all that planning a year before she died."

Palmer and I headed out the back door—he was never one to stay in one place for very long—to take a look at the golf course in his backyard. Naturally, it was one of his own designs, a new one called the Tradition.

"Winnie didn't care much for the desert," he said. Much of Palmer's stardom was rooted in the California desert, the swanky desert of the '60s, in its hot-days-cool-nights heyday. He won six times in the desert, including his last victory, the 1973 Bob Hope Desert Classic. "The social life was a little too fast for her out here, but she would have liked this place, because it's quiet and small. Not a show." He pointed to a sign by a swimming pool, WINNIE'S POOL. "She said, 'If you want to see me out here, you better build me a pool.' She never got to enjoy it."

I joined Palmer as he and David Chapman, the owner of the Tradition, played the club's par-3 course, gambling intensely for small sums that would never be paid. You could see Palmer's joy in stiffing a sand wedge shot from sixty yards and how it was magnified when Chapman yanked one into a bunker. "I've got you now!" Palmer yelled, as if it mattered, and, of course, to him, it did.

One of Palmer's greatest charms is that he's always believed that his golf, or some aspect of it, was improving. In the period I was with him, his driving game, a lifelong obsession for him, actually was getting better. He credited the scientists at Callaway for that. They taught him about launch angles and spin rates and the ideal way to tee up a ball for a driver, higher and farther forward in his stance than he had done before. If you had taught Palmer that stuff, you'd have made a friend for life, too. He didn't need Callaway's money. The company's attention, though, was another thing.

He likes to have people around. One cold weekday afternoon, I was with him in his workshop at Bay Hill, in Florida. He was bending and regripping clubs and checking lofts and lies with his eye. All the while, he was chewing the cud with some of his boys: Jim Deaton, the director of golf at Bay Hill; Dwight Kummer, the course superintendent there; Roy Saunders, Palmer's son-in-law; and Dow Finsterwald, the former tour player who won the '58 PGA Championship at Llanerch, outside Philadelphia, the first televised tournament, the one directed by Frank Chirkinian. (All of golf is connected; it's a reporter's dream.) Finsterwald was with his dog, a golden Lab named Maxfli.

At exactly four p.m.—there is much ritual and order in his life— Palmer ordered his small workshop refrigerator to be opened, and bottles of cold beer were distributed all around. The conversation turned to the clubs to which he belongs. Among many others, he is a member of the Royal and Ancient Golf Club, Pine Valley, and Augusta National. A Masters winner—and he won green coats there four times, in '58, '60, '62, and '64—automatically becomes an honorary Augusta National member. But in '99, the club made Palmer a regular member as well. "I guess they figured I already had the jacket," he said. He is the son of a club pro, a son of the working class, and he has never forgotten it.

Palmer was an owner of the Golf Channel, and one night I joined him at the cable channel's studio, when he was the subject of a live, ninety-minute interview with an endlessly knowledgeable golf host, Peter Kessler. It was something Palmer did annually, and he was going to go through with it, despite the Callaway flap. During the program, a viewer called in with a question: In all his years in pro golf, what was his greatest moment? Palmer chose to answer a slightly different question. He said his fondest moment in golf wasn't from his pro career but from his last days as a rough-hewn, free-swinging kid, when he won the U.S. Amateur, in '54. He defeated a gentleman golfer, Bob Sweeney, in the final, and when the day was over, the social gap between the two men had diminished significantly. Palmer had come to the thirty-sixth hole one up. He hit a good drive and hit his second onto the green. Sweeney's errant tee shot could not be found. Sweeney did not go back to the tee, and the hole was never finished. Joe Dey, the patriarchal executive director of the USGA, approached Palmer and said, "If you don't mind, Mr. Palmer, we'll call this a one-up victory."

It really should have been a two-up victory—technically, Sweeney forfeited the final hole—but Palmer didn't care. He had won the national title. He had just been called Mr. by one of the grand men of the USGA. On that day he became a USGA insider.

And he had been one ever since—until the ERC II driver came in for a test.

Half of Kessler's interview dealt with the club question. The host was trying to bail Palmer out, trying to find a semantic position for his boss that would satisfy both the USGA and Callaway. But Palmer didn't want Kessler's solutions. He tried to say, in numerous ways, that he just wanted people to enjoy golf, in any way they want to enjoy it. It was painful to sit so close to the interview, it was so awkward. As he came off the set at the end of the interview, Palmer was greeted by a little cheering section, his people. "How'd I do?" he asked. His performance was praised. "I need a drink," he said.

In that period, Palmer was on the offensive. It was not clear how he was doing. A few days before the interview with Kessler, he had flown up to USGA headquarters in Far Hills, New Jersey, for a meeting. He brought with him Charlie Mechem, the former LPGA commissioner who had become his unpaid, full-time counselor, as well as Deaton, the Bay Hill pro, and Howdy Giles, his dentist. The USGA was represented by the urologist Trey Holland, its president, and David Fay, its executive director, among others. Palmer urged the USGA to find common ground with the Royal & Ancient on the definition of a nonconforming club. He argued that the Callaway driver did not threaten the game. He offered to step down as the USGA's honorary membership chairman if his position on the Callaway driver put the USGA in an uncomfortable spot. His friend Giles said, "It seems to me the USGA needs Arnold Palmer a lot more than Arnold Palmer needs the USGA." Holland told Palmer that the USGA would always need him, that no person had done more for golf than he had. Then, three weeks later, Holland, addressing the Georgia State Golf Association, spoke of the contradiction of having a USGA spokesperson endorsing a club banned by the USGA. Holland said, "You won't see his name in this year's USGA yearbook. I've taken that out." His comments were reported the next day in *The Atlanta Journal and Constitution,* on the front page of the sports section. By noon they had made it to Palmer. "I like Trey Holland. I don't know what's going on here," Palmer said that day. "My mind's all in a scramble." That night Holland called Palmer and apologized for his indelicate comments in Georgia. He reiterated that the USGA would always need Arnold Palmer. But Palmer was hurt.

I went to Carlsbad, near San Diego, to see Ely R. Callaway, the founder of Callaway Golf, the man whose initials were on the hot driver. He was eighty-one then. "This situation has been devastating Arnold, and it makes me feel very bad," Callaway said. He was a master salesman, and I could not gauge the sincerity of his words. The brawl over the golf club did only good things for the Callaway stock price. It had gone from fifteen dollars on October 18, 2000, the day Palmer spoke at a press conference praising the nonconforming club, to twenty-two dollars three months later. I'm pretty sure Peter Lynch wasn't buying the stock, but still, that was quite a lift, especially in winter.

People wondered if Palmer was in it for the money. There was no way. He had a twelve-year contract with Callaway paying him about $400,000 a year. He had options on about 200,000 shares of Callaway stock that he could exercise at sixteen dollars a share. A lot of money, but not for a man who earned $100,000 a day for corporate outings, who made an estimated $20 million a year in endorsements alone, who was worth north of $200 million.

I'm not implying that Palmer doesn't care about his business life. He has a keen interest in it. One day when I was with him, I told him that I had had dinner the previous night in a California Pizza Kitchen. I had ordered an iced tea and lemonade mixed together from a waitress who was maybe twenty years old. When my computer-generated bill came, the drink was listed as an Arnold Palmer. I asked the waitress if she knew who Arnold Palmer was. She had no idea—to her, it was just the name of a drink when lemonade and iced tea were mixed together. My mother was making it in our house in the 1970s, and Palmer was making it, too. There were certain golf clubs where the combination was known as an Arnold Palmer, but I'd never heard of it beyond that. Palmer slipped a sliver of a cell phone out of his front right pocket, called Charlie Mechem, told the story to him, and said, "Is there a name-rights issue here we should be looking into?" It wasn't too long after that

that Arizona Iced Tea started bottling Arnold Palmers in a tall aluminum can with Palmer's signature and picture right on it.

One night, at the casita in the desert, Palmer was leafing through a lush coffee-table book about his career. We had been talking about the '54 Amateur, and he was looking for a picture of Bob Sweeney, his opponent in the final. He was on the subject of the USGA. "I've been called a cheater," he said. "I've been called Benedict Arnold. This has all been very hard, harder than people know. I believe what I believe, and I believe this driver is good for golf. But I will always be a USGA man. People have to realize that the game comes first. The game is bigger than Callaway, it's bigger than the USGA, it's certainly bigger than me." The sincerity of those words was obvious.

Before he got to Sweeney, he came across a black-and-white picture of Winnie. "She loved her life," he said quietly. "That's what I hope and what I believe."

⛳

My wife lost a good friend in the September 11 attacks, a woman named Catherine who stayed with us for about two weeks when Christine and I were roaming around Europe during our 1991 trip. For the first issue after the attacks, the *SI* managing editor, Bill Colson (he had succeeded Mark Mulvoy), decided to devote the entire issue to the intersection of the terror and sports. I was feeling lost, as so many of us were. I wanted to contribute to the issue but didn't know what to write. A close friend, John McNiff, told me about a well-known Philadelphia golf figure, Davis Sezna, whose son was missing in the debris of the towers. With John's help, the doors to the Sezna family home were opened to me at a time when there was nothing but fright and confusion in their lives, when they did not know whether their son was dead or alive. The following story ran in the issue dated September 24, 2001:

A father was on the golf course, and his son was at work. The morning was crisp, bright, perfect. Twenty-two-year-old Davis G. Sezna, Jr., known as Deeg, was working in the south tower, Two World Trade Center. His father, Davis Sr., was playing at Pine Hill, a public course in southern New Jersey, near from Pine Valley.

"Dad," Deeg would sometimes ask, "do you think someday I'll be Pine Valley material?" Augusta National, Cypress Point, Seminole, Pine Valley. Those are the four sacred corners of the shawl that wraps private-club golf in the United States. For many of its members, Pine Valley is the ultimate sanctuary. Davis Sezna, forty-eight, is a member.

Deeg was employed by another Pine Valley member, Jimmy Dunne, a managing principal at Sandler O'Neill & Partners, a financial-services company. The father made the introduction, but from there the son was on his own. Dunne and Deeg played a round of golf together. Golf reveals a man; that's what Dunne believes. Davis Sr. does too. "Golf's a great interview," Dunne likes to say.

Later Deeg came into the office for a sit-down meeting with Dunne and the firm's other principals. Deeg was wearing a suit. He was serious, energetic, respectful. He was offered a job.

"Can I start on May 14, Mr. Dunne?" Deeg asked. In other words, graduate from Vanderbilt on a Friday, take the weekend off, then begin work on Monday.

"No, you cannot," Dunne answered. "Take the summer off. Kiss a pretty girl. You don't have to call me Mr. Dunne, and you don't have to wear a suit."

Deeg took the summer off. He started work the day after Labor Day. Wore a suit every day. Called his boss Mr. Dunne. He'll make it here doing something, Jimmy Dunne thought. Banker, trader, salesman, something. On September 11, 2001, Deeg's sixth day on the job, he arrived for work a little after seven.

Deeg's father had always worked in golf. He was the owner of a busy public course outside Philadelphia, Hartefeld National, the site of a senior tour event in '98 and '99. He was going into business with the owner of Pine Hill, which is why he was there on September 11, that beautiful Tuesday morning that so abruptly turned grim and gray.

Somebody pulled him off the course when the first plane smashed into the north tower of the World Trade Center. He was watching the terror unfold on TV when the second plane struck his son's building. "I knew Deeg was on the 104th floor," Sezna said. We were talking at his house. "The plane hit, an hour passed, the building crumpled. A friend drove me home."

The Sezna home is in Delaware, in the rolling country-side outside Wilmington, near the Brandywine River, the pastoral land the Wyeths painted for generations. The kitchen dates to the seventeenth century. The backyard was a long, sweeping hill, ending at a pond. The three Sezna boys would hit wedge shots and take divots out of that lawn all summer long. Gail Sezna, their mother, would look the other way. Her father-in-law and her husband were good golfers. Her husband was the 1973 Delaware Open champion. Her sons were being raised in the game, too.

"My dad used to say, 'A golfer is a gentleman,'" Davis Sr. said. There was a group of his friends around, all golfers. "I raised my sons to understand that. The first time I brought Deeg to the course, he was five. As we left, he said, 'Was I a gentleman today, Daddy?'" He dabbed his eyes with a napkin embossed with scallop shells.

This was on Thursday, two days after the attacks. The father had spent the previous day in the detritus of the World Trade Center, searching for his son. Now he was in his backyard, in the "final innings of hope," as he put it.

The visiting men were members of Pine Valley, Seminole, Merion, all clubs to which the father belongs. Sezna, who in addition to being in the golf business was also a restaurateur, was pouring good wine and slicing aged cheddar. It only looked like a late-summer cocktail party. The chatter could not mask the sorrow. The phone rang, and Sezna talked to Tom Fazio, the golf course architect.

"Jimmy Dunne, God bless him, he was there in the rubble with us," Davis told Fazio. Dunne's firm had 125 employees on the 104th floor. Half of them were missing. More than a few were serious golfers or the sons of serious golfers. Dunne is a serious golfer. He wasn't in the office on September 11 because he was attempting to qualify for the U.S. Mid-Amateur, a lifelong dream for him.

The conversation with Fazio came to a close. "They can rip off your arms and legs, Tom, you just don't want them taking your children," he told him. "I love you, Tom Fazio. Give Sue and your kids a big hug from me."

Deeg once got his handicap down to four. Every third year, on a midsummer weekend, he'd play in the two-day Father-Son tournament at Pine Valley. One year, the Seznas were in contention as they stood on the sixteenth tee in the second round. The format was alternate shot. One generation hits a shot, then the other generation plays the next. The son hooked his drive. The father needed to hit a big sweeping hook to reach the green, which is bordered by a pond on the right.

"Why don't you punch a safe one down in front, I'll chip up, and you'll make the putt for par," the son said.

"Nah, I can hook a five-iron on," the father said.

The five-iron shot didn't hook a bit. As it was heading for the water, Deeg said, "How old do I have to be before you'll start listening to me?" He was fifteen. From that double bogey on, his father listened.

Davis showed me a picture of his favorite foursome. Three boys and their father, all in shorts and polo shirts and smiles, standing on the fourteenth tee at Seminole, in South Florida, the Atlantic Ocean behind them, nothing but years of golf in front of them. The father was on the far right, looking proud. He started to identify his boys. "That's Willie next to me," Davis said. "He's a senior in high school, plays to a three. That's Deeg on the left. Between them, that's . . ."

The name never came out. The boy was Teddy, the youngest child of Gail and Davis Sezna. He died in 2000, at age fifteen, on the first Saturday in July in an early-morning boating accident. The father and son were cruising in a thirty-foot motorboat when they ran into a steel light pole. It took two hours for rescuers to find Teddy's body. It took seven hours to get everyone through the receiving line.

On the Saturday after September 11, the father was back in Manhattan, searching for signs of his namesake in hope's final at bat. Somehow the father found the courage, wisdom, and grace to say, "I live for tomorrow. I'm inspired by tomorrow. There will always be tomorrow."

Willie Sezna now has a standing offer to join his father, every summer, in the Pine Valley Father-Son. They'll play in Deeg's memory. They'll play in Teddy's memory. They'll play until the day comes when they can play no more. When that day will be, no one can say. The Seznas know that far too well.

CHAPTER THIRTEEN

LIFERS (2002)

I MET JEFF JULIAN, a vagabond touring pro, only because he was ill. This was at the AT&T tournament at Pebble Beach in February of 2002. He was dying but still playing. He was brimming with life.

At the start of the year, and after the doctors were finally done poking him with needles and making him lie down in an MRI coffin-chamber and asking him to fill tubes with various bodily fluids, Jeff Julian had made a decision. He would do something meaningful to him for the rest of his days. He would continue with his golfing life.

He went to Jacksonville with his golf buddies to prepare for the new season. Coming off a back-nine green one day, somebody cracked a joke. The whole foursome laughed. By the time they reached the next tee, only Julian was still laughing. He couldn't stop. ALS, amyotrophic lateral sclerosis, the disease that killed Lou Gehrig and everyone else who has ever had it, is a horror. The victim's brain can't tell his muscles what to do, and the next thing he knows, he can't stop laughing.

He didn't want anyone feeling sorry for him. This was his attitude: I'm playing in Pebble Beach, one of the sparkly events of the PGA Tour, in one of golf's great meccas. I was with him for the week. He was making new friends by day, taking golf swings on the beach at dusk, drinking Joullian wine and eating heartily at night. He was all over the Monterey Peninsula, having the time of his life, even with a death sentence hanging over his head. We all have death sentences hanging over our heads, Jeff said. The question, of course, is this: What are we going to do in the meantime? The movie of Julian's career highlights was a short. He was forty, and he had played in only fifty-two PGA Tour events, making the cut in only fifteen of them, never finishing better than sixteenth. He had won once on the minor league Nike tour, in '97, and a handful of smaller events throughout New England, where his ancestors have lived for generations. There was a family farm in Vermont, in Norwich, whence Jeff came. His father's father was Alvin "Doggie" Julian, the basketball Hall of Famer who coached the Boston Celtics and at Dartmouth and Holy Cross, where he led Bob Cousy to the NCAA title in 1947. Jeff was an athlete, too, and he had made his way in golf on athletic skill alone. His swing was homemade, all rhythm and touch. You didn't look for him on the practice tee. After dropping out of Clemson in 1982, following his junior year, he spent most of a decade playing golf by day and tending bar by night. He was, he told me with pride, a golf bum. His wife, Kimberly, was often on his bag. In 2001, they had earned $55,132 playing tournament golf. By the standards of the golf bum, that constituted a good year. Learning he had ALS, that was another matter.

At Pebble, Jeff was wearing a ring, a gift from his wife, which was engraved, in Hebrew, with the words, I AM TO MY BELOVED AS MY BELOVED IS TO ME. They kissed after birdies, after bogeys, after sips of wine, after she made a wrong turn. It was as if they were still on their honeymoon. Kim said it was her dream for them to retire in Pebble Beach someday, far in the future. They hadn't known each other all that long. They had met on a Saturday in August in 2000. An opera could be written about that day. Jeff woke up at a friend's house, having missed the cut in a small professional event called the Ozarks Open, in Springfield, Missouri. Later that day, he received a call from his father, Toby: Jeff's mother,

Nancy, had died of a heart attack in her sleep, at age sixty-six. There were no flights out until Sunday morning, so that night Jeff, not wanting to be alone, went to a tournament party at the course. Kimberly Youngblood went too, dragged there by a friend. Jeff admired her French-manicured toes. She admired his hands-as-wings dancing style, which made him look as if he had dropped in from a Grateful Dead concert. They both had young sons, she from a previous marriage, he from a previous relationship. The attraction was mutual, immediate, intense.

Jeff called Kim the following Thursday night, hours after he'd buried his mother. That weekend he made his way to Branson, Missouri, where Kim, nine years younger than Jeff, had lived for most of her life, since long before the town was taken over by Andy Williams, the Lawrence Welk Theater, and the comedian Yakov Smirnoff, the Russian émigré who parlayed a single line—"Vhat a contree"—into a career. Julian came to one of Smirnoff's matinees, not to see the comedian but to see his Statue of Liberty, played by Kim, a role she had been performing twice a day, 150 days a year, for three years.

Six months later, they were making their way to the Norwich town hall to get a sticker for the dump and wound up with a marriage license instead. Two days later, they were married by a justice of the peace at Jeff's mother's grave. All was good. Then, in the late summer of 2001, Jeff started to notice that his speech was slightly slurred and that he was having trouble swallowing.

Carl Vigeland, a superb reporter entrenched in the New England golf scene, provided me with a trove of background on Jeff before I met him. But nothing could fully prepare anybody for what it was like to be in Jeff's company. His speech was labored and slurred (although he expressed himself with great precision), and his strength was so diminished by his disease that Callaway had to put lightweight graphite shafts in his clubs to lighten his workload. But his spirit was overwhelming. Every time he made a birdie at Pebble—he had eleven of them in his fifty-four holes while shooting rounds of 77, 78, and 74—you felt his joy. It was as if golf suddenly had a higher purpose.

Everybody in Jeff's gallery felt it. He had a steadfast following of about a dozen people—his wife, his sisters, other relatives, lifelong friends, new friends, an old girlfriend—and you could see his influence in their faces and hear it in their conversations. A tan man named Brian Anderson followed Jeff for each of his three cold, six-hour rounds. He had heard about him and had to see him play. "When you first see him, you can't believe it," Anderson, an Internet entrepreneur, told me as we walked the course. "He's so filled with life. He's like a movie star. Watching him, you think about where you can be courageous in your own life."

Julian wasn't long off the tee, not by tour standards, hitting drives that went maybe 270 yards. He was never a long hitter, but at Pebble he didn't have a fifth gear. He couldn't muscle a two-iron out of the rough, as he once could, but he played wonderful finesse shots out of bunkers and from the fringe. He played with a calm that was lost on nobody. Late in one round, during a long wait to putt, he had his hands shoved deep into his pockets and was staring at the green as if it were a newly discovered planet. I asked Kim, "What do you think he's thinking about?"

"What he's going to have for dinner," she said.

Deep Thoughts, by Jeff Julian.

Jeff's pro partner at Pebble was Steve Scott, best known for losing to Tiger Woods in thirty-eight holes in the final of the '96 U.S. Amateur despite being two up with three to play. Scott's girlfriend, Kristi Hommel, was his caddie back then. Now they were married, and Kristi was still on the bag. Steve was twenty-five and feeling his way around the pro game. His frustration was obvious. He played every shot as if his life depended on it. Kristi said, "I told Steve, 'Of all the golfers in the field, there must be a reason that we drew Jeff as our partner. With all he's going through, look how smooth his rhythm is, how calm he is. We should try to learn something from that.'" Steve had played in nine tour events as a pro. At Pebble Beach, he made his first cut.

Jeff's amateur partner was a kindly old gent named Pard Erdman, who had played in the tournament dozens of times. He lived on a ranch in Hawaii, and if there was anything in the world that troubled him, you could not see it in his backswing, demeanor, or gait. He and Jeff were ideally suited for one another and often walked the fairways together, shoulder to shoulder with identical strides, saying little. The subject of Jeff's illness never came up. On Sunday of Pebble week, after they had missed the third-round cut, Erdman took Jeff to Cypress Point, where he was a member, for a game. Cypress Point is windswept and aromatic, a jewel. Kim and Pard's wife, Betsy, walked alongside them, as did two of Jeff's sisters. As Jeff and Pard played in, the little group walked along the cliffs, with the Pacific crashing beneath them and the sea air in their lungs. Heaven on earth.

The Julians lived large Pebble week. On Saturday, in the gloaming, Jeff and Kim and I sneaked onto the duney back nine of Pacific Grove, the enchanting municipal course next to the inn where the Julians were staying. In a fast week, we had become friends. We played some holes. As the sun was setting, we talked about Lou Gehrig and his famous, final public remarks. In 1939, Gehrig's disease was eroding his great talent, and he took himself out of the lineup a month into the season, after having played in 2,130 straight games. Soon after, there was a day to honor him at Yankee Stadium. The place was packed with his admirers. Gehrig stood at the microphone and said, "Today I consider myself the luckiest man on the face of the earth." Two years later he was dead. "I understand that," said Julian, who was holding a delicious cabernet in a paper cup. "He was surrounded by his teammates and Babe Ruth and tens of thousands of fans who loved baseball the way he did. I feel that, being able to play golf. So many people have jobs they don't like. I have a job that I love. It doesn't seem fair."

He took his wife's hand and watched the horizon fade from orange to black. He said, "I feel lucky right now because all I can see is the good in people."

⛳

The game's lifers don't often wind up with much, materially, and don't care. For Al Besselink, it was coming down to this: a

$435-a-month room (with three TVs tracking three football games in the fall) in a private home in a working-class neighborhood in Miami, an $11 manicure (including a $2 tip) fortnightly, a money market account containing $5,000 ($30,000 until a recent run of bad luck), and a 2002 PGA Tour money clip (with twelve Benjamins wrapped inside a single). The owner's name was engraved on the clip, all in capitals.

Bessie, as he was known in his 1950s heyday, removed the clip from his front right pocket as we approached the players' gate, wanting to check out the action during the first round of the 2002 Doral tournament.

"Same as the one Tiger Woods carries," he said. He was seventy-seven, and his last cut in a tour event was in 1970, but he still paid his $150 annual dues to be a tour member, and he had the money clip to prove it. A security guard popped his head into the car.

"I'm a player," Bessie said. He was dressed in the manner of an old pro, his blue cotton sweater washed once too often, his black 12D FootJoys freshly shined. We were waved right in.

He had played Doral in the tournament's early days. He played Pebble, L.A., Augusta, Colonial. He played them all. He won in Havana, when Havana was swinging. I asked him when. "I don't know years," he said. "I'm not a geologist." Geologist, genealogist, gerontologist, whatever. He won in Sioux City, in Madrid, in Caracas. He won twenty big tournaments around the world in the '50s and '60s, two hundred when you count the piddling ones. In '53, when he won the first Tournament of Champions, at the Desert Inn in Las Vegas—that place was swinging—he got ten thousand silver dollars in a wheelbarrow and gave half of it to the Walter Winchell–Damon Runyon Cancer Fund. Big deal. It was only money. Besides, he'd bought himself in a pretournament Calcutta for $500 and made $22,500. He was making out all right for the week.

He had lived in South Florida since the late 1940s, when he attended the University of Miami to play on its golf team—a tall, brash kid from New Jersey with thirty-nine months as an Army Air

Corps radio operator. (He's in the university's sports hall of fame.) He knew the Miami of the Elmore Leonard books. He told me where I could find the better bookies, driving ranges, Laundromats, and diners. He had no interest in the bars. He could get you to Gulfstream, the race track, from anywhere, which was saying something, given his eyesight. He had bet the nags all his life.

Doral, he'd never had any luck there. In 1969 he was playing in the tournament and staying at the resort. After his Saturday round, he jumped in a cab and raced over to Hialeah to play the ponies. When he got to the track, he realized he had left his money clip and the $3,500 wedged in it on his bed. He called the resort and asked somebody to secure the money before a housekeeper doing the turndowns mistook it for a tip. "They said, 'No, no, Señor Besselink, we don't see no money on no bed.' I was stupid to call," Bessie said. "But what are you gonna do?" When Ernie Els won the Doral title in 2002, he earned $846,000. Nineteenth paid almost $64,000. Bessie finished nineteenth the year he lost his money clip and the wad in it and won $1,368.

Don't take the story the wrong way. He said he loved Spanish-speaking people. In his neighborhood there was almost nothing but Spanish-speaking people. "Byoo-TEE-ful people," Bessie said. Jews, too—loves 'em. For thirty-five years he represented Grossinger's, the old Jewish resort in the Catskills. "Byoo-TEE-ful people." He was especially fond of blacks. "Teddy Rhodes, Charlie Sifford, they were some of my favorite guys," he said, referring to the men who integrated the tour. Bessie was still tall, several inches over six feet, and big, with a nice head of fluffy white hair. Back in his heyday, his hair was thick and blond and wavy, combed straight back. The writers were always commenting on his hair. The ladies, too. "I won the Joe Louis Invitational in DEE-troit. I gave the champ a pair of blue-and-gray-suede FootJoys. He wore 12D, just like me. He says to one of the guys in his entourage, 'Put these in my locker. Give the boy 200 bucks.' I was the boy. He was byoo-TEE-ful. Those colored people should kiss his ass." What that meant I have no idea, but it was meant as a compliment. Of his best friends, Besselink would say, "Best damn son of a bitch I ever knew."

One day during Doral week, Mike Donald and I took Bessie out for lunch. They were both denizens of the South Florida golf scene. They knew the same courses and the same people. We got together at Miami Shores Country Club, a public course run by their mutual friend Johnny LaPonzina. Bessie was a regular there. Married and divorced three times but never a father, he was reciting his marital history to us. One wife was the daughter of a Texas oilman. Another was the daughter of a prominent Main Line Philadelphia family. The third was the ex-wife of a well-connected Las Vegas builder. "I don't ever hang around with no brokes," he said. "If you're a millionaire, I'll marry you tonight." One of his wives gave him a beautiful watch. Years later, Besselink said, he used it as collateral when he borrowed $5,000 from a friend to pay off a gambling debt. The friend died of a heart attack while engaged in some strenuous indoor activity. The hooker stole the watch.

After lunch we went to the back of the range and hit balls. Mike was hitting one crisp, drawing iron after another, the way pros do. "When you get on the senior tour, I'll caddie for you," Bessie told him. "You're going to make millions. It's going to be so easy, it'll be like stealing—stealing!" Mike watched Besselink hit wedge shots. "You've got great hands," Mike said. There was no shake in them. Bessie hit a low one.

"Now they hit everything high," he said. "I hit it low, with spin." As he played his shots—worn balls, spotty grass, one working eye, two man-made knees—it was evident what an athlete he once must have been.

On another afternoon, Bessie and I went to Gulfstream. He started gambling as a kid, betting his caddie money. "If I couldn't bet, that would be terrible," he said, sounding, for a rare moment, forlorn.

He came to the track with tips for the fifth race and the ninth. At the track he checked in with a guy named Frankie at the $50 window to see what horses Frankie liked. He sought the advice of somebody called the Old Man. "I don't pick horses," Besselink told me. "I get the best information there is, always have." Gulfstream was nearly empty, cold, windy, gray. Gulls swooped lazily over the track. After losing again in the ninth race, Besselink was down $900 for the day. "The Old Man's having a bad day, too," he said. He bet conservatively on the tenth and final race. He took the favorite to win and it did, earning him $300. As we left the track, he bought *The Daily Racing Form* and said, "I'm happy I didn't lose everything."

I drove him home, back to his room with the three TVs. His car was parked in front, an old Oldsmobile. On the backseat were a pillow, many visors and shirts, two pairs of slacks, several towels. In the trunk, amid dozens of clubs, was a big cardboard box stuffed with magazine and newspaper clippings and pictures. Bessie urged me to take the box and read more about his glamorous life, and I did.

It was all true, the whole unlikely life. It was all there in the box. There was a headline: BESSIE SWINGS OFF COURSE TOO. There was a color picture of Terry Moore, the '50s starlet who was introduced to Bessie, the accompanying story said, by Bing Crosby. There were columns on Bessie by Red Smith and Walter Winchell, shots of Bessie with Snead, with Hogan, with Ike, stories referring to oilmen, chairmen, millionaires, to Augusta National and Riviera and the new courses in the California desert. "Always hang around the top of the deck," Bessie had told Mike Donald and me at lunch. That was his code of life, back in the day. As best he could, he was clinging to it.

Ϋ

The players knew Ken Venturi just as we did. They knew his deep voice, his customary sayings, the triumphant moment of his playing career. He had been announcing golf since 1968, and on a Sunday afternoon in 2002, thirty-five years later, it was coming to an end. The CBS golf people (and this was a surprise, given the Ben Wright episode) allowed me to sit in the broadcast tower, beyond the eighteenth green at the Tournament Players Club at Avenel, outside Washington, D.C., during Venturi's final broadcast. As the players came off the final green, many of them paid tribute to him.

For a moment, they put aside their bogeys and frustration and eagerness to split town, looked up at the CBS tower looming above them, and waved goodbye.

The first salute came at about half-past three, thirty minutes into the broadcast. Venturi, working beside his surrogate son, Jim Nantz, their backs to the green just then, didn't notice the gesture. A production assistant tapped his elbow. The announcer popped out of his chair, leaned out an open window, and waved back. He returned to his seat and mouthed the words, "Who was that?" "Joe Durant," the PA whispered, identifying the journeyman pro whom he barely knew.

Venturi is a man who, by his own admission, cries at groundbreakings. When the name Joe Durant reached his ears, he pursed his lips and nodded solemnly, as the news anchors did at the great funerals of the 1960s. Outside the culture of golf, nobody would get Venturi. If you ask him about his reading habits, he assumes you want to know how he reads greens. He has lived his life in the sanctuary of the game. "Kenny's golf," the tour player Jeff Sluman said in a taped tribute. "That's what he's all about."

Nobody ever confused Venturi with Johnny Miller, his counterpart at NBC, whose candor sometimes infuriates the players but who is forever teaching the subtleties of the pro game to his duffer audience with a brilliant torrent of words. Venturi was a recovering stammerer. Talking, oddly enough, was never his strong suit. His commentary—little bursts of a dozen or so loosely connected words—had always been rooted in passion. He became an icon by being in our living rooms one weekend after another, by being reliable, predictable, and comfortable. *He'd like to have that one again. You couldn't walk it out there any better. He'll take his par and walk away quietly. That's class. Touch of class. You could throw a blanket over those two drives.* When Bob Estes won the 2002 Kemper, Venturi said, "You won't find a nicer young man."

Fifteen or so times a year for thirty-five years, Venturi identified the tour's nicest young men—which was amazing because a guy could easily get on his wrong side. The players he liked kicked the sand off their shoes upon leaving a bunker, marked their balls expertly, removed their caps before shaking hands. "He's the most relentlessly consistent person I've ever met," David Feherty, who worked with Venturi for six years, told me. "He either likes you or he doesn't, and the chances are good that he doesn't." Venturi became Venturi by telling us only about the players he did like.

I thought it was odd that he was retiring midseason at an ordinary tour event with an unspectacular field on a course without any history. But I soon realized that it made all the sense in the world to Venturi, who can close his eyes and see the movie of his life on the dark side of his eyelids. He first came to suburban Washington in 1958, to play golf with Eisenhower. They played at Burning Tree, where Venturi has been a member since 1980. He won his U.S. Open down the road from Burning Tree, at Congressional, in 1964, playing the final thirty-six holes in a single day through sweltering heat, reciting in victory the immortal words, "My God, I've won the Open." In 2000 he was the captain of the winning U.S. Presidents Cup team, twenty-five miles southwest of Congressional and Burning Tree at the Robert Trent Jones Golf Club in Lake Manassas, Virginia. "If I hadn't won the Open, I wouldn't have had my career in TV," he told me. "Washington has been very good to me."

Up close, you could see his features the way you could not on TV: his bright blue eyes, silver hair, ruddy skin, thin waist. He was seventy-one then, an age when most golf lifers look shopworn from a life in the sun. But Kenny, as everyone at CBS calls him, still looked as if he could go two rounds in a day. His style was wonderfully antichic. He started wearing Sansabelt trousers in the '60s and remained loyal to the beltless slack ever since, right through the Kemper, loyalty being one of his strong suits.

Frank Chirkinian, long retired as the CBS producer, came to Washington to be with Venturi during the Kemper finale. (Chuck Will, I imagined, was watching at home, although I did not know; we hadn't spoken since the Ben Wright story was published.) For years, in the '70s and '80s and into the '90s, you would see Chirkinian and Venturi and Pat Summerall, all wearing sport coats, holding court at a good hotel bar as another Saturday night on tour came and went. As rat packs go, they may not have been Sinatra, Martin, and Davis, all men Venturi knew, but they had a certain manly flair and they clung to it, even as the rest of the nation began to worship androgyny and shopping malls.

During a break on Sunday's Kemper telecast, Jerry Pate, visiting the booth to pay his respects to his fellow U.S. Open winner, sang a few bars of "Bennie and the Jets," the old Elton John hit, in duet with Nantz. Venturi paid no attention. Later, when the telecast closed with the Sinatra anthem "My Way," his eyes welled up. He wouldn't know Elton, but Sinatra gave away his bride when Venturi married for the second time in 1972. Sinatra paid for that wedding, paid for everything. What Venturi knew, he knew firsthand.

During another commercial break, Gary McCord riffed humorously about verbicide, the willful killing of a verb. Venturi didn't get it, or didn't think it was funny, anyhow. His talent was always to keep things simple. During another commercial the conversation turned to Bobby Clampett's plans to play in a U.S. Open qualifier. "Just drive it in the fairway, hit it on the green, make some putts," Venturi said. "That's all there is to it." In other words, that's what worked for him.

On air, Venturi paid tribute to Pate, a former CBS announcer, by saying, "He's been a great friend, but he still has that beautiful swing." That doesn't mean that most of Venturi's great friends lose their beautiful swings. It's just the way he talks.

With Venturi's retirement, daily tour life lost its last link to an era that was both more glamorous and more rough-and-tumble. Venturi had been prominent in the game for nearly a half century. Francis Ouimet, winner of the 1913 U.S. Open, was his stockbroker. Ouimet's caddie in that Open, Eddie Lowery, was Venturi's backer when he played amateur golf. Venturi was well acquainted with Bobby Jones and Clifford Roberts, the founders of Augusta National. He was taught by Byron Nelson and played often with Ben Hogan. Many of today's players understand and appreciate how much golf Venturi's life spans.

"When I was growing up, the Masters marked the start of the season, and Ken was the voice of the Masters," Joe Durant told me. He knew Venturi the way many players did, from a distance. "I'd stand over a putt and say, 'If he makes this, he wins the Masters.' The voice was Ken's. Then you get out here, and he's watching you play. That's a thrill. Sometimes you think, Boy, I hope he saw that one. Or, Please tell me he didn't see that one. I didn't meet him until I got invited into the broadcast booth. You get to know him because you're playing well. It's something you have to earn."

The best work Venturi ever did, that I know of, was at the Masters in 1996, the year Greg Norman squandered a six-shot lead and Nick Faldo won by five. I'd cite a line, but there aren't any. Venturi was uniquely qualified to cover Norman's collapse. In 1956, Venturi, still an amateur, had a four-shot lead entering the final round at Augusta. He shot 80 and finished second by a stroke to Jackie Burke. He knew the emotion of seeing it all slip away. He praised Norman for the dignity with which he handled the loss. When Venturi captained the U.S. Presidents Cup team, Norman was the headliner on the International side. When the USS *Cole* was attacked a week before the match, and twelve American lives were lost, Venturi urged his team to wear black ribbons. Norman had his teammates do the same. They are similar men, men who understand gestures and symbols. They both would have worn green jackets well.

When Norman was leading the Kemper through two rounds, Venturi was openly rooting for him, at least during the commercials. But the Shark, then forty-seven, faded on the weekend. On the final hole, his approach shot looked like a beauty in the air. "He stiffed it for you," Nantz said to his partner, off air. But the ball took a bad bounce and finished ten paces from the hole, and Norman needed three putts to conclude his weekend's work.

Norman retrieved his ball from the hole, looked up at Venturi and doffed his cap. Venturi stood at his open window and waved back. From a distance of fifty feet, Norman tossed his ball to Venturi. Venturi caught it, signed it, and tossed it back. Norman was deeply disappointed with his weekend play—two rounds of 70, and he could have won the event—but as he came off the green, he remembered Venturi. "That's class," Venturi said, using one of his favorite phrases.

Forty minutes later, Venturi was signing off for the final time, citing something his father, a man who sold net twine to California fishermen, told him as a boy. "The greatest gift in life is to be remembered," Venturi told millions of viewers. "Thank you for remembering me. God bless you and God bless America."

The red light went off. Venturi and Nantz hugged. The CBS crew, mostly working men in T-shirts and shorts, gathered under a tent and made a last toast to their Kenny. Venturi was wearing his CBS blazer. His pattern, for years, was to leave it with one of the production people, and he'd catch up with it at the next event. Now there were no more events. He wore the coat home.

CHAPTER FOURTEEN

LADIES (2003, PART 1)

FOR TWO DAYS, NEAR THE END OF MAY IN 2003, a woman golfer played an ordinary PGA Tour event and turned it into something major. Annika Sorenstam played with the men, from their tees, for their money, and everywhere you went, people were talking about it, including in the men's locker room of the Colonial Country Club in Fort Worth, Texas, where a PGA Tour event has been played since 1946, when the tour was more bawdy and guys drank well into the night.

As Sorenstam, fit and muscular and erect, came off the final green of her second and last round, her eyes were blurry from tears and exhaustion. She had shot an assembly-line 71 in Thursday's opening round of the Bank of America Colonial, an exhibition of control and precision on the fabled par-70 course. She holed a fourteen-footer for par on the last hole of the Friday round for a loose 74 that would have been worse in the hands of a golfer less composed and not as tough. Golf undresses a man—that's what they used to say.

Five over par for two rounds, with scores of cameras, hundreds of reporters, thousands of spectators, and millions of television viewers watching her every shot and fist pump. Annika, then thirty-two, beat some of the boys but too few to make the cut, which she missed by four shots. In the plush men's locker room, a small group of players watched her finish on a gigantic TV. "Give her five more tournaments, she could make a cut," said Esteban Toledo, a Mexican golfer who came up on the game's dirt paths.

In the weeks leading to the tournament, Sorenstam kept saying she was playing in the Colonial for herself, to test her game on a big-time course and against a big-time field. She played against Phil Mickelson, Sergio García, Nick Price, and 107 other male golfers, eleven of whom she ended up beating.

But it turned out to be much more than a solo test flight. After two days and thirty-six holes and 145 shots, she threw her game ball to a random fan in the stands, who jumped up and down jubilantly with it. The guy had Annika Sorenstam's golf ball! She had done something over two rounds that she had not accomplished in more than nine years on the LPGA tour: She had played her way into our imaginations. The support from her massive galleries was heartfelt, and in the fading light of a muggy Friday afternoon she had figured out why. "Because I'm living the dream I want to live," she said, choking on her words. "I'm doing what I want to do." She was thinking about the possible and got us thinking that way, too.

There were many people—and for a day Vijay Singh was their courageous, pig-headed, and lonely spokesperson—who didn't believe a woman should be invited to play in a PGA Tour event. They were outraged. Why I could not understand. After all, the tournament sponsor had twelve exemptions to dole out, and the PGA Tour has no gender constraints in its bylaws. Sorenstam ignored the doubters and kept plugging along.

Throughout her career Sorenstam has been a plugger, a model technician. In the opening round she was that, and she was more. She began her round, on the tenth hole, a two-shotter a little over 400 yards, with a queasy stomach and wobbly knees and perspiring hands and a textbook par. She unleashed a 243-yard four-wood, hit a piercing 139-yard nine-iron, rolled her 16-foot birdie putt smoothly, and tapped it in. It wasn't enough. By the end of the day, the field would average 3.938 on that hole. She made a perfect par, and it set her back. Tour golf is brutal.

But more than she ever had before, Sorenstam exposed her personality to the public. She did a mock stumble after that opening tee shot, not as an actress—there is nothing theatrical in her or her golf game—but to express what she was feeling. The moment was big, bigger than she had expected. She was the first woman to play a PGA Tour event since Babe Didrikson Zaharias competed in the Tucson Open in 1945. This was not a media circus. This was an athlete pushing herself, in a packed arena she had never performed in before. The press came to watch her attempt something real.

Her playing partners, Aaron Barber and Dean Wilson, were warm human beings, male division. (Barber was also playing on a sponsor's exemption.) They say on tour that every shot, good or bad, makes somebody happy, but in the Sorenstam-Barber-Wilson group, that wasn't true. "Remember," Barber said to Wilson before they began play, "we're in this together." He and Wilson were the anti-Singhs. They high-fived Sorenstam when she hit good shots, suffered with her when she hit poor ones, hugged her when it was over.

Her Thursday round was played in a dream state. The spectators following her were mostly older folks, golfers, still and silent when the marshals signaled for quiet. As she prepared to drive on the ninth tee—the last hole of her first round—a little breeze brought down a flurry of fluffy white cottonwood seeds. The picture of tranquility was a fraud. She was even par for the day just then and hit another pure tee shot. She followed it with a sweet-spot seven-iron that pitched near the hole and trickled over the green. Then she putted when she needed to chip. With a tuft of grass behind the ball, any PGA Tour player would have tried to get the ball in the air rather than rolling it. But Sorenstam, unsure of her nerves and her ability, chose the most cautious of shots and ran it eight feet past the hole. She missed the ensuing putt and made a bogey.

Still, it had been a mesmerizing round. A demanding course was playing easy—the fairways and greens were holding—and Annika Sorenstam was in control of her game and her emotions. (She hit thirteen of fourteen fairways and fourteen of eighteen greens in regulation.) "I'll never forget the amount of people and how positive they were," she said after the round. "I'll never forget this day."

Her Friday round was different from the start. Play was sluggish, the day was hot, her swing looked somehow incomplete. Her gallery had almost doubled overnight, the Thursday folks returning, plus schoolchildren and their mothers, and businessmen clenching cigars and cups of beer. Sorenstam made a birdie on the second hole to go even par for the tournament and was in position to make the cut. But then fatigue seemingly set in. Sorenstam later disputed that, but her caddie, Terry McNamara, and her playing partners and her shots disagreed. She pushed a few tee shots, hit a couple of tentative chips and pitches, and in one eight-hole stretch, five through twelve, made five bogeys. There are no birdie holes at Colonial, not when you can't smash it off the tee at will and hit towering approach shots that curve and spin on command and hole all manner of putts. That's not Sorenstam's game. That game, so far, has been the province of the elite male professional.

Sorenstam left Colonial with a new list of things to improve. Her short putting and chipping are below average for a world-class woman player and poor by the standards of the PGA Tour. The myth is that the top women chip and putt as well as the top men. They don't. The modern putting and chipping game is about controlling the big muscles and taking the hands out of the swing, and the top men, with greater physical strength, do that far better than the top women.

After the Sorenstam Colonial, much was said about driving distance. Sorenstam, one of the longest hitters in the LPGA, averaged 268 yards off the tee at Colonial; the field averaged 279. There have always been men who play the PGA Tour successfully hitting about the distance Sorenstam did at Colonial—Loren Roberts, most notably. But they are wizards on the green and around it. Sorenstam has never been, and her tour has never demanded that she become one.

She said she will not be returning to the PGA Tour. "I'm a long way from the leaderboard," she said after Friday's round. She plays tournaments to win, not to maybe make a cut. But the Colonial experience made her a more complete golfer. She played two rounds under a scrutiny more intense, you could argue, than any other golfer has ever faced, and she survived. In fact, she thrived. She came in strong and left stronger. The galleries will side with her from this day forward because at Colonial she dared to try something bold, did it gracefully and well, and let millions of strangers in on the experience.

As she walked up to the eighteenth green during the Friday round, the spectators were applauding her, and she was applauding them. Frank Lickliter, a meat-and-potatoes tour pro, watched for a moment on a clubhouse TV and said, coldly, "Just go home."

Later that night she did go home, but for only one reason: Her score was four strokes too high. She wasn't trying to prove anything to Frank Lickliter at Colonial. She was taking inventory of her game. She was pushing herself. Along the way, she opened the eyes of those willing to see.

ꝑ

By the summer of 2003, when Michelle Wie first became a national grillroom subject, I felt like asking people to calm down. Yes, there was a kid from Hawaii—a thirteen-year-old girl!—who could do what the men could do: She could hit really high and really long. Yeah, she looked like the golfer who, someday, could be the one to break the barrier, who could play with the men. It was true that her entrance onto the world golf stage, in 2003, was spectacular, finishing ninth in an LPGA major and winning the U.S. Women's Public Links Championship. And she was more accomplished at thirteen than another golfing Mozart, Tiger Woods, was at that age. Then there were her stated goals, so audacious and inspiring: to someday, after college, turn professional and become one of the dominant players on the PGA Tour. Plus, she was intent on playing in the Masters, as an amateur. An impressive list. Still: She was a thirteen-year-old girl. I was on my own little island of doubt. She had told me that she looked forward to her birthday and Christmas because they were days off from golf. Nobody else I knew seemed too troubled by that. In fact, everywhere else golf heads were trying to figure out when she would go pro, which brand of clubs and ball she'd play when she did, who would manage her, and how many millions some corporation would guarantee her. I went to see her play in an LPGA event in New Jersey and tried to block all that out. I just wanted to enjoy her precociousness.

One night, I was in the dining room of the Marriott Seaview Resort near Atlantic City when she was loading up at the dessert table. She looked almost like a typical teenager, except that she was still wearing her golf shoes and cap from the first round of the LPGA ShopRite Classic. She looked like a golf nerd, just like Tiger did at thirteen.

On the practice tee, there was nobody who looked like her. She was long and lean, nearly six feet tall, and her swing is one of the best in golf. On the range she was unloading a series of 300-yard drives. No wonder the marketers were salivating. She was an A student, pretty and charming, relaxed in interviews. In a moment, it was obvious why she was generating hysteria. Her father, B.J., was contributing, by having her play week after week.

I asked B.J., a University of Hawaii transportation professor who was then working as Michelle's caddie, if it was too much. He acknowledged that it was. He struck me as a reasonable man. "Next summer we concentrate on one thing—winning the men's U.S. Public Links," he said. That's a men's event by tradition only, not by rule. The winner, by tradition, is invited to play in the Masters and is typically some hotshot male amateur. B.J. Wie saw it as a road to Augusta for Michelle.

Dad, do I call him Hootie or Mr. Johnson?

Wie is the only child of doting parents, both of whom, once low handicappers, gave up golf to devote themselves to their daughter's golfing success. Michelle started hitting balls in earnest at age four, and she played year-round. Her swing is a dream. Her backswing is superwide, like Davis Love's but longer. The downswing is art. There was nothing violent in her swing, as there is in Tiger's. No 150-pound golfer, male or female, has ever made hitting a 300-yard drive look so effortless. "You can't teach that rhythm," Wie's teacher then, Gary Gilchrist, told me. "You're born with it."

Her mistakes were caused by swinging too easily, especially with wedges and, most notably, the putter, her least consistent club. "In ball striking she's already one of the top five out here," said Patricia Meunier-Lebouc, the French golfer who won the Kraft Nabisco Championship, an LPGA major, with Wie playing with her in the final round. "Her putting I don't know about. She makes a big demonstration when she misses. A professional does not do that. But she is a kid."

A competitive kid. At the short, lovely, Bay Course at the Seaview Resort—I first got to know it as a member of the Philadelphia Newspapermen's Golf Association—Wie opened with an even-par 71, one behind Annika Sorenstam and six shots behind the leaders. At her press conference afterward, she was asked if she was happy with her play. "No," she answered. "Not really." Never mind that she was a teenager holding her own against the best women in the world. In Michelle Wie's mind, a score can always be lower. Two years later, she was in the hunt at the U.S. Women's Open and at the U.S. Public Links Championship, a men's event.

I found the Wies candid. Describing debates with her caddie-father over club selection, Michelle said, "We were in different books. We were on different planets." Later B.J. was asked what he thought of the course. "Frankly?" he said. "I don't care for it. Too traditional. It doesn't inspire Michelle." Then the Wies were saying that Michelle would finish college before turning pro. The father said to me, "When teenagers make a lot of money, it doesn't seem to lead to happiness."

Michelle was saying she wanted to attend Stanford. The family values education. Her father has a doctorate in transportation. His father had one in aeronautics. "A high school education is not

enough," the father told me. He said he and his wife were spending more than $50,000 a year on their child's golf education. They
were not saving for college. They figure Michelle's golf skill would
take care of that.

Michelle's mother, Bo, a Honolulu real estate agent, followed
her daughter on every hole she played at the Atlantic City event,
carrying an enormous umbrella in case of rain, which never came.
After a disappointing Saturday round of 72, to make the cut on
the number, Michelle signed autograph after autograph while her
father sprayed mosquito repellent on her bare legs and shoulders.
But the Wies are not living in some never-never land. They made
it clear to me that they know about the life money can buy: private
jets, fancy cars, the best sushi—Tiger Woods's life. While driving
with her parents between tournaments, Michelle joked that she
would not turn pro for anything less than $100 million, the value
of Woods's Nike deal. "The family has an eight-year plan, but I
think a lot is going to happen that's going to make them rethink
it," Gilchrist said.

The whole discussion was giving me a headache. My goal that
week on the Jersey shore in the summer of 2003 was to enjoy watching a thirteen-year-old girl golfer who was like no thirteen-year-
old golfer ever before. It couldn't be done. The story, and the girl,
were changing way too quickly to allow that.

The year 2003 was when Martha Burk, who was trying to get Augusta National to accept a woman member, went to the Masters. I
was assigned to hang out with her for the week. From the beginning, I didn't really understand what all the fuss was about. If a
private club wants to be single-sex, I don't see anything wrong with
that. My wife is a member of an all-female club. I'm a member of
two men's clubs. We both enjoy the occasional refuge. I understand
that Augusta National is a special case, because of the Masters. The
PGA Tour and the USGA and the PGA all have bylaws that re-
quire clubs hosting events to demonstrate that they do not discrimi-

nate. The rules make sense: The clubs derive immense benefit from opening their gates to the paying and TV-watching public for a week. In an age of inclusiveness, awarding these profitable events to discriminatory clubs would send the wrong message. (The Masters gets around the rules only on a technicality—it's not a PGA Tour event; it's an invitational event run by a private club.) Because the Masters is in the public domain, it seems like the host club should be, too. But the club has been all-male from its inception, and it runs one of golf's great events, one that brings much pleasure to millions of people. That's probably why Martha Burk's movement never went anywhere in the end. Nobody I know wants to see the Masters shut down. Augusta National is a private club with a long history as a men's club; if the club wants to have women, that's up to the membership. If the club wants to stage the Masters, that's up to the membership, too. For years, the club was all-white, and the segregation, I'm sure, was rooted in racism. But I don't think a private club's decision to be single-sex is rooted in hatred. In any event, in April of 2003, my assignment was not the tournament, but the circus beyond the gates.

Martha Burk's Masters week began with a Thursday 4:30 a.m. wake-up call she didn't want. (Not that I was there; she told me about it later.) The call came to her home in Washington, D.C. It was from a radio station looking for an interview. "Are you crazy?" Burk, the unpaid chair of the National Council of Women's Organizations, asked the caller. Who would call in the middle of the night like that? Besides, she already had a media event scheduled for the day, a 1:30 p.m. press conference at the Martin Luther King Jr. Center in Atlanta, a step in her march to Augusta.

A few hours later, she was on her way to the airport in a cab with her husband, a retired professor named Ralph Estes—like Burk, a displaced Texan and a bluegrass music fan. The conversation turned to Tony Kornheiser's column in *The Washington Post* from the previous day, which ran with the headline, FOR MARTHA, NOBODY GIVES A HOOTIE. The story described Burk's effort to boost salaries for players in the WNBA, "a league," Kornheiser wrote, "she knows nothing about." Burk took exception to that assessment and wondered why Kornheiser hadn't called her. The cabbie interrupted her. "If you don't mind me butting in on your conversation," he said, "I think Kornheiser knows nothing about sports." Oh, did Martha Burk get a kick out of that.

The Thursday papers ran stories about Hootie Johnson's Wednesday press conference at Augusta National. Many of the questions posed to Hootie were about the club's male-only policy. Many of the questions invoked Martha Burk. None of the answers did. The club chairman waltzed slowly around the questions but closed the session with a doozy: "I do want to make one point. If I drop dead right now, our position will not change on this issue. It's not my issue alone." Scores of media outlets used that bite of sound, and Burk loved it. In her mind, Johnson was admitting that the membership was comfortable with the club's policy. She could use that. Every time Johnson opened his mouth, Burk believed, he gave her cause a present.

In Atlanta on a cold and rainy Thursday afternoon, Burk was introduced to the dozens of reporters and camerapeople on hand by Martin Luther King III, president of the Southern Christian Leadership Conference. In Augusta, 130 miles away, first-round play had been postponed due to torrential rain, proving, Burk said, that God knew about Augusta National's exclusionary policy and "She doesn't like it." She was sixty-one, a grandmother, and dressed stylishly, in black tasseled loafers, a navy silk suit with tapered pants, a lime-green blouse, and off-red lipstick.

Inside the King Center, schoolchildren watched footage of Dr. King's historic march from Selma and heard him preach the searing words "We as a people will get to the promised land!"

Dr. Burk—she has a Ph.D. in psychology—proved herself to be a capable public speaker. She repeatedly referred to the golf club not simply as "Augusta," as most golfers do, but as "Augusta National Incorporated," driving her point home to the assembled media that the club is "registered as a for-profit corporation." As she spoke, her husband watched from a distance and worried. "She should be wearing a coat," he said. The temperature was in the mid-forties. He was more concerned that the name of her Augusta hotel would get out and some deranged person would do her harm. At one point he took a cell phone call regarding his search for a bodyguard for his wife at the rally planned for Saturday in Augusta. Burk was more worried that the Reverend Jesse Jackson would be there. She wanted to portray the Augusta membership issue as a case of discrimination against women, being fought by a coalition of women's groups. She was concerned that if Jackson turned up, *he* would become the story.

About five hours later Burk, Estes, and the small NCWO entourage were checking in to the new Super 8 motel on the outskirts of Augusta. They had four rooms for three nights and two rooms for two nights, at $250 per room per night, prepaid by check. It was a small fortune for Burk's organization, which had only two paid staffers. In the lobby I introduced Burk to another Super 8 guest, Jeff Julian, who was in Augusta to receive the Ben Hogan award from the Golf Writers Association of America, for his courageous play. The ugly grip of ALS had stolen his conventional speech by then but not his spirit. Kim was with him, and his eyes were still filled with life. He was nearing his end. Burk had no idea how close she was to the heart of golf. It was not her fault at all— there was no reason she should—but she just didn't.

The next day, on Friday of Masters week, Burk was holed up in an old house in Augusta's stately Hill section. Jack Batson, an Augusta lawyer and ACLU member, had made his home available to her and her people for the day so that she would have a place to do her interviews. One of the NCWO staffers, a young woman named Rebecca Menso, with a delicate silver ring pierced through her left nostril, had filled out a sheet of paper that divided the workday into sixteen half-hour sessions, each spoken for by a different news organization: ABC News, *The Los Angeles Times, The Philadelphia Inquirer,* and the Golf Channel, among many others.

Christine Brennan, a *USA Today* columnist, came in. She and Burk had never met. When they did, they seemed like long-lost cousins. "Do you realize what today is?" Brennan asked Burk.

"What is it?"

"It was a year ago today the column ran," Brennan said, referring to her story from April 11, 2002, in which she criticized Augusta's all-male membership policy. Reading that piece prompted Burk to write a private letter to Hootie Johnson, who responded last July with a bizarre three-page press release in which he said the club would not be forced "at the point of a bayonet" to add a female member. (No question about it: Hootie brought this whole thing on himself and his club. He should have drowned her with sweet tea. Instead, he diminished the club with his handling of it.) Ever since Hootie fired the opening salvo, the press had been lunching on the story. *The New York Times* nominated its coverage of the saga for a Pulitzer Prize. Demonstrating that he does have fine southern manners when he cares to use them, Hootie called on Brennan, by name, for the first question at his pretournament press conference.

While Brennan and Burk talked, Jack Batson's son William, a sophomore at an Augusta public school called the Richmond Academy, was out on Washington Road, the main thoroughfare to the course, selling anti-Burk T-shirts. The front of the shirt read, IF MARTHA HAD BALLS. . . . The back read, SHE COULD JOIN THE CLUB! Jack Batson struck me as the Atticus Finch of modern Augusta, and William shared his father's liberal bent, but easy money is easy money, and the dark-haired kid and his friends were clearing five dollars on every sale. That Friday, in under an hour, they sold thirty-six shirts at $20 each, earning themselves $180. News photographers, naturally, took pictures. The circus had come to town, all right.

Then came Saturday, rally day, a beautiful day for a protest. Blocked by city officials and the courts from demonstrating near Augusta National's main entrance, Burk and her people were assigned a grassy, five-acre site a half mile down Washington Road. A bus from Atlanta brought about thirty protesters, and there might have been another sixty assembled, which meant that the ratio of media to marchers was about one to one. "Today, we protest with placards," Burk said over a loudspeaker from a small podium. "Tomorrow, women will be protesting with their pocket-books!" Reporters scribbled.

If you wanted a microphone in your face, all you had to do was dress like Elvis, or wear a tuxedo while carrying a sign reading, FORMAL PROTEST, or do anything out of the ordinary. A woman with snowy white hair held up a sign that read, HOOTIE PATOOTIE, SHAME ON YOUTIE! She had attached her placard to an old Wilson Blue Ridge driver, with a steel shaft and leather grip and laminated wooden head. The woman, Lee De Cesare, married for forty-eight years to the Republican mayor of Madeira Beach, Florida, was a quote machine: "My husband said to me, 'You're going to ruin the tournament,' and I said, 'That's what we're trying to do!'"

Actually, the tournament never paid much attention to the protest, and the protesters didn't pay much attention to the tournament. During Masters week, Burk said repeatedly that she wasn't interested in golf. She knew the world was not going to change if Augusta National took in one or two affluent women. But the club was, she said, a symbol of societal constraint. More to the point, its men-only policy gave her a platform to talk about the other women's issues important to her: Title IX, maternity leave, scads of others. But it was Augusta's membership and Martha versus Hootie that we in the press could most easily get our arms around. It was clear that she'd ride it for as long as she could.

Before leaving the rally site, Burk sat in the back seat of a Chevy Suburban, signed a few autographs, and gave a few follow-up interviews to reporters leaning toward her vehicle. Her bodyguard-for-a-day, a bowling ball of a man in a checkered suit, kept everything orderly. Then she drove off, just as they do in the movies, leaving Augusta behind. Her first Masters week had come and gone, and she had never seen a single shot.

CHAPTER FIFTEEN

WATSON AND BRUCE

(2003, PART 2)

FOR MANY OF US OF A CERTAIN AGE—older than Tiger and younger than Jack—Tom Watson represented golf for a decade and a half, from the first days of disco to the last days of the persimmon driver. It wasn't only the wins: the five British Opens, the two green coats, the U.S. Open he stole from Nicklaus out of the beach grass at Pebble in 1982. It was him. *This gap-toothed Huck Finn is a psychology major out of Stanford,* Vin Scully told us again and again. It didn't matter that we really didn't know anything about him. We were given little glimpses and filled in the rest ourselves. He had a chance to win a sixth British Open at St. Andrews in '84, misclubbed on the Road Hole and lost, but he never made an excuse. He quit the Kansas City Country Club on principle in 1990 because the club refused to admit a Jewish businessman. He was a man of integrity. He was a man.

For years the glimpses were enticing. Near the end of his Duel in the Sun against Jack Nicklaus at Turnberry in '77, he turned to the Golden Bear and said, "This is what it's all about, isn't it." He said it, ever sure of himself, as a statement, not a question. The night he won at Muirfield in '80, he and Ben Crenshaw and their gorgeous first wives sneaked onto the course and played shots in the twilight. Then there was that famous dialogue between him and his caddie, Bruce Edwards, the preamble before the holed pitch shot that won Watson his lone U.S. Open title, in '82:

Edwards: "Come on now, get it close."

Watson: "I'm not going to get it close. I'm going to make it."

The truth is that in his heyday, Watson, deeply self-reliant, never needed much help from his caddies. Not from Alfie Fyles, with whom he won his five British Opens and lost at St. Andrews. Not from Leon McClatty when he won at Augusta. Not even from Edwards, with whom he had won dozens of times in a partnership that began in 1973. Watson wanted punctuality and accurate yardages and not much more, not even from Bruce, a buoyant person, kind to me when I was trying to caddie on the PGA Tour in '85, when he and Watson were at the top of their games, kind to everybody he encountered.

Over time, the glimpses of Watson became unattractive. We learned that he didn't handle his public drinking well, that his relationship with his father was strained, that the man who stood up to the country club bigots otherwise followed the crowd, falling into step with the predictable Rush Limbaugh. He broke up with his wife and broke up with his old Ram clubs. (Not passing any judgment here; relationships, even those with inanimate objects, can go stale.) For several years in the early '90s, Edwards went to work for Greg Norman. Over the course of that decade, many of us left Watson—I did, anyway. When his putting stroke went yippy, I don't know many who really cared. (Well, I'm sure Edwards did, and Watson's friend and surrogate father, Sandy Tatum, a former USGA president.) When Watson played journeyman Don Pooley in an epic U.S. Senior Open playoff in 2002, I was rooting for Pooley, which surprised me, because Watson was the golfer of my boyhood, the golfer I tried to swing like, the golfer I wanted to be.

Then came the real U.S. Open, the 2003 edition, at Olympia Fields outside Chicago, and all was forgotten and all was forgiven.

Over the course of a single day, Watson made us remember why we admired him so. In the opening Thursday round, playing on a USGA exemption at age fifty-three, he shot a 65. Nobody shot lower. For once, here was a golfer playing for somebody other than himself. Edwards was on the bag, even though he was already showing signs of ALS, the same disease that was in the process of claiming Jeff Julian. For a day Watson had the national sporting stage again, and he stood up, hat in hand, and made a public pitch for ALS research money. The emotion of the day was captured in the hug Watson and Edwards shared on the eighteenth green and in a single sentence that Watson blurted out later: "I don't care if I shoot 90 tomorrow." Ever a realist, he knew what we did not: Fifty-three-year-old men with unreliable putting strokes do not win U.S. Opens, but anybody can show gratitude to an old friend.

The remaining three days of the championship belonged to Watson and Edwards as they—they—shot rounds of 72, 75, and 72 to finish twenty-eighth. The old couple, owners of each other's secrets, received standing ovations on green after green.

At the urging of his caddie, Watson had put his old Ping putter in his bag at Olympia Fields. Edwards asked Watson how the putter felt.

"Like an old girlfriend," Watson said.

For a moment, the years evaporated—Edwards and Watson were young again, and the only thing ahead of them was the promise of tomorrow.

A month later, in July, Watson was about to leave home and fly overseas for his annual fortnight of links golf—the British Open followed by the British Senior Open. In 2003, the Open was at Sandwich, in England, followed by the fifty-and-over event at Turnberry, in Scotland. Watson was leaving Bruce behind.

"Yeah, you'll probably win over there without me," Edwards told Watson.

"I'll try to do that for you, pal," Watson responded.

Edwards was missing the trip at Watson's urging. The symptoms of his disease were progressing, and being outside for hours at a time in the wind or the rain, a near certainty over two weeks of British seaside golf, could only be bad for his condition. In the warmth of summer in the United States, Edwards was still able to work. After the U.S. Open, Watson had turned the summer of '03 into the Summer of Bruce. First, there was his time-stopping 65 for a share of the first-round lead at Olympia Fields; then there was the U.S. Senior Open at Inverness, where he was the runner-up, again with Edwards on the bag. And in early July, they did it once more with feeling, at the Senior Players Championship, in which Watson again finished second. Every round was a lovefest for Watson and his caddie, with many standing ovations. The galleries knew what was going on.

Watson was playing with heightened emotion and a swing that has been one of the constants in his adult life. At times he putted like the Watson of old, the one who never missed a five-foot comebacker while winning his eight majors. For weeks on end, he did all the things he wanted to do, except win with Bruce. And now he was leaving, off to the British Isles, to play in two major championships without him.

It was Bruce who arranged for his own replacement. In '73 he was eighteen and looking for work as a tour caddie. He was standing in the players' parking lot at a course in St. Louis with another kid caddie, Neil Oxman, when a young touring pro walked by. "That's Tom Watson," Oxman said to Edwards. "Why don't you ask him?" Edwards did, and he got the job. Thirty years later he returned the favor, arranging for Oxman, a Philadelphian and a prominent Democratic political strategist, to work for Watson for the half month abroad. Oxman was fifty then, a friend of mine from Philadelphia. Golf kook does not do him justice. The invitation came out of a dream. Over the years he had caddied in more than 300 PGA Tour and Champions events but never for a winner and never for Watson, one of his heroes.

Their first stop was the Open at Royal St. George's in Sandwich, a course Watson does not like because of its wicked bounces and sideways wind. He opened with a 71, with Oxman holding the umbrella, and closed with a 69, to finish eighteenth. It was a good showing, but Watson arrived at Turnberry, on the west coast of Scotland, for the Senior Open feeling beat up and out of rhythm. He had come to the right place to straighten himself out. Above the course, high on a bluff, sits the Turnberry Hotel, sprawling and sumptuous, the place Watson stayed during the '77 British Open, when he and Jack Nicklaus played the final thirty-six holes together to decide who would take home the claret jug. They shot identical scores the first three rounds. Nicklaus, ten years older than Watson, closed with a 66, while Watson shot a 65 to win by one. Both made birdies on the last, Nicklaus from thirty-five feet, Watson from two. That's as good as golf gets.

And there they were at the end of July, eating and playing together, twenty-six years later. The night before the tournament began, there was a cocktail party to honor them and to commemorate the renaming of the eighteenth hole from Ailsa Hame to Duel in the Sun, as their epic showdown has come to be known, thanks to an uncharacteristic heat wave that swept through southwestern Scotland that year. In a tight little square, four legends of the game stood together—Watson and Nicklaus and Arnold Palmer and Gary Player—each wearing a blue blazer and holding a drink (Watson's was fresh-squeezed orange juice, no ice), laughing about things I'm sure no ordinary mortal could understand. It was what the old guys' tour was meant to be.

At the party a snippet of BBC tape from the '77 Open was played showing Nicklaus lashing his final approach shot out of the right rough as the commentator, Henry Longhurst, described the Golden Bear's "animalistic strength." Watson stood with his second wife, Hilary, and watched himself from half a lifetime ago, when he was boyish and hatless and wearing spectacular checkered slacks. When the footage came to an end, he took a microphone and told the crowd, "I'm trying to resurrect those pants. I think they were last seen on Jesper Parnevik."

At the party and on the course all week, a few people carried the 2002 book *Duel in the Sun,* written by Michael Corcoran, 200-

plus pages about the '77 Open so detailed that it includes a thorough description of those polyester pants with the half-top pockets in front and Reece pockets in back. There were spectators asking the two protagonists to sign the book, and of course they signed. Nicklaus and Watson are old-school when it comes to things like signing autographs, but they're not nostalgists. They played the first two rounds together at Turnberry—Carl Mason of England filled out the threesome—and as they stood on the ninth tee on Friday, waiting to play, the two talked about the wholesale changes they'd make to the course. Out with the old for those two, or so they say. They leave the history to Corcoran and his ilk, the worldwide community of golf kooks, like Oxman and me. (Scotland remains the headquarters.) As they came up eighteen in the first round, the kids working the leaderboard, teenagers who weren't even born when Nicklaus and Watson won their last regular majors, clapped along with everybody else.

You know what they say in golf: If it's not one thing, it's something else. In the first three rounds, Watson's shotmaking was loose, but his putting was extraordinary. "Tom's making everything," Barbara Nicklaus, Jack's wife, told me. I didn't think she would have said that with such admiration in '77.

Edwards, following the scores on the Internet at home in Ponte Vedra, Florida, knew his boss's putter must have been hot. Watson opened with a 66, four under par, and followed with a 67 on a course that had only wispy rough and was playing short. The cocktail party was over. Watson was playing for keeps, and for Bruce.

After two rounds, his playing partner—his other playing partner—was leading the tournament. "Nice chap," Watson said of Mason, who opened 67-64. "He's playing beautifully." As for Oxman, he was doing fine, carrying the bag and giving his man yardages, but not trying to be Bruce.

In the third round, Mason shot a 65 to stay in the lead, while Watson shot a 66, mostly because he again putted well. He was now three behind a man in total control of his game. To have a chance at winning, Watson knew he would have to resurrect the shotmaking that went with the old polyester pants.

He was playing in the penultimate group, and as he stood on the tee of the eighteenth hole—Duel in the Sun, now, his hole— he was a shot behind Mason, who was in the final threesome. Watson hit a two-iron off the tee, a three-iron just over the green and made bogey, his first of the day. He came off the green and told Bob Rosburg of ABC that he was tired of finishing second. Mason came to the eighteenth tee with a two-shot lead.

Nice chap, poor bloke, a fifty-year-old with a face weathered from years of wind and cigarettes and late nights. On Thursday, Mason had heard this exchange between Watson and Nicklaus and took it to heart:

Nicklaus: "Did you ever hit driver off eighteen in '77?"

Watson: "No."

Nicklaus: "Neither did I."

Okay, then, Mason knew how to play the old Ailsa Hame: iron off the tee, to stay short of the two lethal fairway bunkers on the left side of the hole. Except that on the seventy-second hole, he reached the first deadly bunker with his iron, drew a horrid lie, and ended up making a double-bogey six. He and Watson were tied. The winner would be decided in a sudden-death playoff. "Okay, Neil," Watson said to his caddie. "Let's go." The playoff began on the Duel in the Sun. It was Watson's hole. He wasn't bound by what he did there in '77. He could play it as he pleased.

On this fifth time playing it, he took a driver. So did Mason. They both made par and returned to the eighteenth tee yet again. This time Mason drove it into the second fearsome bunker. He blasted out, flubbed his third shot, and finally pitched his fourth on. Watson drove it in the fairway, hit a wedge on, lagged up, and tapped in to win. He had his first British Senior Open, and Oxman had his first win of any kind, but they both knew to whom the victory really belonged.

In his victory speech, Watson, the honorary Scot, the great stoic, choked on his words when he got to Edwards. "I feel he was there today, making things happen when they happened," he said.

I reached Bruce in Ponte Vedra. He sounded wistful, happy that his man won, sad that he wasn't there to see it. The calls and e-mails were coming in fast, one after another. Kim Julian, Jeff's wife, had called. So had players, caddies, family. Oxman, I guessed, would be sending him family heirlooms. Bruce's speech had deteriorated since the U.S. Open. Time was slipping away fast for him, faster for him than most. I wondered if he'd be able to work again for Tom; that is, be beside Tom on the golf course again.

Ỵ

Two months after the British Senior Open, in late September of 2003, I flew to California for the final event of the senior season, the Charles Schwab Cup Championship. If the weather cooperated, Bruce Edwards would work the tournament. The event was played at a nice, simple, old-style course at the Sonoma Golf Club, surrounded by the bleached hills of California wine country. It was fall. The San Francisco 49ers were on TV, the fall grape harvest was at its peak, and there were only a few hundred spectators following Tom Watson and Jim Thorpe as they played together in the last group on the last day. It was warm and dry, and Bruce was working. He was always thin, and now he looked ominously skinny, but he was caddying. The bag was strapped on the back of a golf cart—he was getting weaker daily—but he was caddying.

Thorpe and Watson were playing for the first-place prize, $440,000, but there was no tension at all. It was as if they were playing for Monopoly money. Thorpe was one of golf's free spirits, a muscular, profane, and quick black man who knew horses, cigars, and the best steak house in town, no matter what town he was in that week. He was popular in the players' locker room, in the press tent, and in the caddie trailer, too. Watson appeared relaxed. He had a friendship with Thorpe, and they came off almost every tee together, side by side and chatting away, Bruce occasionally beside them in the cart. Bruce's spirit was undying. When he wanted to exclaim at Sonoma, he thrust his right knee into the air; the words were not there. Watson, for whatever reason, was at ease. Naturally, there would be, as the laws of sport and human beings dictate, a winner and a loser, or a runner-up, anyway, but Watson wasn't worried. He knew something.

Thorpe won the tournament, and Watson took second, and that runner-up finish meant that he was the winner of a season-long points competition that would pay him $1 million from the Charles Schwab Company, to be doled out over ten years. The money was his to do as he pleased. At the awards ceremony, Watson, with his wife, Hilary, on his left arm, and Bruce on her left arm, announced what that would be, that he was donating the entire $1 million to charity, primarily to ALS research, to ALS victims' services, and to a fund for Bruce and his wife and kids. "We're going to find a cure for this damned disease," Watson said.

I thanked Bruce for his years of help and kindness. He mouthed the words, "You're welcome, buddy." I had seen him at tour events for eighteen years, and I knew how true Watson's words about him were: There wasn't a mean bone in his body.

At the end of the year Watson was named the *SI* Golfer of the Year. He wasn't an obvious choice. You could have made a case for Tiger or Vijay or Annika. But, really, it had to be Watson. He had finally lifted the veil, at least a little bit.

For decades, he had been a puzzle. In his hatless, beltless heyday, and for many years after it, he would hit shots into awful places—in hayfields and forests, or against a St. Andrews wall—and immediately flash that inscrutable, lips-only smile. Bruce was usually there, practically trotting to keep up with him. Watson had that dour grin. It was as if he enjoyed torture by golf.

It wasn't that he was a misanthrope; he was nothing like Ben Hogan or Ty Cobb or Richard Nixon. He was good with his playing partners, in press tents, to kids with pens. But for years, while he dressed in garish colors, his emotions ran in shades of gray. To certain players and caddies and sponsors and fans, Watson seemed cold and unreal—like a wax golfer, even as he was doing all that winning.

He needed Bruce. It was Bruce who helped put a human face on his boss. Operating in the shadows, where the best loopers have always worked, he'd have a smoke with Fuzzy or play cards with Jack's caddie or talk college basketball with the CBS suits, and some of the goodwill that flowed toward Bruce would reach his boss. But there was only so much even a relentlessly upbeat man like Bruce could do. Watson remained an enigma.

Then came 2003. A new Watson—easier to read, more satisfying to watch—emerged. At age fifty-four, twenty years past his prime, he turned out to be the year's most significant golfer. Watson, with an assist, as usual, from Edwards, was the best thing in golf in 2003, by far.

It was late in 2002 when Bruce called Watson at home in a farmhouse in Kansas and told him that he had been diagnosed with ALS. Their relationship was rooted in sports, and to discuss life they borrowed metaphors from games. "I just made a quadruple bogey," Bruce said to Watson.

The news seemed to unlock something in Watson. "We'll beat this thing," he said.

Since then, Watson has been fixated on a single goal: saving his caddie's life. The crisis brought a vigor to his game not seen in years. It also humanized one of the game's great figures.

Watson's season began in earnest on the Thursday before Father's Day, when he shot that 65 in the opening round of the U.S. Open. He spotted the field many years and some yards, but nobody was better that day. It wasn't his moment, though. Everybody who was there could feel the love between him and Bruce. It was in their once-unimaginable hug when the round was over and in the forcefulness of Watson's press-conference statements. Bruce's illness had been public knowledge for months, but now Watson, with his superb round, was one of the sports stories of the day, and he used the spotlight to speak of his "pal," his "brother," and the disease. Passionately, and with a precision that revealed a half year of deep reading in medical texts, he talked about the need for ALS research money "to save the life of my friend and others like him."

Watson wasn't always like that, so aware of others. For years he was consumed with two things, golf and hunting, and when his two children were young, he played a limited role in raising them. He and his high-school sweetheart, the former Linda Rubin, had been married for twenty-five years before they divorced in 1998. For years, Watson had been a heavy social drinker, sometimes bombastic at dinner parties. In 2003, that came to a stop. At the big festive dinners at Augusta in April, he was drinking only soda pop. At Turnberry, a victory glass of champagne went to his lips and no further. He wouldn't talk to me about his abstinence, but when he quit, it was cold turkey and by himself. Throughout 2003 he made repeated efforts to begin anew with his son, Michael, then a junior at Southern Methodist, and his daughter, Meg, a Duke grad working in Kansas City, where Watsons have lived for generations. The relationships had been strained because the children are close to their mother, and the divorce was not amicable. That was another subject Watson would not discuss, but others said his attempts to reconnect with his children were heartfelt and profound.

It was the embrace of Bruce Edwards, though, that was the most public sign of the new Tom Watson. Looking at him and Bruce, you could only wonder where the time went and how much time they had left. Watson was trying to make up for lost chances. "People get caught up in their lives, and then life passes you by," Marsha Edwards, Bruce's wife, told me. "Tom woke up."

By the end of the year, Bruce was communicating mostly by e-mail. I asked him what the best times with Tom were. His answer was immediate: the early '80s, when Watson was dominating and they were both young and it looked as if they would win together forever.

I asked Watson the same question. He said he liked what he was doing now more than what he was doing then, that the golf he played in 2003 was the most satisfying of his life. "Back then it was always about me," he said. "Winning for yourself and winning for somebody else—you can't compare the two."

CHAPTER SIXTEEN

EYEBALLS (2004, PART 1)

YOU DON'T OFTEN GET A CHANCE to look Tiger Woods straight in the eye. Usually, he's got his tunnel vision going. Then there's the brim of his hat, curved to keep us out, or so it seems. But there he was on the practice putting green at Augusta National before the first round of the 2004 Masters, at half past one, waiting for his round to begin, his eyes wide open. He was steps away from the first tee and the first shot of the year's first major. He took a long look at the huge leaderboard beside the eighteenth hole and ran his eyes across the hole-by-hole scores of the English golfer Justin Rose's first round. "Five under," Woods said to his caddie, Steve Williams. Woods already trailed by five. People, dozens of them, stared at Woods as he studied the board. You didn't want to be rude, but you couldn't help it. Wherever he is, however he's playing, he's the star. Your eyes go to him.

His own eyes were watery and cloudy, yellowish. If eyes are windows to the soul, Tiger's soul was dog tired on this Thursday afternoon. His eyes looked old. The rest of him looked as if he could go fifteen rounds with anybody.

In 2004, people started talking about golf's Fab Four: Tiger, Vijay Singh, Ernie Els, and Phil Mickelson. I felt the game had only one true star. You could say of Tiger, and of no other golfer, that nothing he does is ordinary. Earlier, while walking off the driving range, he had spotted a broken tee. He had been using a club, maybe a five-iron, as a walking stick. Without breaking stride, he flicked the tee into the air, bounced it once off the face of the club, and swatted it away. Can you do that? That's why we watch him, or one of the reasons.

He played the first two rounds with Casey Wittenberg, in the field as the U.S. Amateur runner-up, and Thomas Bjorn, the Danish Ryder Cupper and a friend. In the 2001 Dubai Desert Classic, Bjorn played four rounds with Woods and defeated him. If you want to earn Tiger's respect, just beat him. Hal Sutton is on that list. Or do something in golf nobody else has done, like Byron Nelson, who won eleven consecutive events in 1945. Lord Byron, at age ninety-two, was sitting by the first tee, part of the welcoming committee. Tiger shook hands with a few greencoats, with Wittenberg and Bjorn, with several representatives of golf's officialdom, but only when he shook hands with Nelson did he take off his hat.

Then it was his turn to play. Maybe he was nervous because he hadn't won a major since the 2002 U.S. Open at Bethpage. Or maybe what Johnny Miller was saying was correct, that Woods's swing was all screwed up. Or maybe he was already worried about trailing Rose by five. Whatever it was, his opening tee shot was horrid. It started left and stayed left, and only a fortunate bounce off a well-placed pine kept it in play. To look at Tiger's face, you would have thought he had just striped one down the middle. He was the picture of calm. But when his approach shot missed the green, he stood over his divot with his club raised high, like Abraham ready to drop the knife. You think it's easy to play golf when everybody's watching you and expecting only miracles? It cannot be.

Coming off the second green, boy Wittenberg tried an audacious thing with Tiger. He tried to chat him up. I've seen guys who could do that, get Woods to talk after an opening bogey. Bjorn could do it, Chris Riley could do it, maybe a couple of others could. Wittenberg could not, not at age nineteen. Woods stared down the fairway, gave a minimal answer, did nothing to extend the conversation. On the third green, when Wittenberg hit an eighteen-inch putt ten feet past the hole, spectators flinched. One man muttered, "Oh, kid." Woods did not move. He was standing off in the shade, leaning on his putter as if it were a cane, not wasting a smidgen of energy or emotion.

People who know Woods say he is frugal, but maybe it's more accurate to say he doesn't like to waste anything. His caddie is the same way. When Tiger was on the practice tee, Williams hunted down loose tees lying on the ground for his man to use. On the fourth tee Woods took a long sip of water from a short plastic bottle and handed it to Williams, who polished off the remaining few ounces before refilling it. Going up the hill to the fourth green, Woods walked like an old man, with short, slow steps, a study in conservation. Walking down the seventh fairway, he ate shelled nuts out of a large plastic bag, refueling.

Storm clouds moved in, and there was a brief, intense rain shower while Tiger played the seventh and eighth holes. He never went to a rainsuit and barely used his umbrella while playing a series of loose shots with the right side of his pale blue shirt darkened by rainwater. (Wittenberg looked as dry as if he had been playing in the desert.) Woods went out in 40 and he was bloodied, but he was soldiering on. He was grim only over his shots and immediately after them. Between holes, he and Bjorn, who was playing even worse, were yukking it up. They marched down the tenth fairway together stride for stride, with the sound of nearby thunder filling their ears. When they were nearly at the bottom of the hill, a horn sounded, suspending play. When it blew, they slapped each other on the arm and laughed out loud. A bet, of some sort, had been settled.

The rain delay lasted two hours, and when they resumed play at a quarter past six, it was in a fading, misty light. After a par on ten, Woods played through Amen Corner with a backhanded tap-in, a tossed club at his caddie, a slight hitch in his walk, his right leg not quite keeping up with his left, and three straight pars. Then on fourteen he marked his ball with a coin and a tee, so he could see it in the twilight. I had never seen a professional golfer do that before, not without play being suspended. All it was was smart. The three golfers finished fourteen, and then play was suspended as they were slowly making their way to the fifteenth tee. (Woods didn't want to start a new hole.) A Masters official asked Tiger if he wanted a ride to the clubhouse in a van. "I'm going to walk and punish myself a little more today," he said. Bjorn asked Woods if he was sure. Woods answered, "Do we deserve a ride?" They walked the wrong way up the tenth fairway together for the second time that day. Woods reached the clubhouse, bounded up the fourteen semicircular steps by twos to the second-floor Masters club room, and then slipped away into the night, past a group of reporters who were talking to Jack Nicklaus.

The next morning, Friday of the 2004 Masters week, brought a new day and the continuation of an old round. It also brought, for Woods and nobody else in the field, white shoes and a white hat. I could not see his eyes. This time his opening tee shot—far out on the golf course, off the fifteenth tee—was perfect. The bleachers around the fifteenth green were already packed. The spectators watched Woods make birdie the easy way, with two putts. The crowd around the seventeenth green was six deep in all directions as he examined a ten-foot par putt, stalking it down as if his life depended on it. Forty out, 35 in, a 75 that could have been an 80, except Woods doesn't shoot 80. He doesn't let anything get too far away from him.

Woods had only about a half hour between the end of his first round and the beginning of his second. He went straight to the practice tee. His caddie was waiting for him with two bags of Nike practice balls in his hands.

"Stevie," Woods called out to him, moving him over to the far right side of the range, at least a hundred feet from the nearest pro. Woods handed Williams two packages of game balls in unmarked white cardboard sleeves. They dumped the practice balls on the ground, squatted like kids over Halloween candy catchers and sorted through them, searching for any strays that might have sneaked in.

He warmed up, went to the putting green, then went to the first tee, where he shook hands with everybody and played his tee shot. Then he played his second round precisely as he had played his first, a million eyeballs on him. The only thing different was where his ball went and how many strokes he needed. Afterward he answered a few questions about his 75–69 start. "You have to take baby steps, slow and steady improvement," he said. And then he began the wait for round three, when he would do his whole thing—his whole idiosyncratic, practiced, repetitive, captivating thing—again.

When I caddied for Al Geiberger, the original Mr. 59, in a half-dozen tournaments in 1985, I could not have imagined a nicer professional golfer. I traveled with him by car and plane, was a guest in his house, and hung out with his kids. At the 1985 Byron Nelson Classic, the tournament host was sitting on the first tee, greeting the competitors, just as he does at the Masters. Al said, "Mr. Nelson, I'd like you to meet my caddie." I was a kid on his bag, nothing more. Al introduced me to Nelson for only one reason: He knew it would make my day.

Al Geiberger won the 1966 PGA Championship and ten other tour events. Twice he was a Ryder Cupper. He won nineteen times as a senior. All the while, he was aware of other people. Among elite athletes, that's not a common trait.

His swing came out of a golfing dream. I once heard Jack Nicklaus say that without the many distractions in Geiberger's life, medical and personal, Geiberger would have been all-world. His problems were the stuff of a grown-up's nightmare: two marriages that ended in divorce, money woes, a series of major surgeries, a father killed in a plane crash, an infant son drowned in a pool.

I was aware that I wasn't seeing his name in the paper much any-more. He was barely playing. The word on the senior tour was that Al Geiberger was done, that he was needed at home in Palm Desert, California, where he lived with his wife, Carolyn, and their two children, both still in high school. It was well known that Carolyn had never been the same since the horrifying death of their first child, Matthew, in 1988. By 2004, Geiberger was sixty-six. His pension payments had kicked in. Most people have retired by that age.

For a long while, I had wanted to do a father-son story about Al and his adopted son, Brent Geiberger, a successful PGA Tour player, but it was one of those pieces I never got to. (Brent's life would make for an interesting nature-versus-nurture study.) Then I heard that Al had recently endured yet another crisis, this one involving his psychological health. Jim Herre suggested I call him and see if he wanted to talk. I had not spoken to him in years.

He sounded as he always did. He has a Californian's voice, like Johnny Miller's. Nothing seems to get him too excited. I asked if now would be a good time to write a story about him. He said that it would, that there was news in his life he wanted to discuss. I waited for him to introduce the tough subjects.

We met on a weekday morning in May of 2004 in a little carry-your-own-tray place called John's, down Highway 111 from Palm Springs and near the Geibergers' remote hilltop house in the California desert. John's is popular with retirees, golfers, and people coming out of the early morning AA meetings at a nearby church hall. Geiberger sat in his customary seat. For years, he had been skinny, but now he was not. He looked bloated. He was as nice and as open as ever.

"I was sitting right here when I had my birthday," he said. *Birthday* referred to the winter morning, three months earlier, when his three oldest sons, plus five old friends, surrounded Geiberger and performed an intervention, to use a phrase of the twelve-step movement. They came in one by one, Brent straight from the L.A. Open. One of the friends was Frank Beard, a former touring pro and recovering alcoholic who was instrumental in setting up the gathering. "At first I thought, This is some coincidence," Geiberger said, "but not for long."

They all knew what the public did not. In Al's lone appearance on the 2003 senior tour, in a March event in Newport Beach, California, he had shot a first-round 74, then topped his opening tee shot in the second round and proceeded to make a series of double and triple bogeys before being gently led off by a tour official. There were other incidents, off the course. Al's sons and friends knew what he had suspected but could not admit: To use the plain language they did, he was a drug addict and needed help.

The evidence had been mounting for a decade. The years 2002 and 2003 were almost lost. His friends and family watched in pain as Geiberger isolated himself more and more. His golf was lousy, his once-vaunted rhythm noticeably off. His behavior at times, to use Al's word, was "loopy." He had been arrested for driving under the influence and inexplicably collapsed twice while walking. He wasn't returning calls, he was missing his children's birthdays, he was playing almost no golf, he was barely leaving the house, his eyes were often bloodshot. In his lethargy he had put an extra thirty pounds on a frame that for years had been so thin he had needed intra-round peanut butter sandwiches to keep his energy up. (Which is why he was known as Skippy.) His interventionists marched him off to the nearby Betty Ford Center.

"Can't I go home first?" he had asked. The answer was unanimous: No. And the only thing he felt was relief.

When I saw Al, he had recently completed a two-month program at Betty Ford, the first month as a resident, the second as an outpatient. He said he had learned more about himself in eight weeks than he had in sixty-six years. All he had left was the rest of his life.

"I've been carrying around all these things—anger, disappointment, frustration, mourning my son's death, trying to be strong for Carolyn—and never addressed the things I need to be happy," he said.

He knew I knew the physical stresses his body had endured over the years, including the emergency removal of his large intestine in 1980. He answered all sorts of personal questions about his health then, in the hope that he might help others. Now he seemed ready to do the same thing again, for the same reason. The difference, he said, was that now he knew his first responsibility was to look out for himself. He had never felt that way before. "You know how on the plane the stewardess says, 'Put on your own breathing mask before helping others'?" he asked me. He was giving me a driving tour of the Betty Ford Center. "That's because you can't help others if you're dead."

He was behind the wheel of a modest Chevy Impala, having given up the showy Mercedes he had been driving. He and Carolyn were selling their expensive, rustic house off a winding dirt road, a nearly four-acre property that required a small battalion of workers to tend to the many horses and dogs, the pool, the septic tank. They were trying to simplify their lives. Al had been making steady progress through a heap of bills sitting on a table in a house that was almost devoid of artifacts from his long professional life. One of the few golf mementos was a letter from Gerald R. Ford, in which the former president described the sorry state of his game.

At the Betty Ford Center, Al came to accept that he was addicted to the sleep medication Ambien, which he took at night to sleep and during the day to deaden his emotional pain. He also came to accept that, even though he was never more than a moderate drinker—he'd have a glass of wine or two with dinner—he was an alcoholic, "because even one drink is one too many for me, in combination with all the Ambien I was taking." He was going to several Alcoholics Anonymous meetings every week and had stopped taking Ambien completely. Like a lot of people in recovery, he had become a pathological truth teller.

"I was taking eight ten-milligram Ambiens a day," he said. "I'd take a pill like some people drink a beer, simply to help me relax." He'd take the drug before rounds, during rounds, after rounds. He knew it was affecting his balance, and therefore his golf, and certainly his relationships, but he needed the relief the drug was giving him. When he could no longer fool doctors into giving him prescriptions, he'd give piles of cash to a man he knew who would buy the drugs at Mexican pharmacies over the border from San Diego. "If the drugs weren't there on the day I was expecting them and I was out, I could be very, very cranky," he said. While on Ambien, he'd have a glass of wine with dinner, his speech would become slurred, and he'd slip off to a place where nobody could reach him.

Brent told me it was inevitable that the man who raised him would someday return to tournament golf. "He loves golf, and he loves being around people," Brent said. "He had this blanket of haze over him for so long. He was buried by the burden of trying to make everything right at home. Now it's as if he's outside the bubble and he can see from the outside in." What Al saw was that it was not up to him to make everything right, that he couldn't make everything right. The pains in his life, and Carolyn's life, were part of his life. He was trying to find a way to cope that didn't include getting high every day.

Al and I went to the practice tee of a club to which the Geibergers belong, a short drive from the Betty Ford Center. Al's son Bryan was there, hitting balls. In 1985, I was his babysitter for a couple of days near Vail, when Al was playing in the Jerry Ford Invitational. While Carolyn and Al were off at fancy cocktail parties, Bryan and I hunted for golf balls, colored ones in particular, and found scores of them. There was a fury in Bryan's swing, as there is in the swings of so many young professionals, Tiger Woods among them. His father's swing still looked silky, but very short because of the extra weight he was carrying. Al mentioned something to Bryan about the position of his left hand at address. He instructed me to take my club back in one smooth move. It's in his nature to do things for other people. He can't help it.

Early the next morning, Al went off to one of his AA meetings. He used to hate getting up early, but now he said he enjoyed it. At the meetings he talks about himself, or doesn't, as he chooses. He said he had found a new life at the meetings, a place where he can give help and get it, too.

⚑

The 2004 U.S. Open at Shinnecock Hills began on the third Saturday in June at half past twelve in the afternoon, when Johnny Miller came on TV and said that Tiger Woods's swing was a mess, that the wind would come up at two p.m. and change everything, and that Phil Mickelson could be the best player in the world for the next three to five years. Of course, two rounds had already been played, and Miller had worked those rounds. But for the Saturday round, millions of people—lounging on the sofa at home, waistband pager finally off, Doritos within easy reach—turned on NBC and got their first real glimpse of Shinnecock and the players there, chiefly through the eyes of a fifty-seven-year-old former tour pro with a little boy's name. They never knew what Johnny Miller was going to say next, and neither did he.

Miller had become famous for some of his biting comments over the years. He raised the ire of Justin Leonard at the 1999 Ryder Cup (he said Leonard "should be home watching on TV") and Craig Parry at Doral in 2004 (he said Parry's swing "would make Ben Hogan puke") and has annoyed scores of other elite golfers, male and female, professional and amateur. He was the first golf commentator to talk about choking, and he seems weirdly fixated on the verb *to puke* in its various conjugated forms. He's better known for that stuff than for winning the '73 U.S. Open and the '76 British Open, when he was skinny and stylish and young.

In the golf magazine surveys conducted to identify the best TV golf analysts—talk about your specialized society—Miller regularly appeared at the top of the heap. These results were dismissed at the other networks. The people there would say a rip-job artist was being rewarded for playing to a sports culture that wanted to see millionaire athletes demeaned. And that likely is part of Miller's popularity. After generations of gentleman talkers, after Henry Longhurst and Dave Marr and Ken Venturi, Miller broke the candor line and helped make TV golf part of the mainstream sportscape.

But there has always been more to his appeal than that. Miller endlessly teaches an unconquerable game, one played by many of his viewers. Part of his odd charm—and charm is his weakest attribute—is that he has no idea how he does it. The stuff simply comes out of his mouth. Unspoken thought? What's that? He's a savant, golf's Rain Man.

The first U.S. Open Miller ever worked was at Shinnecock, in 1995, when Corey Pavin won. On highlight tapes, Pavin has seen himself hit his four-wood second shot on the final hole over and over.

I asked him about it. He knew his audio by heart. "When I hit that shot, Johnny said, 'It's the shot of his life,'" Pavin said. "He was right. He's not afraid to voice an opinion, and usually he's right."

Davis Love told me he learned the most important thing you need to know about U.S. Open golf from Johnny Miller when he heard him say one day, "In a U.S. Open, pars are the good guys. They wear white hats." A light went on for Love: Every time you make a par in a U.S. Open, you're gaining on the field. You don't try to do too much on any one hole.

The NBC tower at Shinnecock was a little green-painted plywood cabin—it looked like a Monopoly piece—about fifteen feet off the ground, perched in the fescue between the ninth and eighteenth fairways, surrounded by a newly planted privet hedge. There was a Porta Potti at the base of the booth used by some of the players, and that's as close as most of them got to Miller during Open week. Miller almost never does on-air interviews, and he's not one to work the practice tee, chatting up the guys. He certainly doesn't go out to dinner with them. (He doesn't go out to dinner with anybody.) His thing is to do his own thing.

But he doesn't wing it. In his booth at Shinnecock, where the walls, ceiling, and floor were covered with green fake-grass carpeting, Miller often had his reading glasses perched on his nose and a thick orange marker in his left hand to highlight statistical data. Hour after hour during one of golf's holy weeks, he had Dan Hicks, the lead announcer, sitting to his left and David Fay, the USGA executive director, sitting beside his right arm. There were only four or five other people in the booth, including me, all very still. The tone was always serious, different from CBS that way.

Miller is a devout Mormon, though that seldom comes through on TV, except for the frequency with which he lauds the games of Stewart Cink, Bernhard Langer, and Scott Simpson, who are also devout Christians. Physically, he's become a different man since he stopped playing, becoming much fuller and stiff. But he still has the everything's-cool tone he's always had, *cool* being one of the words he uses best. He said Shinnecock's Stanford White clubhouse, all shingly and timeworn, was "pretty cool." It made you look at the building in a whole new way.

David Fay told me that Miller was a significant factor in the USGA's decision to sign on with NBC in 1995. Fay believes that Miller lives largely in a cocoon of golf, and that has something to do with why his commentary is so original. He's not bogged down by what the rest of the world is thinking or doing. At his first Open, Miller was talking about some of the other great courses on the East End of Long Island. "On the air Johnny says, 'They've got some ballbusters out here,'" Fay recalled. He giggled at the memory. Fay knew that Miller meant they were courses that will bust your golf ball. Miller's life is golfcentric. Tommy Roy, the executive producer for NBC Sports, told me that Miller has not only the best eye among golf commentators but also the best ear. He routinely hears off-center shots and predicts where the ball is going before the camera gets there. He loves to predict stuff. On that Saturday, the wind starting blowing hard, by Hicks's observation, at 1:57 p.m., right on Miller's timetable.

On U.S. Open Sunday, Miller made it clear that Shinnecock was not playing to his liking. The wind was blowing so hard that the greens had no moisture and, in places, could not hold a well-placed shot or even a well-placed putt. Miller likes U.S. Opens to play to his old strengths: driving it long and straight and hitting irons precise distances. He'd rather see more rough and slower greens. Early in the final-round broadcast Fred Ridley, the president of the USGA, was seated between Hicks and Miller. They were shoulder to shoulder, all cozy. Miller was at Shinnecock Hills, in a manner of speaking, as a guest of the USGA. He told Ridley about how hard the wind blew all Saturday night right through Sunday morning and the havoc it wrought. He said, "You guys got caught by surprise." It wasn't a question, and it wasn't the old gent, smooth-talker thing. Do you think Miller cared? Not one bit.

On a Saturday in June, during the 2004 LPGA Championship, when it was played for the final time at the DuPont Country Club in Wilmington, Delaware, I brought two helpers to work, my daughter, Alina, and her friend Lisa Winder. Two nine-year-old girls, working their first golf event. There wasn't a cloud in the sky.

We started in the players' parking lot, where they saw Nancy Lopez's golf bag, Juli Inkster's courtesy car, and Amy Alcott in the flesh, who cheerfully signed their notebooks and said, "Okay, girls." Moments later the girls were walking by a display of the twenty-three LPGA Hall of Famers, where they found pictures of Lopez and Inkster and Alcott, and also Betsy Rawls and Patty Berg and Carol Mann. "Look," Alina said, "they used to wear skirts!" We walked by the ninth green, where Betsy King, another Hall of Famer, was lining up a putt. I first went to the LPGA Championship in 1987 to write about King. I had a helper that week, too—Christine, my wife, although she wasn't my wife then. We were on our third date. After the golf we went to the Charcoal Pit, the original one. Best burger in all of Delaware.

Both girls have duffer fathers and other ties to golf. For instance, Lisa's cousin is married to Tommy Lamb, a tour caddie who has carried the bag for Jay Haas and Brad Faxon for years. They know about Tiger and Annika and Michelle Wie and a few others. I explained more than once that Wie was not playing. She was in England for the Curtis Cup, awing the Brits, from the overseas reports. My helpers were in denial. Every time they saw a player of Asian descent, one or the other would ask, "Is that Michelle Wie?"

They wanted to follow Annika, so we did. At one point Alina and Lisa were chitchatting obliviously on a cart path between holes when Annika walked right around them. "We could have touched her!" Lisa said. Annika was playing with Lorena Ochoa and Aree Song, two excellent young players. Alina and Lisa decided that Annika was the least uptight of the three, for the following reasons:

1. Only Annika wore her shirttail out. (The other two had their shirts tucked in tight.)
2. Only Annika responded to her good shots with a fist pump. (The others showed little emotion.)
3. Only Annika wore hoop earrings. (The others wore posts or—get this—*no earrings at all!*)

At one point Alina, a curious sort, asked, "Is Annika sarcastic?" "No," I said. "Not that I've ever heard." Alina looked pleased.

Men have been gushing since the Dead Ball era about the pleasures of taking sons to baseball games, but let me tell you, watching your daughter and her friend cotton to ladies' golf is an underreported delight. (Disney will appropriate it, one imagines, soon enough.) I loved watching the girls watching the pro tee shots, squatting under the yellow gallery ropes, moving their chins from one shoulder to the other as their dancing eyes followed a sailing ball.

The girls, notebooks in hand, polled spectators to determine the most popular golfer in the field. There were eleven votes for Sorenstam, one vote for Meg Mallon (my ballot), and one vague vote for Kim, a name that appeared six times on the draw sheet but only once as a first name, by Alina's count.

Ochoa flipped her ball to Lisa coming off the fifteenth green and signed it for her with a red Sharpie after the round. One vote for Lorena.

Alina asked me one especially endearing question: "Why are your drives in the air longer than the lady players' drives?" She knew nothing about my 91.2 stroke average or the crookedness of my tee shots. Have I said anything about the pleasures of having a daughter?

Alina and Lisa watched Sorenstam reel off a string of birdies and take over the tournament, setting up her seventh major win. They saw a legend at the peak of her powers—Roger Maris in '61, when he hit sixty-one. They met the great Betsy King. The Hall of Famer shook their bony little hands and said, "Hello, girls."

Walking to the car, Lisa announced that she wants to become a journalist when she grows up. After the golf we stopped at the Charcoal Pit and got burgers to go and ate them on the road. In my rearview mirror, I saw the future of the game sitting in the back seat, licking ketchup off their lips and singing with the windows rolled all the way down.

CHAPTER SEVENTEEN

Fountainhead

(2004, PART 2)

IN JULY OF 2004, Jim Herre sent me to Scotland, press pass around my neck and clubs on my shoulders, to cover the British Open at Royal Troon. At the merchandise tent by Troon's sixteenth hole, there was a booth where a man was selling nothing but golf books. A well-worn copy of *To the Linksland* was on his shelf. When I identified myself as its typist, he greeted me like a long-lost cousin. I'm so lucky to get that. Most of that response, I've come to realize, is bound in the hopeful nature of the book, the hopeful nature of the game—and the hopeful nature of our better selves.

That 1991 trip—starting on Peter Teravainen's European golf tour, continuing in John Stark's Scotland, ending with my wee second book—was very, very good to me. From it I got a job at *SI,* our son's name (Ian), membership (set up by Neil Oxman) at a remote and wonderful Scottish club, Machrihanish, and friendships that have improved my life immeasurably. Can a writer pay back what he owes his own book? Maybe some are able to. I cannot.

The book came out the week Fred Couples won the 1992 Masters, and since then I have received a steady stream of real letters and e-mails from would-be pilgrims trying to find their way to Machrihanish or the shepherd's course, Auchnafree, or the grave site of young Tom Morris. My correspondents are forever passionate, not just for the game, but also about the prospect of discovering something to call their own. The letter writers are looking for someone to set them down a course. I had pathfinders who performed that favor for me, most notably the honorable James W. Finegan of Philadelphia and other golfing capitals. I find a quiet joy in playing that role for others.

To the Linksland was published in the three great languages of golf: American, Japanese, and Scottish. In the UK edition, *eagle* was changed to *albatross* and *rental car* to *hire car.* The Japanese translator didn't know what to do with the Hebrew word *chai,* a divine golf word. (It means *life* and is represented, in an ancient numerology game by which each Hebrew letter is assigned a numerical value, by the number 18.) Some readers have sought out John Stark, wondering if they could learn Scottish golf from him and if he could draw them a map to Auchnafree. Stark has not minded the calls but has been cagey, as you would expect, about what he said to whom. His first order of business, always, was to measure sincerity. In 1994, shortly before the Open was played at Turnberry, Brad Faxon called Stark, seeking counsel on the ways of links golf. Brad's devotion to the British Open was well known, even though he had never played well in the great championship. Stark was impressed by Brad's Scottish itinerary: He was preparing for the Open at bucolic Machrihanish, a course close to Stark's heart, and Stark talked to him at length. Brad took seventh at Turnberry. What Stark told Brad I cannot tell you: It's a secret.

When I wrote the book, I took a cue in indirection from my Scottish golf mentor and did not reveal the name of the person who put me on to Stark. Now I see no reason to keep it a secret. (If only life offered more second chances.) My matchmaker was Peter Alliss, the former British Ryder Cupper best known today as a witty and erudite television golf commentator.

Some years after the book came out, I saw Alliss at the Masters. I reintroduced myself, reminded him of how he alerted me to Stark, and thanked him for his excellent tip.

"I'll do what I should have done a long time ago," I said. "I'll send you a book."

"Don't send the book," Alliss said cheerfully. "Send a check!"

Peter Teravainen, my old European tour boss, and I have been in sporadic contact over the years. I hadn't seen him since the '97 U.S. Open at Congressional, when I wrote about him for *SI*. That piece ran with a photograph of Peter standing on golf balls, one of his remedies for his often tender back. He was still living in Singapore and playing, when he could, on the Japan tour.

The years brought changes in Peter. He took a paying equipment deal with Dunlop in Japan and didn't complain that the money was impure. He wore stylish clothes when they were given to him. With fifty on the horizon, he went to see a psychologist, Bob Rotella, at considerable cost. "I should've done it years ago," he told me. The idea of Peter learning something about himself from a newcomer in his life seemed odd to me, but the patient reported that his doctor was helping him clear his mind so that he could concentrate only on the shot before him. He expected to apply his new lessons in an effort to win—what else?—money on one of the senior tours, either in Europe or the United States. My application to get back on his bag is pending.

The star of the 2004 Open at Troon was a golfer out of the Teravainen mold, the American Todd Hamilton, who played for years in Japan. He and Peter were regular practice round partners and would visit a Tokyo bar called Motown on Sunday nights, when their workweek was over. Peter spoke of Hamilton with admiration, and I was struck by that, because I know few people stingier with praise than Teravainen, a thrifty New Englander in every sense.

On the Sunday morning of the 2004 British Open, readying myself for the remote possibility that Hamilton would win at Troon, I called Peter in Singapore, notebook open, looking for help. Tiger Woods and Phil Mickelson and Ernie Els and Retief Goosen were all keeping Hamilton company on the leaderboard, but Peter felt Hamilton would pull off the upset. "He won't be scared of anything," Peter said. "He won three times on seaside courses in Japan last year. In his mind, he'll just put himself back there." It was weird, hearing these insights from Peter. Teravainen had always been one to make predictions based on empirical data, on form. That's why he likes to bet on the stock market and at the dog track. But now he was analyzing a player's head. Maybe it takes a journeyman to understand a journeyman. After all, Peter was the player who, when he was trying to win his first event on the European tour, pretended in his mind that he was just trying to make a cut.

Hamilton won by chipping expertly with his hybrid long iron. E-Club sales jumped for a month. I personally sold two or three in August alone.

The day after Hamilton's victory, I drove up to Crieff to visit with Stark. We've exchanged letters and cards, but I hadn't spoken to him since I saw him in September of 1991, in Dornoch, at the end of my golfing adventure. The village of Crieff seemed unchanged. I could not say the same of myself. Then Christine and I were newlyweds; now we had been married thirteen years, with two children, a dog, mortgage payments, club dues, ringing phones, a calendar marked up by various pens. I was thirty-one then. Now I was forty-four. My middle-age life does not allow me to get lost in the game much anymore, as I did in 1991 and in 1985, years I devoted myself to golf. I play early Sunday mornings, at the Scottish pace, holing all the little putts, as Ian Woosnam's father, now dead, taught me. My game's ragged, but my life's okay. One day, a friend and I played fifty-three holes on an ocean-scented Long Island links, and for that day I was transported, but those moments had become rare. It's not that Stark's lessons didn't stick; it's that the mind drifts.

At night during the Open at Troon, in the gloaming, I played golf with my friend Alan Shipnuck or by myself at Prestwick and Turnberry. You can't beat linksland golf. At first, I kept trying to curve my ball into the sea breeze, thinking the wind would negate my hook, but at some point I began an experiment: I tried to hit fade shots *with* the wind, and found that I could. With one good swing, it felt like the summer of '91 again. I was ready to see Stark.

He was shorter and less imposing than he had been, but his eyes were the same and so was his voice. His backroom office in the pro shop of the Crieff Golf Club, where he stirred coffee with a letter opener and talked about Hogan, was now the domain of the head professional. I sort of poked around, wondering if my old hickory-shafted iron, stamped R. Forgan, might still be around. I didn't say a word. Stark, as you might expect, read my mind.

"Sold all the old clubs, I did," he said. "Man in Texas paid me $10,000 for the whole lot of them and off they went, all crated up."

"Smart," I said. What could Stark's grandchildren possibly do with a bunch of old golf clubs with wooden shafts?

Stark had recently expanded Auchnafree from six holes to nine, at the request of the Whitaker family, owners of the land, and we drove off to have a look. There were always people throughout Great Britain, like Peter Alliss and the Whitakers, who knew about Stark, the man who embodied Scottish golf. The only thing *To the Linksland* did was widen the net. But I never knew how Stark felt about his write-up, and I certainly didn't ask. Then we were back in his car, on a dirt-and-pebble road.

"You came to me looking for the soul of golf," Stark said. "I did not tell you what I was thinking: Yer too late—the soul of golf is dead."

He paused, in the manner of an actor, or a master teacher. My heart began to race. What would come next? I stared through his windshield.

"But then I saw your wonder at it all and I thought, 'All right, then.'" Stark looked pleased, or pleased enough.

When the pupil teaches his teacher, it's nothing but dumb luck. I realize that. Still, it was nice to know.

We stopped at a swinging wood-and-wire gate. "Go on," Stark said. "You know what to do. Unlatch it, let me through, and close it back up again. Don't want the sheep escaping."

We made it to the course, laid out by a shepherd, expanded by Stark, maintained by sheep. I got my clubs out of Stark's trunk. (Or should I say *boot?*) Stark used an old fairway wood as a walking stick, and he carried some balls—yellow ones and striped ones, ones he could afford to lose—in a small white plastic shopping bag. My old teacher watched me make some swings.

What we saw there, what we talked about there, I feel I should not say.

·

CHAPTER EIGHTEEN

REUNION (2005)

IN FEBRUARY OF 2005, when the PGA Tour made its annual migration to Florida, it had been twenty years since I ran away to join the circus, or tried to, anyway. When I went to the '85 Honda Classic to caddie for Brad Faxon, the players, some of them, drove there from the previous stop, at Doral in Miami. In 2005, there were players doing the same thing.

But it was a different PGA Tour back then. By 2005, the game was awash in money and glamour. In 1985, when Brad Faxon was nice enough to give me my caddie tryout, the overriding emotion on tour was lust for the game and desperation to find a way to stay in it. At least, that's how it seemed to me.

I think of 1985 as the final year of the old tour. In '86, the Bing Crosby tournament became the AT&T, Jack Nicklaus motivated a million (estimated) middle-aged people to take up the game when he won the Masters at age forty-six, and Greg Norman nearly won everything, setting himself up for birdies with long, straight bombs with a metal driver. Nabisco had made a big play in golf, and in '86 the purses started to fatten substantially. As they did, more players brought out relatives and college friends to caddie. The tour's core of old black migrant caddie-foils—Golf Ball, Killer,

Bebop, dozens of others—started to fade away. At Doral and Honda, I saw only one black caddie. In practice rounds, the caddies were carrying compasses (to establish prevailing wind directions), altimeters (to determine elevation changes), and range finders (to measure distances to the yard). I believe most of them had degrees from MIT.

Tom Kite played at Doral in 2005, at age fifty-five, a senior player trying to play the big tour one last time. He had played at Doral in '85 as a tour star and the defending champion. He first played there in '73 as a tour rookie, just trying to make the cut. Late in his second round of the '05 tournament, he was still doing the same thing.

He knew he needed a birdie-birdie finish to make it to the weekend. He was on his seventeenth hole, a par-5. After a good tee shot, the green was 250 yards away, downwind. He stood in the middle of the fairway—where else would Tom Kite be?—and took it all in, the water in front, the bunkers left, the grassy mounds over the green, the glitzy Doral clubhouse beyond it. He still flew his nine-iron, one of his many finesse clubs, 132 yards, just as he did when he won at Doral in '84. On adjoining fairways the kids were playing that new game, smashgolf, in which a nine-iron goes 165 yards and the ball stops on its skid mark. The Hall of Famer scratched his visored head. He was thinking what everybody was thinking: Go for it or lay up? He was playing in a PGA Tour event. The rush was still there.

He was bunking at the Doral resort, with a room, at his request, nearly on the practice tee. (Where else would it be?) One luscious South Florida night during Doral week, Kite and his wife, Christy, left the Doral compound and ventured off to Miami Beach, looking for a sidewalk dinner amid the Ocean Drive rollerbladers and the shirtless gay bodybuilders and the hot chicks in their short shorts. Can you have millions in the bank and travel by private jet and still be middle class? Going by the Kites, the answer is yep. They don't do chic. (The medallion on Christy's favorite necklace was a kite.) The Kites, a little bemused, took in the whole South

Beach scene, inspected some menus, settled on a place with no wait, and carried on with their thirty-year conversation about golf. On this night the subject was Tom's return to the PGA Tour.

"You know, every golfer who's doing this has an ego," Kite told his wife. "You want to hear clapping for your good shots. You want people to know what you've done in the game." He never needed to be a celebrity. He could not imagine the restricted life Tiger Woods must lead. But what Kite knew about himself was this: You never grow tired of the clapping, and you never lose your desire to play golf's biggest stages. His son understood that. Not David, who played on the University of South Carolina golf team. David's hammy twin brother, Paul, who was studying acting at the University of Evansville, in Indiana, and dreaming of Hollywood.

In a word association game, *ego* does not come up with *Tom Kite*. Even in the early 1990s, when he was the leader in career money, he played the humble card. He started practicing modesty as a pudgy junior member of the Austin Country Club, reading greens through thick glasses and going head-to-head with the club's golden boy, the "gorgeous" (Christy Kite's word) Ben Crenshaw. Their careers were similar, except that Crenshaw in victory was dazzling, and Kite, even with a trophy in hand, still looked like the night clerk at the Holiday Inn where the caddies stayed. But at Doral in the winter of 2005, Kite was doing something Ben Crenshaw never did. He was playing in a regular PGA Tour event with Tiger Woods and Phil Mickelson and Vijay Singh for $5.5 million and the prospect of being on an ESPN highlight tape all night long. At some point in the Tiger Era, Doral morphed from a golf tournament into an event, and golf went from pastime to big league. If Tom Kite wanted to hear clapping, he had come to the right place.

After a long fallow period, Kite started playing well again in June of 2004, when he was the medalist in the thirty-six-hole U.S. Open sectional qualifier, which got him to the U.S. Open at Shinnecock Hills, where he made the cut. Then he was third in the U.S. Senior Open, second in the Senior British Open, and won a senior event, for the first time in nearly two years. His barren stretch wasn't because of ball striking but because of the yips, the often-fatal putting disease. A change to the claw putting grip saved him. His putting was nothing like spectacular, but the seizure at impact he had been having frequently was now irregular.

The '04 highlight was Shinnecock. The New York crowds were so alive, and he played and practiced with his old tour friends, including Davis Love and Brad Faxon. He was at home on the demanding course. He loved the whole thing.

At the end of 2004, Kite was in forty-first place on the all-time money list. Players in the top fifty are allowed a one-year exemption to play the PGA Tour. Kite knew if he didn't claim the exemption for 2005, he'd lose it altogether. He signed up. He wanted to feel the juice again.

In the opening round at Doral, he played solidly and turned in a 70, two under par. In the second round, he was one over for the day through sixteen holes and one under for the tournament. His guess was that the cut would be three under. That's why he was looking to close birdie-birdie. That's why he was staring down the 250-yard approach shot, downwind and over water, wondering what to do.

"I gotta go for it," he said.

"No, you don't," his caddie, Sandy Jones, replied.

He laid up well short of the water, practically holed out his third shot with a sand wedge, and tapped in for his birdie. The greenside stands were filled—Tiger would soon be coming through—and Kite acknowledged his applause with his familiar curled-lips smile, the one I'd seen on TV forever.

Now he was two under. He needed one more birdie and had one more chance to do it. One more birdie and he'd get to three under and would surely make the cut. His putt on his last hole was tracking all the way. It tickled the lip—and stayed out.

The old pro went into the scorer's room, signed his card, and studied the field's scores on a computer. When he came out, I asked him if two under would somehow be good enough to make the cut.

"It's gonna miss by a shot," he said tersely. "It's gonna miss by a shot." He was hot.

He packed up the car and got on the road, headed for the Honda. It might as well have been 1973 again. Tom Kite had found a way to turn back time. Pretty neat trick.

⚑

For a long while, I had had a hankering to get under the strap again. I asked Brad if I could caddie for him at the '05 Honda—a twentieth-reunion gig—and he was up for it, but in the end his caddie vetoed it. The caddie was new to Brad's bag, and a Floridian, and he didn't want to give it up for a week, especially in Florida. Once I understood his perspective, I was embarrassed I had asked.

In '85, I had caddied in the U.S. Open and the British Open and the PGA Championship but not the Masters. That was a yawning gap in my caddie résumé. At the '04 British Open at Troon, I had met a young Scot named Stuart Wilson. He was the British Amateur champion and the low amateur at the Open. The reigning British Amateur winner is invited to play the Masters each year, provided he has not turned pro. In the dead of winter, I wrote and asked Stuart if I could carry his bag at Augusta. I had one outstanding qualification: My price was right. I got the job.

And so early on the Monday morning of the '05 Masters week, I reported to the Augusta National caddie shack—a substantial cinder-block structure, painted Masters green, behind the press building—where I was issued a caddie jumpsuit. The suits, made in Honduras, are bright white, heavy, 65 percent polyester, with zipper fronts, little side pockets for scorecard pencils, and large back ones for yardage books and headcovers. The last time I was so eager to suit up, I was a backup catcher for Rocky's Main Street Luncheonette, thirty-five years earlier.

I went to the back porch of the clubhouse, where there were twenty or twenty-five real caddies, most of them working for players you've heard of, and Butch Harmon, hanging easily with the loopers. The promise of a new week, and the year's first major, filled the warm spring Georgia air. I waited for my man.

Stuart warmed up briefly and without any fuss next to Mark O'Meara, with whom he played his first two rounds at the British Open at Troon. The day was now sunny and hot, and Stuart's parents sat in the stands behind the range. His mother wore a stopgap hat she had made from a nearby newspaper to keep the sun off her fair Scottish skin. Son gave mother a tiny under-the-shoulder wave and said, "That's a wee bit embarrassing." But she was having the time of her life.

He got to the driver quickly, and some of his shots were sailing far right. He said that happened when his left shoulder got too high and stiff at address.

"Do you have a thought that helps with that?" I asked. A caddie has to insinuate himself somehow. Otherwise he's just carrying the bag.

His answer came out of the Scottish golfer's handbook: "It's not a thought, it's a feeling."

He watched O'Meara make a swing or two more before we left the practice tee. "I wanted to say hi, but I never caught his eye," Stuart said. He was wearing a Scottish pin on his shirt, but he didn't need to. You knew he was a Scotsman on manners alone. Interrupting O'Meara, he didn't think that was his place.

I led the way through the crowd to the first tee for a practice round. The course was clogged with people, but a Masters caddie in his white jumpsuit and a bag on his shoulder has an odd sort of authority. Gallery marshals and Pinkerton guards call out, "Caddie coming through," and magically a path clears. Stuart played the first hole by himself, hitting a solid drive that brought him polite applause. He caught up with Adam Scott, the young Australian star, and Tim Clark, a good young player from South Africa, and both could not have been more inviting. Stuart was twenty-seven, quiet, modest. He set up no practice games for himself, and just by bumping around, he found himself playing with Jay Haas, Chris DiMarco, Jerry Kelly, Paul Casey, and Fuzzy Zoeller over the course of the three practice days. Fuzzy, profane and funny, graciously had Stuart hit before him on nearly every tee. Fuzzy, a former Masters winner, was the host, and Stuart was the guest.

I was traveling only on my caddie badge, not my press pass, so I couldn't get into the clubhouse for the peach cobbler or the press room for the player quote sheets, but I was at home in the caddie shack. ("You can only be one thing," a club official had told me at credential time.) I knew that an MBA mentality had corrupted the caddie culture as the PGA Tour became more about science and money and less about artistry and survival. But a week in the caddie shack was a revelation. You could see the looping game was still ultimately fueled by adrenaline and hope. There was no decaf in the caddie shack, and an outside bucket for spent cigarettes was loaded with butts at the end of each day. During the rain delays, the shack was filled with cribbage and backgammon players, newspaper readers, bench sleepers, and a small group, led by Billy Harmon (Jay Haas's caddie and Butch's kid brother), solving the problems of the world.

The Champions Dinner is held each year on Tuesday night in the Augusta National clubhouse. I sat quietly in my white jumpsuit on a bench near the main entrance as the past winners arrived at irregular intervals, driving down Magnolia Lane, leaving their courtesy-car Cadillacs with the club valet, and disappearing inside. (Had I been in my civilian clothes, I'm sure I would have been chased away.) Vijay Singh came in, tying his necktie as he stepped toward the manned door. Byron Nelson, age ninety-three, made the car-to-door walk on two canes but under his own power. The dinner host, Phil Mickelson, arrived wearing glasses and his club coat—only the reigning champion may wear his coat off property—and his charisma as if it were cologne. Best parade I ever saw.

Stuart drew two big-time partners for the first two rounds: Tom Watson, with his two green coats, and Jim Furyk. My friend Neil Oxman was on Watson's bag, and Mike "Fluff" Cowan, a looping legend and a relaxed soul who caddied for Tiger in '97 when he won the Masters by twelve shots, was working for Furyk. Bruce Edwards had died on the eve of the 2004 Masters (and Jeff Julian three months later, on the day of the first round of the British Open).

Neil, a link between Bruce and Watson, was working for Watson in 2005, in between his political campaigns. He was completing his caddie Grand Slam, too. It was a lucky draw for Stuart, and for me, too.

Right from the opening handshakes, the mood was tight. Thursday Furyk was there to win the thing, Watson to see if he could catch lightning and get in the mix, and Stuart to try to make the cut. We started on the back nine. I talked Stuart into a Heavenwood for his second shot on fifteen, the short par-5 with the little pond in front of the green, and he took it. You never know the role prayer plays in your life until you are put to a test. With the ball in the air, I was praying hard. It pitched just short of the green and started rolling down the hill toward the water and stopped only because the grass was soft and wet.

"Roobish swing," Stuart said. At least, I think that's what he said. There were times the accent got in the way, and I had no idea what he was saying. It wasn't just me. At one point, Watson asked Wilson where he was from.

"Ffrrffrr," Stuart said.

"Where?"

"Ffrrffrr," the Scot repeated.

"How do you spell that?"

"F-O-R-F-A-R," Stuart said.

"Okay," Watson said.

When he had the honor, Watson nearly always went to the other side of the tee box after he played, away from the caddies and the other players. You could see him taking in the whole thing: the perfect grass, the caddies dead quiet and still, the mechanical Augusta National leaderboards and their long strings of precise numbers. This is just a guess—does watching a player for parts of three days give a caddie that right?—but Watson seems to want the world at a certain moral attention, everything in its place. Beyond the gates of the club, that's becoming ever harder to find. Within the club, he expects to find everything just so. Dow Finsterwald, winner of Frank Chirkinian's 1958 PGA Championship at Llanerch, was working the tournament as a glorified marshal. In the middle of the first round, when we went from the eighteenth green to the first tee, Watson wanted to know how many groups were waiting on one. When Finsterwald hemmed and hawed, Watson said curtly, "You should know that." He climbed up a little hill.

"Okay, Tommy," Finsterwald said, calling out to him in a belittling voice of his own.

It was too much golf course for Stuart Wilson, the way he was playing. I saw him play beautifully at Troon, which was hard and fast and breezy. Augusta National was long and wet, and the greens, which look so big, are actually tiny, because there are so few places to land the ball. It was too much everything. Unless you have a certain innate golfing genius, like Fuzzy, you're not going to figure out Augusta on your first week there. Because of the rain delays, the days were long and slow.

"It seems like a long time ago you played in the Par-Three Tournament," I said while we waited in a fairway on Saturday of Masters week, finishing our second round.

"It seems like a long time since I was home," Stuart said. He sounded wistful.

He shot rounds of 82 and 82, and when it was finally over, he huddled with his parents and relatives and friends and cried in the arms of his lovely wife.

I returned my white jumpsuit to Mr. Gray Moore, the Augusta National caddie master with a rich southern accent. The Augusta National land was once an indigo plantation, and the jumpsuit was once the uniform of plantation workers throughout the South. Caddies, at Augusta National and elsewhere, started wearing them years ago because the members didn't want to look at the caddies in their raggedy mismatched clothes. I asked Andy Martinez, Tom Lehman's veteran caddie, if he'd eliminate the jumpsuits if he could. "I wouldn't," he said. "I like the tradition."

As I write this, far from Augusta, I have a clear image of the six of us—three players, three caddies—standing on the eighteenth tee late Saturday morning, waiting to play our thirty-sixth hole, the sound of a train whistle sweeping over the tee.

"That's such a quaint sound," Neil Oxman said quietly.

"Very Scottish," I said. In Scotland, as Neil would know, there are often train tracks and passenger trains running alongside golf courses.

"Very southern," Neil said.

He was correct. It was the long, mournful whistle of a freight train.

On Tuesday morning of Masters week, I was driving to the golf course along Broad Street through downtown Augusta, in an old black neighborhood with small houses and tin roofs. At a railroad crossing, red lights started flashing and the long thin wooden crossing guards came down. A freight train came chugging through, whistle blowing. I put the car in park and kept hitting the scan button, skipping past the many Jesus Saves stations, looking for music. In the exact moment I sat there, with the train rolling past my dull, gray Hertz Taurus, an Augusta country station was playing the old Marshall Tucker anthem, "Can't You See?"

Take me Southbound,
all the way to Georgia now,
till the train runs out of track.
Can't you see?
Oh, can't you see?
What that woman been doin' to me?

At the 2005 Masters, Stuart Wilson didn't make the cut, Tom Watson didn't catch lightning and get in the mix, and Jim Furyk didn't win the tournament. Only a very few people cared.

I thought I had come to Augusta to help Stuart Wilson make the cut. I left realizing something else about the trip, and about every trip to Augusta. You come to Augusta to mark the arrival of spring, where it comes early and boldly, but when you've been there a day or two, you find yourself remembering the Deep South as it was. You wear a white jumpsuit or a green club coat or press-tent khakis or a Scottish pin or some other damn emblem that tells everybody the one thing you are. That world, where people know their place is just about dead. For a week in Augusta in

April, for good or for bad (and there's some of both), the old order rules.

At the Honda Classic, Brad and I had a little reunion. I didn't know what I was doing in '85, and I still don't. It's not just caddying, it's everything. I'm one of those people sentenced to a life of always trying to figure things out as they go along, competent, really, at no useful thing. In '85, Brad was twenty-three and I was twenty-four, but I felt he was older and still do. We're friends, and over the course of twenty years we've had scores of little catch-ups at events all over the country and at the British Open. I like Brad, but I'm generally slightly nervous around him. You know, he fired me, for cause. It haunts me still. When we—we?—made the turn on that Thursday morning, all Brad wanted was his scorecard, his driver with the headcover off, a new ball, a banana, and his sweater put away, and I couldn't manage it. Pathetic.

Greg Rita, the looper Brad was talking to about future gigs as we went off the tenth tee that day, in 1985, is still out there, a star caddie who has won often over the years, majors and minors, carrying for Gil Morgan, Curtis Strange, Mark O'Meara, Scott Hoch, John Daly, and other notables. Mike Donald, who was in our group that day, was nearing fifty. He will always have a distinct spot in the annals of the game, for his second-place finish to Hale Irwin in the 1990 U.S. Open after the nineteen playoff holes. But there's way more to him than that—he sees things that most people don't—and I enjoy being with him. We had dinner together during the Honda week. "I never had a regular caddie back then because I never wanted to share the credit," he told me. We were eating outside at some swanky place on a balmy evening. *SI* was paying. (Christine and the kids were at home in the ice and wind and snow; you can never really lose yourself on these trips.) "I figured it would come at my expense." It was all about survival in those days.

Bill Britton, his friend and my old boss, was staying in Mike's apartment near Fort Lauderdale. Bill lived with his wife and kids in New Jersey, where he has a club job, but that winter he was teaching at the Jim McLean Golf School at Doral. These days you find golf's best survivalist stories off the tour.

The kids, like Brad, who were playing the tour in the mid-1980s all had heroes: Nicklaus or Watson or Trevino. Not anymore. They're good, they know they're good, and they want to do it their own way. Similar thing in the writing game. In '85, I sent my bagger manuscript to four gods: Herbert Warren Wind, James Reston, Dan Jenkins, and George Plimpton. They all blurbed generously. Now, with the web and all, you can start your own career. Mentoring is not a growth industry.

I'll always be grateful for my early help. In '86, *Golf Digest* ran an excerpt from *The Green Road Home,* the part about Brad sacking me. That bit has legs. Once, I think it was at the '02 U.S. Open at Bethpage, a guy looked at my press pass and said, "I know you. You're that guy Faxon fired. Whaddya been doing since then?"

Brad's career is more obvious. He's won seven times on tour, been a Ryder Cupper, served on the tour's Policy Board, developed a deserved reputation as a good quote, an all-world putter, a golf course buff, and a player on an endless quest to answer golf's enduring riddles. On a practice tee, somebody once asked him what he was working on. "Not caring," he answered. He hasn't done all he hoped to do, not so far. He was an All-America coming out of Furman in '83, and the practice-green putts he holed on afternoons as a kid were to win U.S. Opens. He hasn't actually faced such a putt, not in real life. Still, at Honda he was number eighteen on the all-time money list. More than that—and in this he's lucky—the game still absorbs him.

Anyway, who can say they've done all they hoped and hope to do? Not Brad, not I, not anyone I know in his mid-forties. Brad once said to me, "Would you ever try to learn everything you can about writing in a week?"

"No."

"Golf's the same way. You just keep at it, trying to get better."

That's when I realized that making a living from a typewriter or from a set of golf clubs is about the same thing. You can't fake the results in either. You're on your own. The writer and the golfer, they both know, deep down, whether they're getting better or not. At forty-three, forty-four, you're young enough to hang on to that useful phrase, *so far.* It pushes you. But you're old enough to feel the pain of passing time and lost chances and buried dreams. I'm not being gloomy. I can't be: The writing life, like the golfing life, is rooted in optimism. I'm just trying to be truthful. Now it's our children with the sun in their hair, their skin slippery with ocean water. In a wave, you lose all sense of time.

Brad and I couldn't figure out what happened to the twenty years. A blink.

"You were wearing a blue alligator shirt, too small for you," he said. He had just finished the first round of this year's Honda Classic, and we were sitting in the players' dining room and nobody was looking to chase me out. Tom Kite sat down with us.

It's embarrassing, the things other people remember. That blue alligator shirt. If I wear a shirt with a logo now, it's out of laundry desperation.

"Thursday was windy and hot," Brad said, "and on Friday you were red and crispy." The memory is painful, all the way around. All you can do is laugh, right?

Three people I met in my first month in the circus left a mark on me: Brad and Mike Donald—and Chuck Will. We had met at the '85 Players Championship, when I was an out-of-work caddie looking for a one-week job as a CBS spotter.

"Michael Barnblatt?"

"Michael Bamberger."

"If I wanted you, Bamberger, I would have asked for you, you asshole."

From '85 to '95, we had become close, without ever doing all that much together. A few games of golf. Some lunches. Conversations here and there at tour events or in Philadelphia, where we both live. We were close because—tell me if you get this—we loved golf the same way. Two things, really: the click of a well-struck shot, and the kooky lifers the game attracts.

Then came the Ben Wright story. We saw it very differently. My job was to find out where the truth lay between the man on

TV and the woman newspaper reporter. In my book, the final was Valerie Helmbreck 10, Ben Wright 0. He said the things she said he said. Trying to get out a jam, a perspiring Ben Wright got on national TV and essentially called Helmbreck a liar. When CBS fired him, it wasn't for his comments but for trashing the woman to save himself. I never lost a minute of sleep over anything about the story, except this: Chuck and I talked shortly before the story ran, and not since. He felt I had wronged his guy. I felt I had nothing to apologize for.

Chuck spends his winters in South Florida, in a condo on the ocean near the Palm Beach Par-Three course. During the '05 Honda week, I figured it was time to do something. We had met twenty years earlier and had stopped talking almost ten years earlier. Too much time had passed. I checked into a hotel down the street from him and called. (Not caddie digs; thank you again, *SI*. I wanted to be able to say I was in the neighborhood. His wife answered, and Chuck came right to the phone.

His first words were "I thought you died." We then spoke for ninety minutes. We talked about Brad, Mike Donald, Bill Britton, Beaufort the caddie, others. The list of people we know in common is long.

In his CBS days, nobody ever knew how old he was. Chuck was ageless. He retired at the end of 1998, he told me, at age seventy-two. "I'm in my eightieth year," he said, his fancy way of saying that he was seventy-nine. I had no idea. His voice had not changed.

"You know, I stopped getting the magazine because I didn't want to read what you wrote," he said. Candor was never a problem for him. "People would say, 'Why aren't you friends with Michael anymore? He took the job there, and they made him write that story.'"

I told him that was absolutely untrue. I said the story was important for only one reason: The man with the power, with the big job at the national network, was willing to squash the woman he saw as vulnerable. If I didn't want to write stories like that, I wouldn't want to be a reporter at all. I don't know if Chuck got that. I think he did.

I asked him if I could come by during Honda week, take him out for lunch or breakfast. "No, no, no, we're not going to do that," he said. He asked about my wife and children, then talked cheerfully about his final plans. "I've instructed Kathleen, my beautiful bride, who remains twenty-nine years younger than I, to buy a first-class ticket to San Francisco, carrying my remains with her in a box or urn. I want her to get in a car, drive south to the Seal Rock lookout, to that little parking spot there, and, with Cypress Point right behind her, distribute me into the Pacific, with the barking seals." When he's not using profanity, that's exactly how he speaks.

I said, "Can I take you out for a cup of coffee?" He had always lived on black coffee.

"No, no. No," he said.

"Why?"

"I used to call you the Hatchet Man. Your name would come up, and I'd say, 'You mean the hatchet man?' But all the times I said that, it didn't mean I didn't love you."

We fell silent for a moment.

"Why can't we get coffee?" I asked.

"You and I need more time," Chuck said.

In golf, when you lose your game, you say, "Where does it go when it goes?" Time's the same—except it never comes back. Our friendship was founded on golf. Chuck, old enough to be my father, knew we weren't going to fix our ten-year-old divot over a cup of coffee.

He said we would play golf in the spring, at home, when the days would once again be long and warm.

CREDITS

The sections on Brad Faxon in Chapter 1 were first published, in different form, in *The Green Road Home,* Contemporary Books, 1986. Copyright © Michael Bamberger.

The section on the Bellport golf course in Chapter 1 was first published, in different form, in the May/June 2001 issue of *Travel & Leisure Golf* as "First Course, First Love." Used by permission.

The section on Howard Rexford in Chapter 2 was first published, in different form, in *The Philadelphia Inquirer* on August 20, 1989. Used by permission.

The section on the Thompson brothers in Chapter 2 was first published, in different form, in *The Philadelphia Inquirer* on August 29, 1989. Used by permission.

Chapters 3 and 4 first appeared in the book *To the Linksland,* Viking, 1992. Copyright © 2005 Michael Bamberger.

The section on Michael Murphy in Chapter 5 was first published in the May 1994 issue of *Golf Digest.* Copyright © 2005 The Golf Digest Companies. All rights reserved. Used by permission.

The section on Sam Snead in Chapter 5 was first published in the September 1994 issue of *Golf Digest.* Copyright © 2005 The Golf Digest Companies. All rights reserved. Used by permission.

The section on Marc Wilson in Chapter 5 was fist published in the April 1995 issue of *Golf Digest.* Copyright © 2005 The Golf Digest Companies. All rights reserved. Used by permission.

The section on Yogi Berra in Chapter 6 was first published, in different form, in *The Philadelphia Inquirer* on July 8, 1992. Used by permission.

The section on Tom Doak in Chapter 6 was first published, in different form, in *The Philadelphia Inquirer* on July 23, 1992. Used by permission.

The section on the Green Hills golf course in Chapter 6 was first published, in different form, in *The Philadelphia Inquirer* on August 24, 1993. Used by permission.

The section on Irish-Italian Day at the Rolling Green Golf Club in Chapter 6 was first published, in different form, in *The Philadelphia Inquirer* on May 20, 1993. Used by permission.

The section on snapper soup in Chapter 6 was first published, in different form, in *The Philadelphia Inquirer* on May 23, 1993. Used by permission.

The section on Ken Hill in Chapter 6 was first published, in different form, in *The Philadelphia Inquirer* on August 13, 1993. Used by permission.

The section on Howdy Giles in Chapter 6 was first published, in different form, in *The Philadelphia Inquirer* on July 25, 1993. Used by permission.

The section on Arnold Palmer in Chapter 6 was first published, in different form, in *The Philadelphia Inquirer* on June 18, 1994. Used by permission.

The section on Bill Clinton in Chapter 6 was first published, in different form, in *The Philadelphia Inquirer* on August 31, 1994. Used by permission.

The section on Brad Faxon in Chapter 6 was first published, in different form, in *The Philadelphia Inquirer* on August 14, 1995. Used by permission.

The section on Tiger Woods in Chapter 6 was first published, in different form, in *The Philadelphia Inquirer* on August 28, 1995. Used by permission.

The section on Mark McCumber in Chapter 7 was first published by *Sports Illustrated* on October 30, 1995, as "McCumber's Rules." All rights reserved.

The section on Ben Wright in Chapter 7 was first published by *Sports Illustrated* on December 4, 1995, as "Living with a Lie." All rights reserved.

Chapter 8 was first published in the book *Every Shot I Take*, by Davis Love III, published by Simon & Schuster, 1997. Copyright © Davis Love III and Michael Bamberger. Used by permission.

The section on Tiger Woods in Chapter 9 was first published by *Sports Illustrated* on April 21, 1997, as "All Is Changed." All rights reserved.

The section on Peter Teravainen in Chapter 9 was first published by *Sports Illustrated* on June 23, 1997, as "On Strange Turf." All rights reserved.

The section on Jeff Maggert in Chapter 9 was first published by *Sports Illustrated* on June 14, 1999, as "Fresh Start." All rights reserved.

The section on Mike Donald in Chapter 9 was first published by *Sports Illustrated* on August 9, 1999, as "Lifer." All rights reserved.

The section on Jean Van de Velde in Chapter 9 was first published by *Sports Illustrated* on August 23, 1999, as "Back in the Saddle." All rights reserved.

The section on Elmore Just in Chapter 10 was first published by *Sports Illustrated* on August 28, 2000, as "Wooden Soldier." All rights reserved.

The letter to the members of the Merion Golf Club in Chapter 11 was first published by the Merion Golf Club in June 2000. Used by permission. All rights reserved.

The section on Tom Watson's 2003 golf season in Chapter 15 was first published by *Sports Illustrated* on December 29, 2003, as "A Crisis Brought Out His Best." All rights reserved.

The section on Tiger Woods in Chapter 16 was first published by *Sports Illustrated* on April 19, 2004, as "Keeping an Eye on Tiger." All rights reserved.

The section on Al Geiberger in Chapter 16 was first published by *Sports Illustrated* on June 15, 2004, as "Lost and Found." All rights reserved.

The section on Johnny Miller in Chapter 16 was first published by *Sports Illustrated* on June 28, 2004, as "Johnny on the Spot." All rights reserved.

The section on Alina Bamberger and Lisa Winder in Chapter 16 was first published by *Sports Illustrated* on June 21, 2004, as "Discovering the LPGA." All rights reserved.

Chapter 17 was first published as an afterword to the 2005 Gotham edition of *To the Linksland*. Copyright © Michael Bamberger. Used by permission.

The section on Tom Kite in Chapter 18 was first published by *Sports Illustrated* on March 14, 2005, as "What's He Trying to Prove?" All rights reserved.

The section on caddying at Augusta National in Chapter 18 was first published by *Sports Illustrated* on April 11, 2005, as "A Week Inside the Ropes." All rights reserved.

The section on Brad Faxon in Chapter 18 was first published by *Sports Illustrated* on March 28, 2005, as "Marking Time." All rights reserved.